Lectures From Columbo to Almora

Himalayan Series—No. XV

Lectures From Colombo to Almora

By

The Swami Vivekananda.

उत्तिष्ठत जाग्रत  प्राप्य वरान्निबोधत ।

Katha Upa. I. iii. 4

Arise! Awake! and stop not till the goal is reached.

—*Swami Vivekananda.*

REVISED AND ENLARGED EDITION.

PRINTED BY JUGGOBUNDHU GHOSE, AND PUBLISHED BY THE PRABUDDHA BHARATA PRESS, MAYAVATI, ALMORA, HIMALAYAS.

1908

[[illegible] *Rupees.*] [*Foreign, 75 cents, or 4 Shillings*

LECTURES FROM COLOMBO TO ALMORA.

by Swami Vivekananda

CONTENTS.

FIRST PUBLIC LECTURE IN THE EAST

(COLOMBO).

After his memorable propaganda in the West, Swami Vivekananda landed at Colombo on the afternoon of January 15th, 1897, and was given a right royal reception by the Hindu community there. The following address of welcome was then presented to him :—

To

SRIMAT VIVEKANANDA SWAMI.

Revered Sir,

In pursuance of a resolution passed at a public meeting of the Hindus of the city of Colombo, we beg to offer you a hearty welcome to this Island. We deem it a privilege to be the first to welcome you on your return home from your great mission in the West.

We have watched with joy and thankfulness the success with which the mission has, under God's blessing, been crowned. You have proclaimed to the nations of Europe and America, the Hindu ideal of a universal religion, harmonising all creeds, providing spiritual food for each soul according to its needs, and lovingly drawing it unto God. You have preached the Truth and the Way, taught from remote ages by a succession of Masters whose blessed feet have walked and sanctified the soil of India, and whose gracious presence and inspiration have made her through all her vicissitudes, the Light of the World.

To the inspiration of such a Master, Sri Ramakrishna Paramahamsa Deva, and to your self-sacrificing zeal, western nations owe the priceless boon of being placed in living contact with the spiritual genius of India, while to many of our own countrymen, delivered from the glamour of western civilisation, the value of our glorious heritage has been brought home.

By your noble work and example you have laid humanity under an obligation difficult to repay, and you have shed fresh lustre upon our Motherland. We pray that the grace of God may continue to prosper you and your work, and

We remain, Revered Sir,
Yours faithfully,

for and on behalf of the Hindus of Colombo,

P. COOMARA SAWMY,

Member of the Legislative Council of Ceylon,
Chairman of the Meeting.

A. KULAVEERASINGHAM,

Colombo, January 1897. *Secretary.*

The Swami gave a brief reply, expressing his appreciation of the kind welcome he had received. He took advantage of the opportunity to point out that the demonstration had not been made in honour of a great politician, or a great soldier, or a millionaire, but of a begging Sannyasi, showing the tendency of the Hindu mind towards religion. He urged the necessity of keeping religion as the backbone of the national life, if the nation were to live, and disclaimed any personal character for the welcome he had received, but insisted upon its being the recognition of a principle.

On the evening of the 16th, the Swami gave the following public lecture in the Floral Hall:—

What little work has been done by me has not been from any inherent power that resides in me, but from the cheers, the good-will, the blessings, that have followed my path in the West from this our very beloved, most sacred, dear Motherland. Some good has been done, no doubt, in the West, but specially to myself, for what before was the result of an emotional nature perhaps, has gained the certainty of conviction, and attained the power and strength of demonstration. Formerly, I thought as every Hindu thinks, and as the Hon. President has just pointed out to you, that this is the *Punya Bhumi*, the land of Karma. To-day I stand here and say, with the conviction of truth, that it is so. If there is any land on this earth that can lay claim to be the blessed *Punya Bhumi*, to be the land to which all souls on this earth must come to account for Karma, the land to which every soul that is wending its way Godward must come to attain its last home, the land where humanity has attained its highest towards gentleness, towards generosity, towards purity, towards calmness, above all the land of introspection and of spirituality,—it is India. Hence have started the founders of religions from the most ancient times, deluging the earth again and again with the pure and perennial waters of spiritual truth. Hence have proceeded the tidal waves of philosophy that have covered the earth, East or West, North or South, and hence again must start the wave which is going to spiritualise the material civilisation of the world. Here is the life-giving water with which must be quenched the burning fire of materialism, which is burning the core of the hearts of millions, in other lands. Believe me, my friends, this is going to be.

So much I have seen, and so far those of you who are students of the history of races are already aware of this fact. The debt which the world owes to our Motherland is immense. Taking country with country, there is not one race on this earth to which the world owes so much as to the patient Hindu, the mild Hindu. "The mild Hindu" sometimes is used as an expression of reproach, but if ever a reproach concealed a wonderful truth it is in the term, the "mild Hindu," who has always been the blessed child of God. Civilisations have arisen in other parts of the world. In ancient times and in modern times, great ideas have emanated from strong and great races. In ancient and in modern times, wonderful ideas have been carried forward from one race to another. In ancient and in modern times, seeds of great truth and power have been cast abroad by the advancing tides of national life, but mark you, my friends, it has been always with the blast of war trumpets, and with the march of embattled cohorts. Each idea had to be soaked in a deluge of blood; each idea had to wade through the blood of millions of our fellow-beings; each word of power had to be followed by the groans of millions, by the wails of orphans, by the tears of widows. This, in the main, other nations have taught; but India has for thousands of years peacefully existed. Here activity prevailed when even Greece did not exist, when Rome was not thought of, when the very fathers of the modern Europeans lived in the forests and painted themselves blue. Even earlier, when history has no record, and tradition dares not peer into the gloom of that intense past, even from then until now, ideas after ideas have marched out from her, but every word has been spoken with a blessing behind it, and peace before it. We, of all nations of the world have never been a conquering race, and that blessing is on our head, and therefore we live. There was a time when at the sound of the march of big Greek battalions, the earth trembled. Vanished from off the face of the earth, with not even a tale left behind to tell, gone is that ancient land of the Greeks. There was a time when the Roman Eagle floated over everything worth having in this world; everywhere Rome's power was felt and pressed on the head of humanity; the earth trembled at the name of Rome. But the Capitoline Hill is a mass of ruins, the spider weaves its web where the Cæsars ruled. There have been other nations equally glorious that have come and gone, living a few hours of exultant and of exuberant dominance, and of a wicked national life, and then vanishing like ripples on the face of the waters. Thus have these nations made their mark on the face of humanity. But we live, and if Manu came back to-day he would not be bewildered, and would not find himself in a foreign land. The same laws are here, laws adjusted and thought out through thousands and thousands of years; customs, the outcome of the acumen of ages and the experience of centuries, that seem to be eternal; and as the days go by, as blow after blow of misfortune has been delivered upon them, they seem to have served one purpose only, that of making them stronger and more constant. And to find the centre of all this, the heart from which the blood flows, the main-spring of the national life, believe me when I say after my experience of the world, that it is here. To the other nations of the world, religion is one among the many occupations of life. There is politics, there are the enjoyments of social life, there is all that wealth can buy or power can bring, there is all that the senses can enjoy; and among all these various occupations of life, and all this searching after something which can give yet a little more whetting to the cloyed senses—among all these, there is perhaps a little bit of religion. But here, in India, religion is the one and the only occupation of life. How many of you know that there has been a Chino-Japanese war? Very few of you, if any. That there are tremendous political movements and socialistic movements trying to transform Western society, how many of you know? Very few indeed, if any. But that there was a Parliament of Religions in America, and that there was a Hindu Sannyasin sent over there, I am astonished to find that even the cooly knows of it. That shows the way the wind blows, where the national life is. I used to read books written by globe-trotting travellers, especially foreigners, who deplored the ignorance of the Eastern masses, but I found out that it was partly true and at the same time partly untrue. If you ask a ploughman in England, or in America, or France, or in Germany to what party he belongs, he can tell you whether he belongs to the Radicals or the Conservatives, and for whom he is going to vote. In America he will say whether he is Republican or Democrat, and even knows something about the silver question. But if you ask him about his religion, he will tell you that he goes to church, and belongs to a certain denomination. That is all he knows, and he thinks it is sufficient.

Now, when we come to India, if you ask one of our ploughmen, "Do you know anything about politics?" He will reply, "What is that?" He does not understand about socialistic movements, the relation between capital and labour, and all that, he has never heard of such things in his life; he works hard and earns his bread. But you ask, "What is your religion?" he replies, "Look here, my friend, I have marked it on my forehead." He can give you a good hint or two on questions of religion. That has been my experience. That is our nation's life. Individuals have each their own peculiarities, and each man has his own method of growth, his own life marked out for him, by the infinite past life, by all his past Karma as we Hindus say; into this world, with all the past on him, the infinite past ushers the present, and the way in which we use the present is going to make the future. Thus, everyone born into this world has a bent, a direction towards which he must go, through which he must live, and what is true of the individual is equally true of the race. Each race, similarly, has a peculiar bent, each race has a peculiar *raison d'être*, each race has a peculiar mission to fulfil in the life of the world. Each race has to make its own result, to fulfil its own mission. Political greatness or military power is never the mission of our race; it never was, and, mark my words, it never will be. But there has been the other mission given to us, which is to conserve, to preserve, to accumulate, as it were, into a dynamo, all the spiritual energy of the race, and that concentrated energy is to pour forth in a deluge on the world, whenever circumstances are propitious. Let the Persian or the Greek, the Roman, the Arab, or the Englishman march his battalions, conquer the world, and link the different nations together, and the philosophy and spirituality of India is ever ready to flow along the new-made channels into the veins of the nations of the world. The Hindu's calm brain must pour out its own quota to give to the sum-total of human progress. India's gift to the world, is the light spiritual.

Thus, in the past, we read in history, that whenever there arose a great conquering nation uniting the different races of the world, binding India with the other races, taking her out, as it were, from her loneliness, and from her aloofness from the rest of the world, into which she again and again cast herself, that wherever such function has been brought about, the result has been the flooding of the world with Indian spiritual ideas. At the beginning of this century, Schopenhauer, the great German philosopher, studying, from a not very clear translation of the Vedas made from an old translation into Persian, and thence by a young Frenchman into Latin, says, "In the whole world there is no study so beneficial and so elevating as that of the Upanishads. It has been the solace of my life, it will be the solace of my death." This great German sage foretold, that "The world is about to see a revolution in thought more extensive and more powerful than that which was witnessed by the Renaissance of Greek Literature," and to-day his predictions are coming to pass. Those who keep their eyes open, those who understand the workings in the minds of the different nations of the West, those who are thinkers and study the different nations, will find the immense change that has been produced in the tone, the procedure, in the methods, and in the literature of the world by this slow, never-ceasing permeation of Indian thought. But there is another peculiarity, as I have already hinted to you. We never preached our thoughts with fire and sword. If there is one word in the English language to represent the gift of India to the world, if there is one word in the English language to express the effect which the literature of India produces upon mankind, it is this one word, "fascination." It is the opposite of anything that takes you suddenly; it throws on you, as it were, a charm imperceptibly. To many, Indian thought, Indian manners, Indian customs, Indian philosophy, Indian literature, are repulsive at the first sight, but let them persevere, let them read, let them become familiar with the great principles underlying these ideas, and it is ninety-nine to one that the charm will come over them, and fascination will be the result. Slowly and silently, as the gentle dew that falls in the morning, unseen, unheard, yet producing a most tremendous result, has been the work of this calm, patient, all-suffering, spiritual race, upon the world of thought.

Once more history is going to repeat itself. For to-day, under the blasting light of modern science, when old, and apparently strong and invulnerable beliefs have been shattered to their very foundations, when special claims laid upon the allegiance of mankind by different sects have been all blown into atoms and have vanished into air—when the sledge-hammer blows of modern antiquarian researches are pulverising like masses of porcelain all sorts of antiquated orthodoxies—when religion in the West is only in the hands of the ignorant, and the knowing ones look down with scorn upon anything belonging to religion, here comes to the fore the philosophy of India, which displays the highest religious aspirations of the Indian mind, where the grandest philosophical facts have been the practical spirituality of the people. This naturally is coming to the rescue, the idea of the oneness of all, the Infinite, the idea of the Impersonal, the wonderful idea of the eternal soul of man, of the unbroken continuity in the march of beings, and the infinity of the universe. The old sects looked upon the world as a little mud-puddle, and thought that time began but the other day. It was there in our old books, and only there that the grand idea of the infinite range of time, space and causation, and above all, the infinite glory of the spirit of man governed all the search for religion. When the modern tremendous theories of evolution and conservation of energy and so forth, are dealing death blows to all sorts of crude theologies, what then can hold any more the allegiance of cultured humanity but the most wonderful of convincing, broadening, and ennobling ideas, that can only be found in that most marvellous product of the soul of man, the wonderful voice of God, the Vedanta.

At the same time, I must remark, that what I mean by our religion working upon the nations outside of India, comprises only the principles, the background, the foundation upon which that religion is built. The detailed workings, the minute points which have been worked out through centuries of social necessity, little ratiocinations about manners and customs and social well-being, do not rightly find a place in the category of religion. We know, that in our books, a clear distinction is made between two sets of truths. The one set is that which abides for ever, being built upon the nature of man, the nature of the soul, the soul's relation to God, the nature of God, perfection, and so on; there are also the principles of cosmology, of the infinitude of creation, or more correctly speaking—projection, the wonderful law of cyclical procession, and so on;—these are the eternal principles founded upon the universal laws in nature. The other set comprises the minor laws, which guides the working of our everyday life. They belong more properly to the Puranas, to the Smritis, and not to the Srutis. These have nothing to do with the other principles. Even in our own nation these minor laws have been changing all the time. Customs of one age, of one Yuga, have not been the customs of another, and as Yuga comes after Yuga, they will still have to change. Great Rishis will appear and lead us to customs and manners that are suited to new environments.

The great principles underlying all this wonderful, infinite, ennobling, expansive view of man and God, and the world, have been produced in India. In India alone, man has not stood up to fight for a little tribe God, saying "My God is true and yours is not true; let us have a good fight over it." It was only here that such ideas did not occur, as fighting for little gods. These great underlying principles being based upon the eternal nature of man, are as potent to-day for working for the good of the human race, as they were thousands of years ago, and they will remain so, so long as this earth remains, so long as the law of Karma remains, so long as we are born as individuals and have to work out our own destiny by our individual power.

And above all, what India has to give to the world, is this. If we watch the growth and development of religions in different races, we shall always find this, that each tribe at the beginning has a god of its own. If the tribes are allied to each other, these gods will have a generic name, as for example, all the Babylonian gods had. When the Babylonians were divided into many races, they had the generic name of Baal, just as the Jewish races had different gods with the common name of Moloch: and at the same time you will find, that one of these tribes becomes superior to the rest, and lays claim to its own king as the king over all. Therefrom, it naturally follows that it also wants to preserve its own god as the god of all the races. Baal-Merodach, said the Babylonians, was the greatest god; all the others were inferior. Moloch-Yavah was the superior over all other Molochs; and these questions had to be decided by the fortunes of battle. The same struggle was here also. In India the same competing gods had been struggling with each other for supremacy, but the great good fortune of this country and of the world was, that there came out in the midst of the din and confusion, a voice which declared, ***Ekam sat viprá bahudhá vadanti*** (That which exists is One; sages call It by various names). It is not that Siva is superior to Vishnu, not that Vishnu is everything and Siva is nothing, but it is the same one whom you call either Siva or Vishnu, or by a hundred other names. The names are different, but it is the same one. The whole history of India you may read in these few words. The whole history has been a repetition in massive language, with tremendous power, of that one central doctrine. It was repeated in the land, till it had entered into the blood of the nation, till it began to tingle with every drop of blood that flowed in their veins, till it became one with the life, part and parcel of the material of which they were composed, and thus, the land was transmuted into the most wonderful land of toleration, giving the right to welcome the various religions as well as all sects, into the old mother-country.

And herein is the explanation of the most remarkable phenomenon that is only witnessed here, of all the various sects, apparently hopelessly contradictory, yet living in such harmony. You may be a dualist, and I may be a monist. You may believe that you are the eternal servant of God, and another may declare that he is one with God Himself; yet both of them are good Hindus. How is that possible? Read then—***Ekam sat viprá bahudhá vadanti*** (That which exists is One; sages call It by various names). Above all others, my countrymen, this is the one grand truth that we have to teach to the world. Even the most educated people of other countries turn up their noses at an angle of forty-five degrees and call our religion, idolatry. I have seen that, and they never stopped to think what a mass of superstition there was in their own heads. It is so still everywhere, this tremendous sectarianism, the low narrowness of the mind. The thing which a man has, is the only thing worth having; the only life worth living is his own little life of dollar-worship and mammon-worship; the only little possession worth having is his own property, and nothing else. If he can manufacture a little clay nonsense or invent a machine, that is to be admired beyond the greatest possessions. That is the case over the whole world, in spite of education and learning. But education has yet to be in the world, and civilisation—civilisation has begun nowhere yet, ninety-nine decimal nine per cent of the human race are more or less savages, even now. We may read of these things in books, and we hear of toleration in religion and all that, but very little is there yet in the world; take my experience for that; ninety-nine per cent do not even think of it. There is tremendous religious persecution yet, in every country in which I have been, and the same old objections are raised against learning anything new. The little toleration that is in the world, the little sympathy that is yet in the world, for religous thought, is practically here, in the land of the Aryas, and nowhere else. It is here that Indians build temples for Mohammedans and Christians; nowhere else. If you go to other countries and ask Mohammedans, or people of other religions to build a temple for you, see how they will help. They will instead try to break down your temple and you too, if they can. The one great lesson therefore that the world wants most, that the world has yet to learn from India, is the idea, not only of toleration, but of sympathy. Well has it been said in the *Mahimna Stotra*—"As the different rivers, taking their start from different mountains, running straight or crooked, at last come unto the ocean, so, O Siva, the different paths which men take through different tendencies, various though they appear, crooked or straight, all lead unto Thee." Though they may take various roads, all are on the way. Some may run a little crooked, others may run straight, but at last, they will all come unto the Lord, the One. Then and then alone, is your Bhakti and Siva complete, when you not only see Him in the Lingam, but you see Him everywhere. He is the sage, he is the lover of Hari, who sees Hari in everything and in everyone. If you are a real lover of Siva, you must see Him in everything, and in everyone. You must see that every worship is given unto Him, whatever may be the name or the form; that all knees bending towards the Kaaba, or kneeling in a Christian Church, or in a Buddhist Temple, are kneeling to Him, whether they know it or not, whether they are conscious of it or not; that in whatever name or form they are offered, all these flowers are laid at His Feet, for He is the one Lord of all, the one Soul of all souls. He knows infinitely better what this world wants, than you or I. It is impossible that all difference can cease; it must exist; without variation life must cease. It is this clash, the differentiation of thought, that makes for light, for motion, for everything. Differentiation, infinitely contradictory, must remain, but it is not necessary that we should hate each other, therefore. It is not necessary therefore, that we should fight each other. Therefore, we have again to learn the one central truth that was only preached here, in our Motherland, and that once more has to be preached from India. Why? Because, not only is it in our books, but it runs through every phase of our national literature, and is in the national life. Here and here alone, is it practised every day, and any man whose eyes are open can see that it is practised here and here alone. Thus we have to teach religion. There are other and higher lessons that India can teach, but they are only for the learned. The lessons of mildness, gentleness, forbearance, toleration, sympathy, and brotherhood, everyone may learn, whether man, woman or child, learned or unlearned, without respect of race, caste or creed. "They call Thee by various names; Thou art One."

VEDANTISM.

The following address of welcome from the Hindus of Jaffna was presented to Swami Vivekananda:—

SRIMAT VIVEKANANDA SWAMI.

REVERED SIR,

We, the inhabitants of Jaffna professing the Hindu religion, desire to offer you a most hearty welcome to our land, the chief centre of Hinduism in Ceylon, and to express our thankfulness for your kind acceptance of our invitation to visit this part of Lanka.

Our ancestors settled here from Southern India, more than two thousand years ago, and brought with them their religion, which was patronised by the Tamil kings of Jaffna; but when their government was displaced by that of the Portuguese and the Dutch, the observance of religious rites was interfered with, public religious worship was prohibited, and the Sacred Temples including two of the most far-famed Shrines, were razed to the ground by the cruel hand of persecution. In spite of the persistent attempts of these nations to force upon our forefathers the Christian religion, they clung to their old faith firmly, and have transmitted it to us as the noblest of our heritages. Now, under the rule of Great Britain, not only has there been a great and intelligent revival, but the sacred edifices have been, and are being, restored.

We take this opportunity to express our deep-felt gratitude for your noble and disinterested labours in the cause of our religion in carrying the light of truth, as revealed in the Vedas, to the Parliament of Religions, in disseminating the truths of the Divine Philosophy of India in America and England, and in making the Western world acquainted with the truths of Hinduism and thereby bringing the West in closer touch with the East. We also express our thankfulness to you for initiating a movement for the revival of our ancient religion in this materialistic age, when there is a decadence of faith and a disregard for search after spiritual truth.

We cannot adequately express our indebtedness to you for making the people of the West know the catholicity of our religion, and for impressing upon the minds of the *savants* of the West the truth, that there are more things in the Philosophy of the Hindus than are dreamt of in the Philosophy of the West.

We need hardly assure you that we have been carefully watching the progress of your Mission in the West, and always heartily rejoicing at your devotedness and successful labours in the field of religion. The appreciative references made by the press, in the great centres of intellectual activity, moral growth, and religious inquiry in the West, to you and to your valuable contributions to our religious literature, bear eloquent testimony to your noble and magnificent efforts.

We beg to express our heart-felt gratification at your visit to our land and to hope that we, who, in common with you, look to the Vedas as the foundation of all true spiritual knowledge, may have many more occasions of seeing you in our midst.

May God, who has hitherto crowned your noble work with conspicuous success, spare you long, giving you vigour and strength to continue your noble Mission.

We remain, Revered Sir,
Yours faithfully,
for and on behalf of the Hindus of Jaffna.

An eloquent reply was given, and on the following evening, the Swami lectured on *Vedantism*. A report of which is here appended :—

The subject is very large and the time is short; a full analysis of the religion of the Hindus is impossible in one lecture. I will, therefore, present before you the salient points of our religion in as simple language as I can. The word Hindu, by which it is the fashion now-a-days to style ourselves, has lost all its meaning, for this word merely meant those who lived on the other side of the river Indus (in Sanskrit Sindhu). This name was murdered into Hindu, by the ancient Persians, and all people living on the other side of the river Sindhu were called by them Hindus. Thus this word has come down to us, and during the Mohammedan rule we took up the word ourselves. There may not be any harm in using the word, of course, but, as I have said, it has lost its significance, for, you may mark that all the people who live on this side of the Indus, in modern times do not follow the same religion as they did in ancient times. The word, therefore, covers not only Hindus proper, but Mohammedans, Christians, Jains, and other peoples who live in India. I, therefore, would not use the word Hindu. What word should we use then? The other words which alone we can use, are either the Vaidiks, followers of the Vedas, or better still, the Vedantists, followers of the Vedanta. Most of the great religions of the world owe allegiance to certain books, which they believe are the words of God, or some other supernatural beings, and which are the basis of their religion. Now of all these books, according to the modern *savants* of the West, the oldest are the Vedas of the Hindus. A little understanding, therefore, is necessary about the Vedas.

This mass of writing called the Vedas is not the utterance of persons. Its date has never been fixed, can never be fixed, and, according to us, the Vedas are eternal. There is one salient point which I want you to remember, that all the other religions of the world claim their authority as being delivered by a personal God or a number of personal beings, angels, or special messengers of God, unto certain persons; while the claim of the Hindus is, that the Vedas do not owe their authority to anybody, they are themselves the authority, being eternal—the knowledge of God. They were never written, never created, they have existed throughout time; just as creation is infinite and eternal, without beginning and without end, so is the knowledge of God, without beginning and without end. And this knowledge is what is meant by the Vedas (*Vid* to know). The mass of knowledge called the Vedanta was discovered by personages called Rishis, and the Rishi is defined as a *Mantra Drashta*, a seer of thought; not that the thought was his own. Whenever you hear that a certain passage of the Vedas came from a certain Rishi, never think that he wrote it, or created it out of his mind; he was the seer of the thought which already existed; it existed in the universe eternally. This sage was the discoverer; the Rishis were spiritual discoverers.

This mass of writing, the Vedas, is divided principally into two parts, the *Karma Kanda* and the *Jnana Kanda*—the work portion and the knowledge portion, the ceremonial and the spiritual. The work portion consists of various sacrifices ; most of them of late have been given up as not practicable under present circumstances; but others remain to the present day in some shape or other. The main ideas of the *Karma Kanda*, which consist of the duties of man, the duties of the student, of the householder, of the recluse, and the various duties of the different stations of life, are followed, more or less, down to the present day. But the spiritual portion of our religion is in the second part, the *Jnana Kanda*, the Vedanta, the end of the Vedas, the gist, the goal of the Vedas. The essence of the knowledge of the Vedas was called by the name of Vedanta, which comprises the Upanishads ; and all the sects of India, whether Dualists, qualified Dualists, Monists, or the Sivites, Vaisnavites, Saktas, Souras, Ganapattyas—if there is any sect in India which dares to come within the fold of Hinduism, it must acknowledge the Upanishads of the Vedas. They can have their own interpretations, and can interpret them in their own way, but they must obey the authority. That is why we want to use the word Vedantist instead of Hindu. All the philosophers of India who are orthodox have to acknowledge the authority of the Vedanta, and all our present-day religions, however crude some of them may appear to be, however inexplicable some of their purposes may seem, one who understands them, and studies them, can trace them back to the ideas of the Upanishads. So deeply have these Upanishads sunk into our race, that those of you who study the symbology of the crudest religion of the Hindus, will be astonished to find sometimes figurative expressions of the Upanishads —the Upanishads become symbolised after a time into figures and so forth. Great spiritual and philosophical ideas in the Upanishads are to-day with us, converted into household worship in the form of symbols. Thus the various symbols now used by us, all come from the Vedanta, because in the Vedanta they are used as figures, and these ideas spread among the nation and permeated it throughout, until they became part of their everyday life, as symbols.

Next to the Vedanta come the Smritis. These also are books written by sages, but the authority of the Smritis is subordinate to that of the Vedanta, because they stand in the same relation with us, as the Scriptures of the other religions stand with regard to them. We admit that the Smritis have been written by particular sages ; in that sense they are the same as the Scriptures of other religions, but these Smritis are not final authority. If there is anything in a Smriti which contradicts the Vedanta, the Smriti is to be rejected ; its authority is gone. These Smritis, we see again, have varied from time to time. We read that such and such Smriti should have authority in the *Satya Yuga*, such and such in the *Tretá Yuga*, some in the *Dwápara Yuga*, and some in the *Kali Yuga*, and so on. As essential conditions changed, as various circumstances came to have their influence on the race, manners and customs had to be changed, and these Smritis, as mainly regulating the manners and customs of the nation, had also to be changed from time to time. This is a point I specially ask you to remember. The principles of religion that are in the Vedanta are unchangeable. Why? Because they are all built upon the eternal principles that are in man and nature ; they can never change. Ideas about the soul, going to heaven, and so on, can never change ; they were the same thousands of years ago, they are the same to-day, they will be the same millions of years to come. But those religious practices which are based entirely upon our social position and correlation, must change with the changes in society. Such an order, therefore, would be good and true at a certain period and not at another. We find accordingly, that certain food should be allowed at one time and not at another, because the food was suitable for that time; but climatic and other things change, various other circumstances require to be met, so the Smriti changed the food and other things. Thus it naturally follows, that if in modern times our society requires changes to be made, they must be met, and sages will come and show us the way how to meet them; but not one jot of the principles of our religion will be changed; they will remain intact.

Then there are the *Puranas*. *Purânam Panchalakshanam*, which means, the Puranas are of five characteristics,—that which treats of history, of cosmology, with various symbological illustration of philosophical principles and so forth. These were written to popularise the religion of the Vedas. The language in which the Vedas are written is very ancient, and even among scholars very few can trace the date of these books. The Puranas were written in the language of the people of that time, what we call modern Sanskrit. They were then meant, not for scholars, but for the ordinary people; and ordinary people cannot understand philosophy. Such things were given unto them in concrete form, by means of the lives of saints and kings and great men, and historical events that happened to the race, &c. The sages made use of these things, to illustrate the eternal principles of religion.

There are still other books, the *Tantras*. These are very much like *Puranas* in some respects, and in some of them there is an attempt to revive the old sacrificial ideas of the *Karma Kanda*.

All these books constitute the Scriptures of the Hindus. When there is such a mass of sacred books in a nation and in a race, which has devoted the greatest part of its energies to the thought of philosophy and spirituality, (for nobody knows for how many thousands of years), it is quite natural that there should be so many sects; indeed it is a wonder that there are not thousands more. These sects differ very much from each other in certain points. We shall not have time to understand the differences between these sects, and all the spiritual details about them; therefore, I shall take up the common ground, the principles of all these sects, which every Hindu must believe.

The first, is the question of the creation, that this Nature, *Prakriti*, *Maya*, is infinite, without beginning. It is not that this world was created the other day, not that a God came and created the world, and since that time has been sleeping; for that cannot be. The creative energy is still going on. God is eternally creating—is never at rest. Remember the passage in the Gita where Krishna says: "If I remain at rest for one moment this universe will be destroyed." If that creative energy which is working all around us, day and night, stops for a second, the whole thing falls to the ground. There never was a time when that energy did not work throughout the universe, but there is the law of cycles, *Pralaya*. Our Sanskrit word for creation properly translated, should be *projection, and not creation*. For the word creation in the English language has unhappily got that fearful, that most crude idea of something coming out of nothing, creation out of non-entity, and non-existence becoming existence, which, of course, I would not insult you by asking you to believe. Our word, therefore, is projection. The whole of this Nature exists, it becomes finer, subsides, and then after a period of rest, as it were, the whole thing is again projected forward, and the same combination, the same evolution, the same manfestations appear, and remain playing, as it were, for a certain time, only again to break into pieces, to become finer and finer, until the whole thing subsides, and again comes out. Thus it goes on backwards and forwards, with a wave-like motion throughout eternity. Time, space and causation are all within this Nature. To say, therefore, that it had a beginning, is utter nonsense. No such question can occur as to its beginning, or its end. Therefore, wherever in our Scriptures the words beginning and end are used, you must remember that it means the beginning and the end of one particular cycle ; no more than that.

What makes this creation : God. What do I mean by the use of the English word, God ? Certainly not the word as ordinarily used in English; a good deal of difference. There is no other suitable word in English. I would rather confine myself to the Sanskrit word, *Brahman*. He is the general cause of all these manifestations. What is this *Brahman ?* He is eternal, eternally pure, eternally awake, the almighty, the all-knowing, the all-merciful, the omnipresent, the formless, the partless. He creates this universe. If He is always creating and holding up this universe, two difficulties arise. We see that there is partiality in the universe. One person is born happy, and another unhappy; one is rich and another is poor; this shows partiality. Then, there is cruelty also, for here the very condition of life is death. One animal tears another to pieces, and every man tries to get the better of his own brother. This competition, cruelty, horror, and sighs rending hearts day and night, is the state of things in this world of ours. If this be the creation of a God, that God is worse than cruel, worse than any devil that man ever imagined. Ay ! says the Vedanta,' it is not the fault of God that this partiality exists, that this competition exists. Who makes it ? We ourselves. There is a cloud shedding its rain on all fields alike. But it is only the field that is well-cultivated, which gets the advantage of the shower; another field, which has not been tilled or taken care of, cannot get that advantage. It is not the fault of the cloud. The mercy of God is eternal and unchangeable; it is we that make the differentiation. But how can this difference of some being born happy and some unhappy be explained ? They do nothing to make that difference ! Not in this life, but they did in their last birth, and this difference is explained by the action in the previous life.

We now come to the second principle on which we all agree, not only all Hindus, but all Buddhists, and all Jains. We all agree that life is eternal. It is not that it has sprung out of nothing, for that cannot be. Such a life would not be worth having. Everything that has a beginning in time must end in time. If life began but yesterday, it must end to-morrow, and annihilation is the result. Life must have been existing. It does not now require much acumen to see that, for all the sciences of modern times have been coming round to our help, illustrating from the material world the principles embodied in our Scriptures. You know it already, that each one of us is the effect of the infinite past; the child is ushered into the world, not as something flashing from the hands of nature, as poets delight so much to depict, but he has the burden of an infinite past; for good or evil he comes to work out his own past deeds. That makes the differentiation. This is the law of Karma. Each one of us is the maker of his own fate. This law knocks on the head at once all doctrines of predestination and fate, and gives us the only means of reconciliation between God and man. We, we, and none else, are responsible for what we suffer. We are the effects, and we are the causes. We are free therefore. If I am unhappy, it has been of my own making, and that very thing shows that I can be happy if I will. If I am impure, that is also of my own making, and that very thing shows that I can be pure if I will. The human will stands beyond all circumstance. Before it, the strong, gigantic, infinite will and freedom in man, all the powers, even of nature, must bow down, succumb, and become its servants. This is the result of the law of Karma.

The next question, of course, naturally would be, what is the soul? We cannot understand God in our Scriptures without knowing the soul. There have been attempts in India, and outside of India too, to catch a glimpse of the beyond by studying external nature, and we all know what an awful failure has been the result. Instead of giving us a glimpse of the beyond, the more we study the material world the more we tend to become materialised. The more we handle the material world, even the little spirituality which we possessed before, vanishes. Therefore, that is not the way to spirituality, to knowledge of the Highest; but it must come through the heart, the human soul. The external workings do not teach us anything about the beyond, about the Infinite, it is only the internal that can do so. Through soul, therefore, the analysis of the human soul alone, can we understand God. There are differences of opinion as to the nature of the human soul among the various sects in India, but there are certain points of agreement. We all agree, that souls are without beginning and without end, and immortal by their very nature; also, that all powers, blessing, purity, omnipresence, omniscience are buried in each soul. That is a grand idea we ought to remember. In every man and in every animal, however weak or wicked, great or small, resides the same omnipresent, omniscient soul. The difference is not in the soul, but in the manifestation. Between me and the smallest animal, the difference is only in manifestation, but as a principle he is the same as I am, he is my brother, he has the same soul as I have. This is the greatest principle that India has preached. The talk of the brotherhood of man becomes in India the brotherhood of universal life, of animals, and of all life down to the little ants,—all these are our bodies. Even as our Scripture says,—"Thus the sage, knowing that the same Lord inhabits all bodies, will worship every body as such." That is why in India there have been such merciful ideas about the poor, about animals, about everybody and every thing else. This is one of the common grounds about our ideas of the soul.

Naturally we come to the idea of God. One thing more about the soul. Those who study the English language are often deluded by the words, soul and mind. Our *Atman* and soul are entirely different things. What we call *Manas*, the mind, the western people call soul. The West never had the idea of soul until they got it through Sanskrit Philosophy, some twenty years ago. The body is here, beyond that is the mind, yet the mind is not the *Atman;* it is the fine body, the *Sukshma Sharira*,—made of fine particles, which goes from birth to death, and so on; but behind the mind is the *Atman*, the Soul, the Self of man. It cannot be translated by the word Soul or Mind, so we have to use the word *Atman*, or, as Western philosophers have designated it by the word, Self. Whatever word you use, you must keep it clear in your mind, that the *Atman* is separate from the mind, as well as from the body, and that this *Atman* goes from birth and death, accompanied by the mind—the *Sukshma Sharira*. And when the time comes that it has attained to all knowledge, and manifested itself to perfection, then this going from birth to death ceases for it. Then it is at liberty either to keep that mind, or the *Sukshma Sharira*, or to let it go for ever, and remain independent and free throughout all eternity. The goal of the soul is freedom. That is no peculiarity of our religion. We also have heavens, and hells too, but these are not infinite, for in the very nature of things they cannot be. If there were any heavens, they would be only repetitions of this world of ours on a bigger scale, with a little more happiness, and a little more enjoyment, but that is all the worse for the soul. There are many of these heavens. Persons who do good works here with the thought of reward, when they die, are born again as gods in one of these heavens, as Indra and others. These gods are the names of certain states. They also had been men, and by good work they have become gods, and those different names that you read of, such as Indra, and so on, are not the names of the same person. There will be thousands of Indras. Nahusha was a great king, and when he died he became Indra. It is a position; one soul becomes high and takes the Indra position, and remains in it only a certain time; he then dies and is born again as man. But the human body is the highest of all. Some of the gods may try to go higher and give up all ideas of enjoyment in heavens, but, as in this world, wealth and position and enjoyment delude the vast majority, so, do most of the gods become deluded also, and after working out their good Karma, they fall down and become human beings again. This earth, therefore, is the *Karma Bhumi;* it is this earth from which we attain to liberation. So, even these heavens are not worth attaining to. What is then worth having? *Mukti*, freedom. Even in the highest of heavens, says our Scripture, you are a slave; what matters it if you are a king for twenty thousand years? So long as you have a body, so long as you are a slave to happiness, so long as time works on you, space works on you, you are a slave. The idea, therefore, is to be free of external and internal nature. Nature must fall at your feet, and you must trample on it, and be free and glorious, by going beyond. No more is there life, therefore, no more is there death; no more enjoyment, therefore, no more misery. It is bliss unspeakable, indestructible, beyond everything. What we call happiness and good here, are but particles of that eternal Bliss. And this eternal Bliss is our goal.

The soul is also sexless; we cannot say of the *Atman* that it is a man or a woman. Sex belongs to the body alone. All such ideas, therefore, as man or woman, are a delusion when spoken with regard to the Self, and are only proper when spoken of the body. So are the ideas of age; It never ages; the ancient One is always the same. How did It come down to earth? There is but one answer to that in our Scriptures. Ignorance is the cause of all this bondage. It is through ignorance that we have become bound; knowledge will cure it, by taking us to the other side. How will that knowledge come? Through love, Bhakti. By the worship of God, by loving all beings as the temples of God; He resides within them. Thus, with that intense love will come knowledge, and ignorance will disappear, the bonds will break, and the soul will be free. There are two ideas of God in our Scriptures; the one, the personal, and the other, the impersonal. The idea of the Personal God is, that He is the omnipresent creator, preserver, and destroyer of everything, the eternal Father and Mother of the universe, but One who is eternally separate from us and from all souls; and liberation consists in coming near to Him and living in Him. Then there is the other idea of the Impersonal, where all those adjectives are taken away as superfluous, as illogical, and there remains an impersonal, omnipresent Being who cannot be called a knowing being, because knowledge only belongs to the human mind. He cannot be called a thinking being, because that is a process of the weak only. He cannot be called a reasoning being, because reasoning is a sign of weakness. He cannot be called a creating being, because none creates except in bondage. What bondage has He? None works except for the fulfilment of desires; what desires has He? None works except it is to supply some wants; what wants has He? In the Vedas it is not the word "He" that is used, but "It'; " for "He" would make an invidious distinction, as if He were a man. "It" the impersonal, is used, and this impersonal "It," is preached. This system is called the Advaita.

And what are our relations with this Impersonal Being? That we are He. We and He are one. Every one is but a manifestation of that Impersonal, the basis of all being, and misery consists in thinking of ourselves as different from this Infinite, Impersonal Being; and liberation consists in knowing our unity with this wonderful Impersonality. These, in short, are the two ideas of God that we find in our Scriptures. Some remarks ought to be made here. It is only through the idea of the Impersonal God that you can have any system of ethics. In every nation the truth has been preached from the most ancient times—love your fellow-beings as yourselves—I mean love human beings as yourselves. In India it has been preached, 'love all beings as yourselves'; we make no distinction between men and animals. But no reason was forthcoming, no one knew why it would be good to love other beings as ourselves. And the reason why is there, in the idea of the Impersonal God; you understand it—when you learn that the whole world is one—the oneness of the universe—the solidarity of all life,—that in hurting any one I am hurting myself, in loving any one I am loving myself. Hence we understand why it is that we ought not to hurt others. The reason for ethics, therefore, can only be had from this ideal of the Impersonal God. Then there is the question of the position of the Personal God in it. I understand the wonderful flow of love that comes from the idea of a Personal God, I thoroughly appreciate the power and potency of Bhakti on men to suit the needs of different times. What we now want in our country, however, is not so much of weeping, but a little strength. What a mine of strength is in this Impersonal God, when all superstitions have been thrown overboard, and man stands on his feet with the knowledge that I am the Impersonal Being of the world! What can make me afraid? I care not even for nature's laws. Death is a joke to me. Man stands on the glory of his own Soul, the Infinite, the Eternal, the Deathless—that Soul which no instruments can pierce, which no heat can dry, or fire burn, no water melt, the Infinite, the Birthless, the Deathless, without beginning and without end, before whose magnitude the suns and moons and all their systems appear like drops in the ocean, before whose glory space melts away into nothingness, and time vanishes into non-existence. This glorious Soul we must believe in. Out of that will come power. Whatever you think, that you will be. If you think yourselves weak, weak you will be; if you think yourselves strong, strong you will be; if you think yourselves impure, impure you will be; if you think yourselves pure, pure you will be. This teaches us not to think ourselves as weak, but as strong, omnipotent, omniscient. No matter that I have not expressed it yet; it is in me. All knowledge is in me, all power, all purity, and all freedom. Why cannot I express this knowledge? Because I do not believe in it. Let me believe in it and it must and will come out. This is what the idea of the Impersonal teaches. Make your children strong from their very childhood, teach them not weakness, nor forms, but make them strong, let them stand on their feet, bold, all-conquering, all-suffering, and first of all, let them learn of the glory of the Soul. That, you get alone in the Vedanta,—and there alone. It has ideas of love and worship and other things which we have in other religions, and more besides; but this idea of the Soul is the life-giving thought, the most wonderful. There and there alone, is the great thought that is going to revolutionise the world and reconcile the knowledge of the material world with religion.

Thus I have tried to bring before you the salient points of our religion—the principles. I have only to say a few words about the practice and the application. As we have seen, under the circumstances existing in India, naturally many sects must appear. As a fact, we find that there are so many sects in India, and at the same time we know this mysterious fact that these sects do not quarrel with each other. The Sivite does not say that every Vaishnavite is going to be damned, nor the Vaishnavite that every Sivite will be damned. The Sivite says, this is my path, and you have yours; at the end we must come together. They all know that in India. This is the theory of *Ishtam*. It has been recognised in the most ancient times that there are various forms of worshipping God. It is also recognised that different natures require different methods. Your method of coming to God may not be my method, possibly it might hurt me. Such an idea as that there is but one way for everybody is injurious, meaningless, and entirely to be avoided. Woe unto the world when everyone is of the same religious opinion and takes to the same path. Then all religions and all thought will be destroyed. Variety is the very soul of life. When it dies out entirely creation will die. When this variation in thought is kept up, we must exist; and we need not quarrel because of that variety. Your way is very good for you, but not for me. My way is good for me but not for you. My way is called in Sanskrit, my *Ishtam*. Mind you, we have no quarrel with any religion in the world. We have each our *Ishtam*. But when we see men coming and saying, "this is the only way," and trying to force it on us in India, we have a word to say; we laugh at them. For such people who want to destroy their brothers because they seem to follow a different path towards God,—for them to talk of love is absurd. Their love does not count for much. How can they preach of love who cannot bear another man to follow a different path from their own? If that is love, what is hatred? We have no quarrel with any religion in the world, whether it teaches men to worship Christ, Buddha or Mahomet, or any other prophet. "Welcome, my brother," the Hindu says, "I am going to help you; but you must allow me to follow my way too. That is my *Ishtam*. Your way is very good, no doubt, but it may be dangerous for me. My own experience tells me what food is good for me, and no army of doctors can tell me that. So I know from my own experience what path is the best for me." That is the goal, the *Ishtam*, and therefore we say that if a temple, or a symbol, or an image, helps you to realise the Divinity within, you are welcome to it. Have two hundred images if you like. If certain forms and formularies help you to realise the Divine, God speed you; have, by all means, whatever forms, and whatever temples, and whatever ceremonies bring you nearer to God. But do not quarrel about them; the moment you quarrel, you are not going Godward, you are going backward, towards the brutes.

These are a few ideas in our religion. It is one of inclusion of every one, exclusion of none. Though our castes and our institutions are apparently linked with our religion, they are not so. These institutions have been necessary to protect us as a nation, and when this necessity for self-preservation will no more exist, they will die a natural death. But, the older I grow, the better I seem to think of these time-honoured institutions of India. There was a time when I used to think that many of them were useless and worthless, but the older I grow, the more I seem to feel a diffidence in cursing any one of them, for each one of them is the embodiment of the experience of centuries. A child of but yesterday, destined to die the day after to-morrow, comes to me and asks me to change all my plans, and if I hear the advice of that baby and change all my surroundings according to his ideas, I myself should be a fool, and no one else. Much of the advice that is coming to us from different countries is similar to this. Tell these wiseacres: I will hear you when you have made a stable society yourselves. You cannot hold on to one idea for two days, you quarrel and fail; you are born like moths in the spring and die like them in five minutes. You come up like bubbles and burst like bubbles too. First form a stable society like ours. First make laws and institutions that remain undiminished in their power through scores of centuries. Then will be the time to talk on the subject with you, but till then, my friend, you are only a giddy child.

I have finished what I had to say about our religion. I will end by reminding you of the one pressing necessity of the day. Praise be to Vyasa, the great author of the Mahabharata, that in this *Kali Yuga* there is one great work. The *Tapas* and the other hard Yogas that were practised in other *Yugas* do not work now. What is needed in this Yuga is giving, helping others. What is meant by *Dânam*? The highest of gifts is the giving of spiritual knowledge, the next, is the giving of secular knowledge, and the next, is the saving of life; the last, is giving food and drink. He who gives spiritual knowledge, saves the soul from many and many a birth. He who gives secular knowledge opens the eyes of human beings towards spiritual knowledge, and far below these, rank all other gifts, even the saving of life. Therefore, it is necessary that you learn this, and note that all other kinds of work are of much less value than that of imparting spiritual knowledge. The highest and greatest help is that given in the dissemination of spiritual knowledge. There is an eternal fountain of spirituality in our Scriptures, and nowhere on earth except in this land of renunciation do we find such noble examples of practical spirituality. I have had a little experience of the world. Believe me, there is much talking in other lands, but the practical man of religion, who has carried it into his life, is here and here alone. Talking is not religion; parrots may talk, machines may talk nowadays. But show me the life of renunciation, of spirituality, of all-suffering, of love infinite. This kind of life indicates a spiritual man. With such ideas and such noble practical examples in our country, it would be a great pity if the treasures in the brains and hearts of all these great Yogins, were not brought out to become the common property of every one, rich and poor, high and low; not only in India, but they must be thrown broadcast all over the world. This is one of our greatest duties, and you will find that the more you work to help others, the more you help yourselves. The one vital duty incumbent on you if you really love your religion, if you really love your country, is that you must struggle hard to be up and doing, with this one great idea of bringing out the treasures from your closed books, and delivering them over to their rightful heirs. And above all, one thing is necessary. Aye, for ages we have been saturated with awful jealousy; we are always getting jealous of each other. Why has this man a little precedence, and not I; even in the worship of God we want precedence, to such a state of slavery have we come. This is to be avoided. If there is any crying sin in India at this time it is this slavery. Every one wants to command and no one wants to obey; and this is owing to the absence of that wonderful *Brahmacharya* system of yore. First, learn to obey. The command will come by itself. Always first learn to be a servant, and

REPLY TO THE ADDRESS OF WELCOME AT PAMBAN.

On the arrival of Swami Vivekananda at Pamban, he was met by His Highness the Raja of Ramnad, who accorded him a hearty welcome. Preparations had been made at the landing wharf for a formal reception, and here, under a pandal which was decorated with great taste, the following address on behalf of the Pamban people was read :—

MAY IT PLEASE YOUR HOLINESS.

We greatly rejoice to welcome Your Holiness with hearts full of deepest gratitude and highest veneration—gratitude for having so readily and graciously consented to pay us a flying visit in spite of the numerous calls on you, and veneration for the many noble and excellent qualities that you possess and for the great work you have so nobly undertaken to do, and which you have been discharging with conspicuous ability, utmost zeal and earnestness.

We truly rejoice to see that the efforts of Your Holiness in sowing the seeds of Hindu philosophy in the cultured minds of the great Western nation, are being crowned with so much success, that we already see all around, the bright and cheerful aspect of the bearing of excellent fruits in great abundance, and most humbly pray that Your Holiness will, during your sojourn in Aryavartha, be graciously pleased to exert yourself even a little more than you did in the West, to awaken the minds of your brethren in this our motherland, from their dreary life-long slumber and make them recall to their minds the long-forgotten gospel of truth.

Our hearts are so full of the sincerest affection, greatest reverence, and highest admiration for Your Holiness—our great spiritual leader, that we verily find it impossible to adequately express our feelings, and therefore beg to conclude with an earnest and united prayer to the merciful Providence, to bless Your Holiness with a long life of usefulness, and to grant you every thing that may tend to bring about the long-lost feelings of universal brotherhood.

The Raja added to this a brief personal welcome, which was remarkable for its depth of feeling, and then the Swami replied to the following effect :—

Our sacred motherland is a land of religion and philosophy—the birthplace of spiritual giants—the land of renunciation, where and where alone, from the most ancient to the most modern times, there has been the highest ideal of life open to man.

I have been in the countries of the West; have travelled through many lands, of many races, and each race and each nation appears to me to have a particular ideal—a prominent ideal running through its whole life, and this ideal is the backbone of the national life. Not politics nor military power, not commercial supremacy nor mechanical genius, furnishes India with that backbone, but religion, and religion alone, is all that we have and mean to have. Spirituality has been always in India.

Great indeed are the manifestations of muscular power, and marvellous the manifestations of intellect expressing themselves through machines by the appliances [illegible] influence which spirit exerts [illegible] world.

The [illegible] India has always been most active. To-day, we are [illegible] the Hindu is mild and passive, and [illegible] the people of other lands. I discard the idea that India was ever passive. Nowhere has activity been more pronounced than in this [illegible], and the great proof of this activity is that our most ancient and magnanimous race still lives and at every decade in its glorious career seems to take on fresh youth—undying and imperishable. This activity manifests here in religion. But it is a peculiarity in human nature, that it judges others according to its own standard of activity. Take, for instance, a shoemaker. He understands only shoemaking and thinks there is nothing in this life except the manufacturing of shoes. A bricklayer understands nothing but bricklaying and proves this alone in his life from day to day. And there is another reason which explains this. When the vibrations of light are very intense, we do not see them, because we are so constituted that we cannot go beyond our own plane of vision. But the Yogi with his spiritual introspection is able to see through the materialistic veil of the vulgar crowds.

The eyes of the whole world are now turned towards this land of India for spiritual food, and India has to provide it for all the races. Here alone is the best ideal for mankind, and Western scholars are now striving to understand this ideal which is enshrined in our Sanskrit Literature and Philosophy, and which has been the characteristic of India all through the ages.

Since the dawn of history, no missionary went out of India to propagate the Hindu doctrines and dogmas, but now a wonderful change is coming over us. Sri Bhagavân Krishna says, "Whenever virtue subsides and immorality prevails, then I come again and again to help the world." Religious researches disclose to us the fact, that there is not a country possessing a good ethical code but has borrowed something of it from us, and there is not one religion possessing good ideas of the immortality of the soul but has derived it directly or indirectly from us.

There never was a time in the world's history when there was so much robbery and high-handedness, and tyranny of the strong over the weak, as at this latter end of the nineteenth century. Everybody should know that there is no salvation except through the conquering of desires, and that no man is free who is subject to the bondage of matter. This great truth all nations are slowly coming to understand and appreciate. As soon as the disciple is in a position to grasp this truth, the words of the *Guru* come to his help. The Lord sends help to His own children in His Infinite mercy which never ceaseth and is ever flowing in all creeds. Our Lord is the Lord of all religions. This idea belongs to India alone, and I challenge any one of you to find it in any other Scripture of the world.

We Hindus have now been placed, under God's providence, in a very critical and responsible position. The nations of the West are coming to us for spiritual help. A great moral obligation rests on the sons of India to fully equip themselves for the work of enlightening the world on the problems of human existence. One thing we may note, that whereas you will find that good and great men of other countries take pride in tracing back their descent to some robber-baron who lived in a mountain fortress and emerged from time to time to plunder passing wayfarers, we Hindus, on the other hand, take pride in being the descendants of Rishis and sages, who lived on roots and fruits in mountains and caves, meditating on the Supreme. We may be degraded and degenerated now, but however degraded and degenerated we may be, we can become great if we only begin to work in right earnest on behalf of our religion.

Accept my hearty thanks for the kind and cordial reception you have given me. It is impossible for me to express my gratitude to H. H. the Raja of Ramnad for his love towards me. If any good work has been done by me and through me, India owes much to this good man, for it was he who conceived the idea of my going to Chicago, and it was he who put that idea into my head and persistently urged me on to accomplish it. Standing beside me, he with all his old enthusiasm is still hoping for me to do more and more work. I wish there were half a dozen more such Rajas to take interest in our dear motherland, and work for her amelioration in the spiritual line.

ADDRESS AT THE RAMESVARAM TEMPLE ON REAL WORSHIP.

A visit was subsequently paid to the Ramesvaram Temple, where the Swami was asked to address a few words to the crowd of people who had assembled there. This he did in the following terms :—

It is in love that religion exists and not in ceremony; in the pure and sincere love in the heart. Unless a man is pure in body and mind, his coming into a temple and worshipping Siva is useless. The prayers of those that are pure in mind and body will be answered by Siva, and those that are impure, and yet try to teach religion to others, will fail in the end. External worship is only a symbol of internal worship; but internal worship and purity are the real things. Without them, external worship would be of no avail. Therefore, you must all try to remember this. People have become so degraded in this *Kali Yuga* that they think they can do anything, and then they can go to a holy place, and their sins will be forgiven. If a man goes with an impure mind into a temple, he adds to the sins that he had already, and goes home a worse man than what he left it. *Tirtha* (place of pilgrimage) is a place which is full of holy things and holy men. But if holy people live in a certain place, and if there is no temple there, even that is a *Tirtha*. If unholy people live in a place where there may be a hundred temples, the *Tirtha* has vanished from that place. And it is most difficult to live in a *Tirtha*, for if sin is committed in any ordinary place it can easily be removed, but sin committed in a *Tirtha* cannot be removed. This is the gist of all worship, to be pure and to do good to others. He who sees Siva in the poor, in the weak, and in the diseased, really worships Siva; and if he sees Siva only in the image, his worship is but preliminary. He, who has served and helped one poor man seeing Siva in him, without thinking of his caste, or creed, or race, or anything, with him Siva is more pleased than with the man who sees Him only in temples.

A rich man had a garden and two gardeners. One of these gardeners was very lazy and did not work; but when the owner came to the garden, the lazy man would get up and fold his arms and say, "How beautiful is the face of my master," and dance before him. The other gardener would not talk much, but would work hard, and produce all sorts of fruits and vegetables which he would carry on his head, to his master who lived a long way off. Of these two gardeners, who would be the more beloved by his master? Siva is that master, and this world is His garden, and there are two sorts of gardeners here: the one who is lazy, hypocritical, and does nothing, only talking about Siva's beautiful eyes and nose and other features; and the other, who is taking care of Siva's children, all those that are poor and weak, all animals, and all His creation. Which of these would be the more beloved of Siva? Certainly, he that serves His children. He who wants to serve the father must serve the children first. He who wants to serve Siva must serve His children—must serve all creatures in this world first. It is said in the Shastra that those who serve the servants of God are His greatest servants. So you will bear this in mind. Let me tell you again, that you must be pure and help any one who comes to you as much as lies in your power. And this is good Karma. By the power of this, the heart becomes pure (*Chitta Suddhi*), and then Siva who is residing in every one, will become manifest. He is always in the heart of every one. If there is dirt and dust on a mirror, we cannot see our image. So ignorance and wickedness are the dirt and dust that are on the mirror of our hearts. Selfishness is the chief sin, thinking of ourselves first. He who thinks 'I will eat first, I will have more money than others, and I will possess everything'; he who thinks 'I will get to heaven before others, I will get *Mukti* before others,' is the selfish man. The unselfish man says 'I will be last, I do not care to go to heaven, 'I will even go to hell, if by doing so I can help my brothers.' This unselfishness is the test of religion. He who has more of this unselfishness is more spiritual and nearer to Siva. Whether he is learned or ignorant, he is nearer to Siva than anybody else, whether he knows it or not. And if a man is selfish, even though he has visited all the temples, seen all the places of pilgrimage, and painted himself like a leopard, he is still further off from Siva.

REPLY TO THE ADDRESS OF WELCOME AT RAMNAD.

At Ramnad the following address was presented to Swami Vivekananda by the Rajah :—

His most Holiness

Sri Paramahamsa, Yathi-Rája, Digvijaya-Kolâhala Sarvamata-Sampratipanna, Parama-Yogeeswara, Srimat Bhagaván Sree Rama Krishna Paramahamsa Kara-kamala-Sanjátha, Rajadhiraja-Sevitha, SREE VIVEKANANDA SWAMI.

May it Please Your Holiness.

We, the inhabitants of this ancient and historic Samasthanam of Sethu Bandha Râmeswar, otherwise known as Ramânathapuram or Ramnad, beg, most cordially, to welcome you to this, our motherland. We deem it a very rare privilege to be the first to pay your Holiness our heart-felt homage on your landing in India, and that, on the shores sanctified by the footsteps of that great Hero and our revered Lord—Sree Bhagaván Ramachandra.

We have watched with feelings of genuine pride and pleasure the unprecedented success which has crowned your laudable efforts in bringing home to the master-minds of the West, the intrinsic merits and excellence of our time-honoured and noble religion. You have, with an eloquence that is unsurpassed and in language plain and unmistakable, proclaimed to and convinced the cultured audiences in Europe and America, that Hinduism fulfils all the requirements of the ideal of a universal religion, and adapts itself to the temperament and needs of men and women of all races and creeds. Animated purely by a disinterested impulse, influenced by the best of motives and at considerable self-sacrifice, your Holiness has crossed boundless seas and oceans to convey the message of truth and peace, and to plant the flag of India's spiritual triumph and glory, in the rich soil of Europe and America. Your Holiness has, both by precept and practice, shown the feasibility and importance of universal brotherhood. Above all, your labours in the West have indirectly and to a great extent tended to awaken the apathetic sons and daughters of India to a sense of the greatness and glory of their ancestral faith, and to create in them a genuine interest in the study and observance of their dear and priceless religion.

We feel we cannot adequately convey in words our feelings of gratitude and thankfulness to your Holiness for your philanthropic labours towards the spiritual regeneration of the East and the West. We cannot close this address without referring to the great kindness which your Holiness has always extended to our Rajah, who is one of your devoted disciples, and the honour and pride he feels by this gracious act of your Holiness in landing first on his territory, is indescribable.

In conclusion, we pray to the Almighty to bless your Holiness with long life, and health and strength to enable you to carry on the good work that has been so ably inaugurated by you.

With respects and love,
We beg to subscribe ourselves,

Your Holiness's most devoted and obedient disciples and servants.

Ramnad,
25th January 1897.

D

The Swami's reply follows *in extenso*:—

The longest night seems to be passing away, the sorest trouble seems to be coming to an end at last, the seeming corpse appears to be awaking, and a voice is coming to us,—away back where history and even tradition fails to peep into the gloom of the past, coming down from there, reflected as it were, from peak to peak of the infinite Himalaya of knowledge, and of love, and of work, India, this motherland of ours,—a voice is coming unto us, gentle, firm, and yet unmistakable in its utterances, and is gaining volume as days pass by, and behold, the sleeper is awakening! Like a breeze from the Himalayas, it is bringing life into the almost dead bones and muscles, the lethargy is passing away, and only the blind cannot see, or the perverted will not see, that she is awakening, this motherland of ours, from her deep long sleep. None can resist her any more; never is she going to sleep any more; no outward powers can hold her back any more; for the infinite giant is rising to her feet.

Your Highness and gentlemen of Ramnad, accept my heart-felt thanks for the cordiality and kindness with which you have received me. I feel that you are cordial and kind, for, heart speaks unto heart better than any language of the mouth; spirit speaks unto spirit in silence, and yet in most unmistakable language, and I feel it in my heart of hearts. Your Highness of Ramnad, if there has been any work done by my humble self in the cause of our religion and our motherland, in the Western countries, if any little work has been done in rousing the sympathies of our own people, by drawing their attention to the inestimable jewels that they know not, are lying deep buried, about their own home,—if, instead of dying of thirst and drinking dirty ditch water elsewhere, out of the blindness of ignorance, they are being called to go and drink from the eternal fountain, which is flowing perennially by their own homes—if anything has been done to rouse our people towards action, to make them understand that in everything, religion and religion alone is the life of India, and when that goes India will die, in spite of politics, in spite of social reforms, in spite of Kubera's wealth poured upon the head of every one of her children,—if anything has been done towards this end, India and every country where any work has been done, owe much of it to you, Rajah of Ramnad. For it was you who gave me the idea first, and it was you who persistently urged me on towards the work. You, as it were, intuitively understood what was going to be, and took me by the hand, helped me all along, and have never ceased to encourage me. Well is it therefore, that you should be the first to rejoice at my success, and meet it is that I should first land in your territory on my return to India. Great works are to be done, wonderful powers have to be worked out, we have to teach other nations many things, as has been said already by your Highness. This is the motherland of philosophy, of spirituality, and of ethics, of sweetness, gentleness, and love. These still exist, and my experience of the world leads me to stand on firm ground, and make the bold statement, that India is still the first and foremost of all the nations of the world in these respects. Look at this little phenomenon. There have been immense political changes within the last four or five years. Gigantic organisations undertaking to subvert the whole of existing institutions in different countries and meeting with a certain amount of success, have been working all over the Western world. Ask our people if they have heard anything about them? They have heard not a word about them. But that there was a Parliament of Religions in Chicago, and that there was a Sannyâsin sent over from India to that Parliament, and that he was very well received, and since that time has been working in the West, the poorest beggar has known. I have heard that our masses are dense, that they do not want any education, and that they do not care for any information. I had at one time a foolish leaning towards that opinion myself, but I find experience is a far more glorious teacher than any amount of speculation, or any amount of books written by globe-trotters and hasty observers. This experience teaches me that they are not dense, that they are not slow, that they are as eager and thirsty for information as any race under the sun; but then each nation has its own part to play, and naturally, each nation has its own peculiarity and individuality, with which it is born. Each represents, as it were, one peculiar note in this harmony of nations, and this is its very life, its vitality. In it, is the backbone, the foundation, and the bedrock of the national life, and here in this blessed land, the foundation, the backbone, the life-centre is religion and religion alone. Let others talk of politics, of the glory of acquisition of immense wealth poured in by trade, of the power and spread of commercialism, of the glorious fountain of physical liberty, but these the Hindu mind does not understand and does not want to understand. Touch him on spirituality, on religion, on God, on the soul, on the Infinite, on spiritual freedom, and I assure you, the lowest peasant in India is better informed on these subjects than many a so-called philosopher in other lands. I have said, gentlemen, that we have yet something to teach to the world. This is the very reason, the *raison d'être*, that this nation should live on, in spite of hundreds of years of persecution, in spite of nearly a thousand years of foreign rule and foreign oppression. This nation still lives; the *raison d'être* is, because it still holds to God, to the treasure-house of religion and spirituality.

In this land, religion and spirituality are still the fountains which will have to overflow and flood the world, to bring in new life and new vitality to the Western and other nations, which are now almost borne down, half-killed and degraded by political ambitions and social scheming. From out of the many voices, consonant and dissentient, from out of the medley of sounds filling the Indian atmosphere, rises up supreme, striking, and full, one note, and that is renunciation. Give up! That is the watchword of the Indian religions. This world is a delusion of two days. The present life is of five minutes. Beyond is the Infinite, beyond this world of delusion; let us seek that. This continent is illumined with brave and gigantic minds and intelligences who even think of this so-called infinite universe as only a mudpuddle; beyond and still beyond they go. Time, even infinite time is to them but non-existence. Beyond and beyond time they go. Space is nothing to them; beyond that they want to go, and this going beyond the phenomenal is the very soul of religion. The characteristic of my nation is this transcendentalism, the struggle to go beyond, this daring to tear the veil off the face of nature and have at any risk, at any price, a glimpse of the beyond. That is our ideal, but of course all the people in a country cannot give up entirely. Do you want to enthuse them, then here is the way to do so. Your talks of politics, of social regeneration, your talks of money-making, and commercialism—all these will roll off like water from a duck's back. This spirituality, then, is what you have to teach the world. Have we to learn anything else, have we to learn anything from the world? We have, perhaps to gain a little in material knowledge, in the power of organisation, in the ability to handle powers, organising powers, in bringing the best results out of the smallest of causes. This perhaps to a certain extent we may learn from the West. But if any one preaches in India the ideal of eating and drinking and making merry, if any one wants to apotheosise the material world into a God, that man is a liar; he has no place in this holy land, the Indian mind does not want to listen to him. Aye, in spite of the sparkle and glitter of Western civilisation, in spite of all its polish and its marvellous manifestation of power, standing upon this platform, I tell them to their face, that it is all vain. It is vanity of vanities. God alone lives. The soul alone lives. Spirituality alone lives. Hold on to that.

Yet, perhaps, some sort of materialism, toned down to our own requirements, would be a blessing to many of our brothers who are not yet ripe for the highest truths. This is the one mistake made in every country and in every society, and it is a greatly regrettable thing that in India, where it was always understood, the same mistake of forcing the highest truths on to people who are not ready for them, has been made of late. My method need not be yours. The Sannyâsin, as you all know, is the ideal of the Hindu's life, and every one by our Shastras is compelled to give up. Every Hindu who has tasted the fruits of this world must give up in the latter part of his life, and he who does not is not a Hindu, and has no more right to call himself a Hindu. We know that this is the ideal—to give up after seeing and experiencing the vanity of things. Having found out that the heart of the material world is a mere hollow, containing only ashes, give it up and go back. The mind is circling forward, as it were, towards the senses, and that mind has to circle backwards; the *Pravritti* has to stop and the *Nivritti* has to begin. That is the ideal. But that ideal can only be realised after a certain amount of experience. We cannot teach the child the truth of renunciation; the child is a born optimist; his whole life is in his senses; his whole life is one mass of sense-enjoyment. So there are child-like men in every society, who require a certain amount of experience, of enjoyment, to see through the vanity of it, and then renunciation will come to them. There have been ample provision made for them in our Books; but unfortunately, in later times, there is a tendency to bind every one down by the same laws as those by which the Sannyasin is bound, and that is a great mistake. But for that a good deal of the poverty and the misery that you see in India need not have been. A poor man's life is hemmed in and bound down by tremendous spiritual and ethical laws for which he has no use. Hands off! Let the poor fellow enjoy himself a little, and then he will raise himself up and renunciation will come to him of itself. Perhaps in this line, we can be taught something by the western people, but we must be very cautious in learning these things. I am sorry to say that most of the examples one meets nowadays, of men who have imbibed the western ideas, are more or less failures. There are two great obstacles on our path in India, the Scylla of old orthodoxy, and the Charybdis of modern European civilisation. Of these two, I vote for the old orthodoxy, and not for the Europeanised system; for the old orthodox man may be ignorant, he may be crude, but he is a man, he has a faith, he has strength, he stands on his own feet; while the Europeanised man has no backbone, he is a mass of heterogeneous ideas picked up at random from every source—and these ideas are unassimilated, undigested, unharmonised. He does not stand on his own feet, and his head is turning round and round. Where is the motive power of his work?—in a few patronising pats from the English people. His schemes of reforms, his vehement vituperations against the evils of certain social customs have, as the mainspring, some European patronage. Why are some of our customs called evils? Because the Europeans say so. That is about the reason he gives. I would not submit to that. Stand and die in your own strength; if there is any sin in the world, it is weakness; avoid all weakness, for weakness is sin, weakness is death. These unbalanced creatures are not yet formed into distinct personalities; what are we to call them—men, women or animals? While those old orthodox people were staunch and were men. There are still some excellent examples, and the one I want to present before you now, is your Rajah of Ramnad. Here, you have a man than whom there is a no more zealous Hindu throughout the length and breadth of this land; here, you have a prince than whom there is no prince in this land better informed in all affairs, both oriental and occidental, who takes from every nation whatever he can that is good. "Learn good knowledge with all devotion from the lowest caste. Learn the way to freedom, even if it comes from a Pariah, by serving him. If a woman is a jewel, take her in marriage even if she comes from a low family of the lowest caste." Such is the law laid down by our great and peerless legislator, the divine Manu. This is true. Stand on your own feet, and assimilate what you can; but learn from every nation, take what is of use to you, but remember that as Hindus everything else must be subordinated to our own national ideals. Each man has a mission in life, which is the result of all his infinite past Karma. Each of you was born with a splendid heritage, which is the whole of the infinite past life of your glorious nation. Millions of your ancestors are watching, as it were, every action of yours, so be alert. And what is the mission with which every Hindu child is born? Have you not read the proud declaration of Manu regarding the Brahmana where he says, that the birth of the Brahmana is—"for the protection of the treasury of religion." I should say that *that* is the mission not only of the Brahmana, but of every child, whether boy or girl, who is born in this blessed land,—"for the protection of the treasure of religion." And every other problem in life must be subordinated to that one principal theme. That is also the law of harmony in music. There may be a nation whose theme of life is political supremacy; religion and everything else must become subordinate to that one great theme of its life. But here is another nation whose great theme of life is spirituality and renunciation, whose one watchword is, that this world is all vanity and a delusion of three days; and everything else, whether science or knowledge, enjoyments or powers, wealth, name or fame, must be subordinated to that one theme. The secret of a true Hindu's character lies in the subordination of his knowledge of European sciences and learning, of his wealth, position, and name, to that one principal theme which is inborn in every Hindu child—the spirituality and purity of the race. Therefore, between these two, the case of the orthodox man who has the whole of that life-spring of the race, spirituality, and the other man, whose hands are full of western imitation-jewels but has no hold on the life-giving principle, spirituality,—of these, I do not doubt that every one here will agree that we should choose the first, the orthodox, because there is some hope in him. He has the national theme and something to hold to, so he will live, but the other will die. Just as in the case of individuals, if the principle of life is undisturbed, if the principal function of that individual life is present, any injuries received as regards other functions are not serious—other functions never become constant. So long as this principal function of our life is not disturbed, nothing can destroy our nation. But mark you, if you give up that spirituality, leaving it aside to go after the materialising civilisation of the West, the result will be that in three generations you will be an extinct race; because, the backbone of the nation will be broken, the foundation upon which the national edifice has been built will be undermined, and the result will be annihilation all round.

Therefore, my friends, the way out is, that first and foremost we must keep a firm hold on spirituality—that inestimable gift handed down to us by our ancient forefathers. Did you ever hear of a country, where the greatest kings tried to trace their descent, not to kings, not to robber-barons living in old castles, who plundered poor travellers, but to semi-naked sages who lived in the forest? Did you ever hear of such a land? This is the land. In other countries great priests try to trace their descent to some king, but here, the greatest kings would trace their descent to some ancient priest. Therefore, whether you believe in spirituality or not, for the sake of the national life, you have to get a hold on spirituality and keep to it. Then stretch the other hand out and gain all you can from other races, but everything must be subordinated to that one ideal of life; and out of that a wonderful, glorious, future India will come—I am sure it is coming—a greater India than ever was. Sages will spring up greater than all the ancient sages, and your ancestors will not only be satisfied, but I am sure, they will be proud, from their positions in other worlds, to look down upon their descendants, so glorious, and so great. Let us all work hard, my brethren, this is no time for sleep. On our work depends the coming of the India of the future. She is there ready waiting. She is only sleeping. Arise, and awake and see her seated here, on her eternal throne, rejuvenated, more glorious than she ever was—this motherland of ours. The idea of God was nowhere else ever so fully developed as in this motherland of ours, for the same idea of God never existed anywhere else. Perhaps you are astonished at my assertion, but show me any idea of God from any other scriptures equal to ours; they have only clan-Gods, the God of the Jews, the God of the Arabs, and of such and such a race, and their God is fighting the Gods of the other races. But the idea of that beneficent, most merciful God, our father, our mother, our friend, the friend of our friends, the soul of our souls, is here and here alone. And may He who is the Siva of the Sivaites, the Vishnu of the Vaisnavites, the Karma of the Karmis, the Buddha of the Buddhists, the Jina of the Jains, the Jehovah of the Christians and the Jews, the Allah of the Mohammedans, the Lord of every sect, the Brahman of the Vedántists, He, the all-pervading, whose glory has been known only in this land,—may He bless us, may He help us, may He give strength unto us, energy unto us, to carry this idea into practice. May that which we have listened to and studied become food to us, may it become strength in us, may it become energy in us to help each other; may we, the teacher and the taught, not be jealous of each other! Peace, peace, peace, in the name of Hari.

REPLY TO THE ADDRESS OF WELCOME AT PARAMAKUDI.

Paramakudi was the first stopping-place after leaving Ramnad, and there was a demonstration on a large scale, including the presentation of the following address:—

SREEMAT VIVEKANANDA SWAMI.

We, the citizens of Paramakudi, respectfully beg to accord to your Holiness a most hearty welcome to this place after your successful spiritual campaign of nearly four years in the Western world.

We share with our countrymen the feelings of joy and pride at the philanthropy which prompted you to attend the Parliament of Religions held at Chicago, and lay before the representatives of the religious world the sacred but hidden treasures of our ancient land. You have by your wide exposition of the sacred truths contained in the Vedic literature, disabused the enlightened minds of the West of the prejudices entertained by them against our ancient faith, and convinced them of its universality and adaptability for intellects of all shades and in all ages.

The presence amongst us of your Western disciples is proof positive that your religious teachings have not only been understood in theory but have also borne practical fruits. The magnetic influence of your august person reminds us of our ancient holy Rishis, whose realisation of the Self by asceticism and self-control made them the true guides and preceptors of the human race.

In conclusion we most earnestly pray to the All-Merciful, that your Holiness may long be spared to continue to bless and spiritualise the whole of mankind.

With best regards,
We beg to subscribe ourselves,
Your Holiness's most obedient and devoted
Disciples and Servants.

In the course of his reply the Swami said,—

It is almost impossible to express my thanks for the kindness and cordiality with which you have received me. But, if I may be permitted to say so, I will add that love for my country, and especially for my countrymen, will be the same whether they receive me with the utmost cordiality, or spurn me from the country. For we read in the Gita that Sri Krishna says—men should work for work's sake only, and love for love's sake. The work that has been done by me in the Western world has been very little; there is no one present here who could not have done a hundred times more work in the West than has been done by me. And I am anxiously waiting for the day when mighty minds will arise, gigantic spiritual minds, who will be ready to go forth from India to the ends of the world, to teach spirituality and renunciation, those ideas which came from the forests of India, and belong to Indian soil alone. There come periods in the history of the human race when, as it were, whole nations are seized with a sort of world-weariness, when they find that all their plans are slipping between their fingers, that old institutions and systems are crumbling into dust, that their hopes are all blighted, and everything seems to be out of joint. Two attempts have been made in the world to found social life; the one was upon religion, and the other was upon social necessity. The one was founded upon spirituality, the other upon materialism, the one upon transcendentalism, the other upon realism. The one looks beyond the horizon of this little material world and is bold enough to begin life there, even apart from the other. The other, the second, is content to take its stand on the things of the world and expects to find a firm footing. Curiously enough, it seems that at times the spiritual side prevails, and then the materialistic side, in wavelike motions following each other. In the same country there will be different tides; at one time the full flood of materialistic ideas prevails; and everything in this life—prosperity, the education which procures more pleasure, more food—will become glorious at first and then, that will degrade and degenerate. Along with the prosperity, will rise to white heat all the inborn jealousies and hatreds of the human race. Competition and merciless cruelty will be the watchword of the day. To quote a very commonplace and not very elegant English proverb, "Everyone for himself, and the devil take the hindmost" becomes the motto of the day. Then people think that the whole scheme of life is a failure. And the world would be destroyed did not spirituality come to the rescue, and lend a helping hand to the sinking world. Then the world gets new hope, and finds a new basis for a new building, and another wave of spirituality comes, which in time again declines. As a rule, spirituality brings a class of men who lay exclusive claim to the special powers of the world. The immediate effect of this is a reaction towards materialism, which opens the door to scores of exclusive claims, until the time comes when not only all the spiritual powers of the race, but all its material powers and privileges are centered in the hands of a very few; and these few, standing on the necks of the masses of the people, want to rule them. Then society has to help itself, and materialism comes to the rescue. If you look at India, our motherland, you will see that the same thing is going on now. That you are here to-day to welcome one who went to Europe to preach Vedanta, would have been impossible had not the materialism of Europe opened the way for it. Materialism has come to the rescue of India in a certain sense, by throwing open the doors of life to everyone, by destroying the exclusive privileges of caste, by opening up to discussion the inestimable treasures which were hidden away in the hands of a very few, who have even lost the use of them. Half has been stolen and lost, and the other half which remains, is in the hands of men who, like dogs in the manger, do not eat themselves and will not allow others to do so. On the other hand, the political systems that we are struggling for in India, have been in Europe for ages, have been tried for centuries, and have been found wanting. One after another, the institutions, systems, and everything connected with political governments have been condemned as useless, and Europe is restless, does not know where to turn. The material tyranny is tremendous. The wealth and power of a country are in the hands of a few men who do not work, but manipulate the work of millions of human beings. By this power they can deluge the whole earth with blood. Religion and all things are under their feet; they rule and stand supreme. The western world is governed by a handful of Shylocks. All those things that you hear about—constitutional government, freedom, liberty and parliaments—are but jokes. The West is groaning under the tyranny of the Shylocks, and the East is groaning under the tyranny of the Priests; each must keep the other in check. Do not think that one alone is to help the world. In this creation of the impartial Lord, He has made equal every particle in the universe. The worst, most demoniacal man, has some virtues which the greatest saint has not, and the lowest worm may have certain things which the highest man has not. The poor labourer, who you think has so little enjoyment in life, has not your intellect, cannot understand the Vedanta Philosophy and so forth, but compare your body to his, and you will see, his body is nothing like so sensitive to pain as yours. If he gets severe cuts on his body, they heal up more quickly than yours would. His life is in the senses, and he enjoys there. His life is one of equilibrium and balance. Whether on the ground of materialism, or of intellect, or of spirituality, the compensation that is given by the Lord to every one impartially, is exactly the same. Therefore we must not think that we are the saviours of the world. We can teach the world a good many things, and we can learn a good many things from it, too. We can teach the world, only what it is waiting for. The whole of western civilisation will crumble to pieces in the next fifty years if there is no spiritual foundation. It is hopeless and perfectly useless to attempt to govern mankind with the sword. You will find that the very centres from which such ideas as government by force sprang up, are the very first centres to degrade and degenerate and crumble to pieces. Europe, the centre of the manifestation of material energy, will crumble into dust within fifty years, if she is not mindful to change her position, to shift her ground and make spirituality the basis of her life. And what will save Europe is the religion of the Upanishads. Apart from the different sects, philosophies and scriptures, there is one underlying doctrine, the belief in the soul of man, the Atman, common to all our sects, and that can change the whole tendency of the world. With Hindus, Jains and Buddhists, in fact everywhere in India, there is the idea of a spiritual soul which is the receptacle of all power. And you know full well, that there is not one system of philosophy in India which teaches you that you can get power, or purity, or perfection from outside, but they all tell you that these are your birthright, your nature. Impurity is a mere super-imposition, under which your real nature has become hidden. But the real *you* is already perfect, already strong. You do not require any assistance to govern yourself; you are already self-restrained. The only difference is in knowing it or not knowing it. Therefore the one difficulty has been summed up in the word, *avidya*. What makes the difference between God and man, between the saint and the sinner? Only ignorance. What is the difference between the highest man and the lowest worm that crawls under your feet? Ignorance; that makes all the difference. For inside that little crawling worm is lodged infinite power, and knowledge, and purity, the infinite divinity of God Himself. It is unmanifested; it will have to be manifested. This is the one great truth India has to teach to the world, because it is nowhere else. This is spirituality, the science of the soul. What makes a man stand up and work? Strength. Strength is goodness, weakness is sin. If there is one word that you find come out like a bomb from the Upanishads, bursting like a bombshell upon masses of ignorance, it is the word, fearlessness. And the only religion that ought to be taught, is the religion of *fearlessness*. Either in this world or in the world of religion, it is true that fear is the sure cause of degradation and sin. It is fear that brings misery, fear that brings death, fear that breeds evil. And what causes fear? Ignorance of our own nature. Each of us is heir-apparent to the Emperor of Emperors; we are of the substance of God Himself. Nay, according to the Advaita you are God Himself and you have forgotten your own nature in thinking of yourselves as little men. We have fallen from that nature and thus make differences—I am a little better than you, or you than I, and so on. This idea of oneness is the great lesson India has to give, and, mark you, when this is understood it changes the whole aspect of things, because you look at the world through other eyes than you have been doing before. And this world is no more a battle-field where each soul is born to struggle with every other soul, and the strongest gets the victory and the weakest goes to death. It becomes a play-ground where the Lord is playing like a child, and we are His playmates, His fellow-workers. This is only a play, however terrible, hideous and dangerous it may appear. We have mistaken its aspect. When we have known the nature of the soul, hope comes to the weakest, to the most degraded, to the most miserable sinner. Only, declares your Shastra, despair not. For you are the same whatever you do, and you cannot change your nature. Nature itself cannot destroy nature. Your nature is pure. It may be hidden for millions of æons, but at last it will conquer and come out. Therefore the Advaita brings hope to every one and not despair. Its teaching is not through fear; it teaches, not of devils who are always on the watch to snatch you if you miss your footing,—it has nothing to do with devils,—but says that you have taken your fate in your own hands. Your own Karma has manufactured for you this body, and nobody did it for you. The Omnipresent Lord has been hidden through ignorance, and the responsibility is on yourself. You have not to think that you were brought into the world without your choice, and left in this most horrible place, but to know that you have yourself manufactured your body, bit by bit, just as you are doing it this very moment. You yourself eat; nobody eats for you. You assimilate what you eat; no one does it for you. You make blood, and muscles and body out of the food; nobody does it for you. So you have done all the time. One link in a chain explains the infinite chain. If it is true for one moment that you manufacture your body, it is true for every moment, that has been or will come. And all the responsibility of good and evil is on you. This is the great hope. What I have done, that I can undo. And at the same time our religion does not take away from mankind, the mercy of the Lord. That is always there. On the other hand, He stands besides this tremendous current of good and evil; He the bondless, the ever-merciful, is always ready to help us to the other shore, for His mercy is great, and it always comes to the pure in heart.

Your spirituality, in a certain sense, will have to form the basis of the new orders of society. If I had more time, I could show you how the West has yet more to learn from some of the conclusions of the Advaita, for in these days of materialistic science the ideal of the Personal God does not count for much. But yet, even if a man has a very crude form of religion, and wants temples and forms, he can have as many as he likes; if he wants a Personal God to love, he can find here the noblest ideas of a Personal God such as were never attained anywhere else in the world. If a man wants to be a rationalist and satisfy his reason—it is also here that he can find the most rational ideas of the Impersonal.

REPLY TO THE ADDRESS OF WELCOME AT SIVAGANGA AND MANAMADURA.

At Manamadura, the following address of welcome from the Zemindars and citizens of Sivaganga and Manamadura, was presented to the Swami :—

To Sri Swami Vivekananda.

Most Revered Sir,—

We, the Zemindars and citizens of Sivaganga and Manamadura, beg to offer you a most hearty welcome. In the most sanguine moments of our life, in our wildest dreams, we never contemplated that you, who were so near our hearts, would be in such close proximity to our homes. The first wire intimating your inability to come to Sivaganga, cast a deep gloom on our hearts, and but for the subsequent silver lining to the cloud our disappointment would have been extreme. When we first heard that you had consented to honour our town with your presence, we thought we had realised our highest ambition. The mountain promised to come to Mahomet, and our joy knew no bounds. But when the mountain was obliged to withdraw its consent, our worst fears were roused that we might not be able even to go to the mountain, you were graciously pleased to give way to our importunities.

Despite the almost insurmountable difficulties of the voyage, the noble self-sacrificing spirit with which you have conveyed the grandest message of the East to the West, the masterly way in which the mission has been executed and the marvellous and unparalleled success which has crowned your philanthrophic efforts, have earned for you an undying glory. At a time, when Western bread-winning materialism was making the strongest inroads on Indian religious convictions, when the sayings and writings of our sages were beginning to be numbered, the advent of a new master like you has already marked an era in the annals of religious advancement, and we hope that in the fulness of time you will succeed in disintegrating the dross that is temporarily covering the genuine gold of Indian Philosophy, and casting it in the powerful mint of your intellect will make it current coin throughout the whole globe. The Catholicity with which you were able triumphantly to bear the flag of Indian Philosophic thought among the heterogeneous religionists assembled in the Parliament of Religions, enables us to hope that at no distant date you, just like your contemporary in the political sphere, will rule an empire over which the sun never sets, only with this difference, that hers is an empire over matter, and yours will be over mind. As she has beaten all records in political history by the length and beneficence of her reign, so we earnestly pray to the Almighty that you will be spared long enough to consummate the labour of love that you have so disinterestedly undertaken, and thus to outshine all your predecessors in spiritual history.

We are,

Most Revered Sir,

Your most dutiful and devoted Servants.

The Swami's reply was to the following effect :—

I cannot express the deep debt of gratitude which you have laid upon me by the kind and warm welcome which has just been accorded to me by you. Unfortunately I am not just now in a condition to make a very big speech, however I may wish it. In spite of the beautiful adjectives which our Sanskrit friend has been so kind as to apply to me, I have a body after all, foolish though it may be, and the body always follows the promptings, conditions and laws of matter. As such, there is such a thing as fatigue and weariness as regards the material body. It is a great thing to see the wonderful amount of joy and appreciation expressed in every part of the country, for the little work that has been done by me in the West. I look at it only in this way: I want to apply it to those great souls who are coming in the future. If the little bit of work that has been done by me receives such approbation from the nation, what must be the approbation that the spiritual giants, the world-movers coming after us, will get from this nation? India is the land of religion; the Hindu understands religion, and religion alone. Centuries of education have always been in that line, and the result is, that it is the one concern in life, and you all know well that it is so. It is not necessary that every one should be a shopkeeper; it is not necessary even that every one should be a schoolmaster; it is not necessary that every one should be a fighter, but in this world there will be different nations producing the harmony of result. Well, perhaps we are fated by Divine Providence to play the spiritual note in this harmony of nations, and it rejoices me to see that we have not yet lost the grand traditions which have been handed down to us by the most glorious forefathers of whom any nation can be proud. It gives me hope, it gives me adamantine faith in the destiny of the race. It cheers me, not for the personal attention paid to me, but to know that the heart of the nation is there, and is still sound. India is still living; who says she is dead? But the West wants to see us active. If they want to see us active on the field of battle they will be disappointed —that is not our field; just as we would be disappointed if we hoped to see a military nation active on the field of spirituality. But let them come here and see that we are equally active and how the nation is living, and is as alive as ever. We should dispel the idea that we have degenerated at all. So far so good. But now I have to say a few harsh words, which I hope you will not take unkindly. For the complaint has just been made that European Materialism has well nigh swamped us. It is not all the fault of the Europeans, but a good deal our own. We, as Vedântists must always look at things from an introspective viewpoint, from its subjective relations. We, as Vedântists, know for certain that there is no power in the universe to injure us unless we first injure ourselves. One-fifth of the population of India have been Mahommedans. Just as before that, going further back, two-thirds of the population in ancient times had become Buddhists; one-fifth are now Mahommedans. Christians are already more than a million. Whose fault is it? One of our historians says in ever-memorable language—Why should these poor wretches starve and die of thirst when the perennial fountain of life is flowing by? The question is, what did we do for these people who forsook their own religion? Why should they have become Mahommedans? I heard of an honest girl in England who was going to become a street-walker. When a lady asked her not to do so, her reply was, "That is the only way I can get sympathy, I can find none to help me now, but let me be a fallen, down-trodden woman, and then perhaps merciful ladies will come and take me to a home and do everything they can for me." We are weeping for these renegades now, but what did we do for them before? Let every one of us ask ourselves, what have we learnt; have we taken hold of the torch of truth, and if so, how far did we carry it? We did not help them then. This is the question we should ask ourselves. That we did not do so was our own fault, our own Karma. Let us blame none, let us blame our own Karma. Materialism, or Mohammedanism, or Christianity, or any other ism in the world could never have succeeded but that you allowed them. No bacilli can attack the human frame until it is degraded and degenerated by vice, bad food, privation, and exposure; the healthy man passes scatheless through masses of poisonous bacilli. And yet there is time to change our ways. Give up all those old discussions, old fights about things which are meaningless, which are nonsensical in their very nature. Think of the last six hundred or seven hundred years of degradation, when grown-up men by the hundreds have been discussing for years, whether we should drink a glass of water with the right hand or the left, whether the hand should be washed three times or four times, whether we should gargle five or six times. What can you expect from men who pass their lives in discussing such momentous questions as these; and writing most learned philosophies on them! There is a danger of our religion getting into the kitchen. We are neither Vedântists, most of us now, nor Paurânics, nor Tântrics. We are just "Don't-touchists." Our religion is the kitchen. Our God is the cooking-pot, and our religion is "Don't touch me, I am holy." If this goes on for another century, every one of us will be in a lunatic asylum. It is a sure sign of softening of the brain when the mind cannot grasp the higher problems of life; all originality is lost, the mind has lost all its strength, its activity, and its power of thought, and just tries to go round and round the smallest curve it can find. This state of things has first to be thrown overboard, and then we must stand up, be active and strong; and then we shall recognise our heritage to that infinite treasure, the treasure our forefathers have left for us, a treasure that the whole world requires to-day. The world will die if this treasure is not distributed. Bring it out, distribute it broadcast. Says Vyâsa, giving is the one work alone in this *Kali Yuga*, and of all the gifts, giving spiritual life is the highest gift possible; the next gift is secular knowledge; the next, saving the life of man, and the last, giving food to the needy. Of food we have given enough; no nation is more charitable than we. So long as there is a piece of bread in the home of the beggar he will give half of it. Such a phenomenon can be observed only in India. We have enough of that, let us go for the other two, the gifts of spiritual and secular knowledge. And if we were all brave and had stout hearts, and with absolute sincerity put our shoulders to the wheel, in twenty-five years the whole problem would be solved, and there would be nothing left here to fight about, but the whole Indian world would be once more Aryan. This is all I have to tell you now. I am not given much to talking about plans; I rather prefer to do and show, and then talk about my plans. I have my plans, and mean to work them out if the Lord wills it, and if life is given to me. I do not know whether I shall succeed or not, but it is a great thing to take up a grand ideal in life and then give up one's whole life to it. For what otherwise is the value of life, this vegetating, little, low, life of man? Subordinating it to one high ideal is the only value that life has. This is the great work to be done in India. I welcome the present religious revival, and I should be foolish if I lost the opportunity of striking the iron while it is hot.

REPLY TO THE ADDRESS OF WELCOME AT MADURA.

The Swami was presented with an address of welcome by the Hindus of Madura, which read as follows :—

Most Revered Swami.

We the Hindu Public of Madura beg to offer you our most heartfelt and respectful welcome to our ancient and holy city. We realise in you a living example of the Hindu Sannyasin, who renouncing all worldly ties and attachments calculated to lead to the gratification of the self, is worthily engaged in the noble duty of living for others and endeavouring to raise the spiritual condition of mankind. You have demonstrated in your own person that the true essence of the Hindu Religion, is not necessarily bound up with rules and rituals, but that it is a sublime philosophy capable of giving peace and solace to the distressed and afflicted.

You have taught America and England to admire that philosophy and that religion which seeks to elevate every man in the best manner suited to his capacities and environments. Although your teachings have for the last three years been delivered in foreign lands, they have not been the less eagerly devoured in this country and they have not a little tended to counteract the growing materialism imported from a foreign soil.

India lives to this day, for it has a mission to fulfil in the spiritual ordering of the universe. The appearance of a soul like you at the close of this cycle of the *Kali Yuga*, is to us a sure sign of the incarnation in the near future of great souls through whom that mission will be fulfilled.

Madura, the seat of ancient learning, Madura the favoured city of the God Sundareswara, the holy Dwadasantakshetram of Yogis, lags behind no other Indian city in its warm admiration of your exposition of Indian Philosophy and in its grateful acknowledgments of your priceless services for humanity.

We pray that you may be blessed with a long life of vigour and strength and usefulness.

The Swami replied in the following terms :—

I wish I could live in your midst for several days, and fulfil the conditions that have just been pointed out by your most worthy Chairman, of relating to you my experiences in the West, and the result of all my labours there for the last four years. But, unfortunately, even Swamis have bodies; and the continuous travelling and speaking that I have had to undergo for the last three weeks, make it impossible for me to deliver a very long speech this evening. I will therefore satisfy myself with thanking you very cordially for the kindness that has been shown to me, and reserve other things for some day in the future, when under better conditions of health, we shall have time to talk over more various subjects than we can do in so short a time this evening. Being in Madura, as the guest of one of your well-known citizens and noblemen, the Rajah of Ramnad, one fact comes prominently to my mind. Perhaps most of you are aware that it was the Rajah who first put the idea into my mind of going to Chicago, and it was he who all the time supported it with all his heart and influence. A good deal, therefore, of the praise that has been bestowed upon me in this address, ought to go to this noble man of Southern India. I only wish that instead of becoming a Rajah he had become a Sannyâsin, for that is what he is really fit for.

Wherever there is a thing really needed in one part of the world, the complement will find its way there and supply it with new life. This is true in the physical world, as well as in the spiritual. If there is a want of spirituality in one part of the world, and at the same time that spirituality exists elsewhere, whether we consciously struggle for it or not, that spirituality will find its way to the part where it is needed, and balance the inequality. In the history of the human race, not once or twice, but again and again, it has been the destiny of India in the past to supply spirituality to the world; and, as such, we find that wherever either by mighty conquest or by commercial supremacy, different parts of the world have been kneaded into one whole race, and bequests have been made from one corner to the other, each nation, as it were, poured forth its own quota, either political, social, or spiritual. India's contribution to the sum-total of human knowledge has been spirituality, philosophy. These she contributed even long before the rising of the Persian Empire; the second time was during the Persian Empire; for the third time, during the ascendency of the Greeks; and now for the fourth time during the ascendency of the English, she is going to fulfil the same destiny once more. As Western ideas of organisation and external civilisation are penetrating and pouring into our country, whether we will have them or not, so, Indian spirituality and philosophy are deluging the lands of the West. None can resist it, and no more can we resist some sort of material civilisation from the West. A little of it, perhaps, is good for us, and a little spiritualisation is good for the West; thus the balance will be preserved. It is not that we ought to learn everything from the West, or that they have to learn everything from us, but each will have to supply and hand down to future generations what it has, for the future accomplishment of that dream of ages, the harmony of nations, an ideal world. Whether that ideal world will ever come I do not know, whether that social perfection will ever be reached, I have my own doubts about it; but, whether it comes or not, each one of us will have to work for the idea as if it will come to-morrow, and as if it only depends on his work, and his alone. Each one of us will have to believe that every one else in the world has done his work, and the only work remaining to be done to make the world perfect has to be done by himself. This is the responsibility we have to take upon ourselves. In the meanwhile in India there is a tremendous revival of religion. There is danger ahead, as well as glory, for, revival sometimes breeds fanaticism, sometimes goes to the extreme, so that often it is not even in the power of those who start the revival to control it when it has gone beyond a certain length. It is better, therefore, to be forewarned. We have to find our way between the Scylla of old superstitious orthodoxy, and the Charybdis of materialism,—of Europeanism, of soullessness, of the so-called reform,—which has penetrated to the foundation of Western progress. These two have to be taken care of. In the first place we cannot become Westerns, therefore imitating the Westerns is useless. Suppose you can imitate the Westerns, that moment you will die, you will have no more life in you. In the second place, it is impossible. A stream is taking its rise, away beyond where time began, flowing through millions of ages of human history; do you mean to get hold of that stream, and push it back to its source, to a Himalayan glacier? Even if that were practicable it would not be possible for you to be Europeanised. If you find it is impossible for the European to throw off the few centuries of culture which there is in the West, do you think it is possible for you to throw off the culture of shining scores of centuries? It cannot be. We must also remember that in every little village-god, and every little superstitious custom, is that which we are accustomed to call our religious faith. Local customs are infinite and contradictory; which are we to obey, and which not to obey? The Brâhman in Southern India, for instance, would shrink in horror at the sight of another Brâhman eating meat; a Bráhman in the North thinks it a most glorious and holy thing to do—he kills goats by the hundred in sacrifice. If you put forward your custom they are equally ready with theirs. Various are the customs all over India, but they are local. The greatest mistake made is, that ignorant people always think that this local custom is the essence of our religion.

But beyond this there is a still greater difficulty. There are two sorts of truths we find in our Shastras, one that is based upon the eternal nature of man—the one that deals with the eternal relation of God, soul, and nature; the other, with local circumstances, environments of the time, social institutions of the period, and so forth. The first class of truths is chiefly embodied in our Vedas, our scriptures; the second in the Smritis, the Purânas, etc. We must remember that for all periods the Vedas are the final goal and authority, and if the Purânas differ in any respect from the Vedas, that part of the Purânas is to be rejected without mercy. We find then, that in all these Smritis the teachings are different. One Smriti says, this is the custom, and this should be the practice of this age. Another one says, this is the practice of this age, and so forrh. This is the *âchâra* which should be the custom of the *Satya Yuga*, and this is the *âchâra* which should be the custom of the *Kali Yuga*, and so forth. Now this is one of the most glorious doctrines that you have, that eternal truths, being based upon the nature of man, will never change so long as man lives; they are for all times, omnipresent, universal virtues. But the Smritis speak generally of local circumstances, of duties arising from different environments, and they change in the course of time. This you have always to remember, that because a little social custom is going to be changed you are not going to lose your religion, not at all. Remember these customs have already been changed. There was a time in this very India when, without eating beef, no Brâhman could remain a Brâhman; you read in the Vedas how, when a Sannyâsin, a king, or a great man came into a house, the goat and the bullock were killed; how in time it was found that as we were an agricultural race, killing the best bulls meant annihilation of the race. Therefore the practice was stopped, and a voice was raised against the killing of cows. Sometimes we find existing then, what we now consider the most horrible customs. In course of time other laws had to be made. These in turn will have to go, and other Smritis will come. This is one fact we have to learn, that the Vedas being eternal will be one and the same throughout all ages, but the Smritis will have an end. As time rolls on, more and more of the Smritis will go, Sages will come, and they will change and direct society into better channels, into duties and into paths which are the necessity of the age, and without which it is impossible that society can live. Thus we have to guide our course, avoiding these two dangers, and I hope that every -ne of us here will have breadth enough, and at the same time faith enough, to 'erstand what that means, and that what I suppose is, the inclusion of everything, not the exclusion. I want the intensity of the fanatic plus the extensity of the materialist. Deep as the ocean, broad as the infinite skies, that is the sort of heart we want. Let us be as progressive as any nation that ever existed, and at the same time as faithful and conservative towards our traditions as Hindus alone know how to be. In plain words, we have first to learn the distinction between the essentials and the non-essentials in everything. The essentials are eternal, the non-essentials have value only for a certain time, and if after a time they are not replaced by something essential, they are positively dangerous. I do not mean that you should stand up and revile all your old customs and institutions. Certainly not; you must not revile even the most evil one of them. Revile none. Even those customs that are now appearing to be positive evils, have been positively life-giving in times past, and if we have to remove these, we must not do so with curses, but with blessings and gratitude for the glorious work these customs have done for the preservation of our race. And we must also remember that the leaders of our societies have never been either generals or kings, but Rishis. And who are the Rishis? The Rishi as he is called in the Upanishads, is not an ordinary man, but a *Mantra drashtâ*. He is a man who sees religion, to whom religion is not merely book-learning, not argumentation, nor speculation, nor much talking, but actual realisation, a coming face to face with truths which transcend the senses. This is Rishihood, and that Rishihood does not belong to any age, or time, or even to sects or caste. Vâtsyâyana says, truth must be realised—and we have to remember that you, and I, and every one of us will be called upon to become Rishis, and we must have faith in ourselves, we must become world-movers, for everything is in us. We must see Religion face to face, experience it, and thus solve our doubts about it; and then standing up in the glorious light of Rishihood each one of us will be a giant, and every word falling from our lips will carry behind it that infinite sanction of security, and before us evil will vanish by itself, without the necessity of cursing any one, without the necessity of abusing any one, without the necessity of fighting any one in the world. May the Lord help us, each one of us here, to realise the Rishihood, for our own salvation and for that of others.

THE MISSION OF THE VEDANTA.

On the occasion of his visit to Kumbhakonam, the Swamiji was presented with the following address by the local Hindu community:—

REVERED SWAMIN,—

On behalf of the Hindu inhabitants of this ancient and religiously important town of Kumbhakonam, we request permission to offer you a most hearty welcome on your return from the Western World to our own holy land of great temples and famous saints and sages. We are highly thankful to God for the remarkable success of your religious mission in America and in Europe, and for His having enabled you to impress upon the choicest representatives of the world's great religions assembled at Chicago, that both the Hindu Philosophy and Religion are so broad and so rationally catholic as to have in them the power to exalt and to harmonise all ideals of God and of human spirituality.

The conviction that the cause of Truth is always safe in the hands of Him who is the life and soul of the universe, has been for thousands of years part of our living faith; and if to-day we rejoice at the results of your holy work in Christian lands, it is because the eyes of men in and outside of India are thereby being opened to the inestimable value of the *Spiritual* heritage of the *pre-eminently religious* Hindu nation. The success of your work has naturally added great lustre to the already renowned name of your great Guru; it has also raised us in the estimation of the civilised world; more than all, it has made us feel that we too, as a people, have reason to be proud of the achievements of our past, and that the absence of telling aggressiveness in our civilisation is in no way a sign of its exhausted or decaying condition. With clear-sighted, devoted, and altogether unselfish workers like you in our midst, the future of the Hindu nation cannot but be bright and hopeful. May the God of the universe who is also the great God of all nations, bestow on you health and long life, and make you increasingly strong and wise in the discharge of your high and noble function as a worthy teacher of Hindu Religion and Philosophy.

A Second address was also presented by the Hindu students of the town.

The Swami then delivered the following address on the Mission of the Vedanta:—

A very small amount of religious work performed brings a large amount of result." If this statement of the Gita wanted an illustration, I am finding every day the truth of that great saying in my humble life. My work has been very insignificant indeed, but the kindness and the cordiality of welcome that have met me at every step of my journey from Colombo to this city, are simply beyond all expectation. Yet, at the same time, it is worthy of our traditions as Hindus, it is worthy of our race; for here we are the Hindu race, whose vitality, whose life-principle, whose very soul, as it were, is in religion. I have seen a little of the world, travelling among the races of the East and the West; and everywhere I find among nations, one great ideal, which forms the backbone, so to speak, of that race. With some it is polities, with others it is social culture; others again may have intellectual culture and so on for their national background. But this, our motherland, has religion and religion alone for its basis, for its backbone, for the bedrock upon which the whole building of its life has been based. Some of you may remember that in my reply to the kind address which the people of Madras sent over to me in America, I pointed out the fact that a peasant in India has, in many respects, a better religious education than many a gentleman in the West, and to-day, beyond all doubt, I myself am verifying my own words. There was a time when I did feel rather discontented at the want of information among the masses of India, and the lack of thirst among them for information, but now I understand it. Where their interest lies, there they are more eager for information than the masses of any other race that I have seen or have travelled among. Ask our peasants about the momentous political changes in Europe, the upheavals that are going on in European society, and they do not know anything of them, nor do they care to know; but the peasants, even in Ceylon, detached from India in many ways, cut off from a living interest in India—I found the very peasants working in the fields there, were already acquainted with the fact that there had been a Parliament of Religions in America, and that an Indian Sannyasin had gone over there and that he had had some success. Where, therefore, their interest is, there they are as eager for information as any other race; and religion is the one and the sole interest of the people of India. I am not just now discussing whether it is good to have the vitality of the race in religious ideals or in political ideals, but so far it is clear to us, that for good or for evil, our vitality is concentrated in our religion. You cannot change it. You cannot destroy it and put in its place another. You cannot transplant a large growing tree from one soil to another and make it immediately take root there. For good or for evil, the religious ideal has been flowing into India for thousands of years; for good or for evil, the Indian atmosphere has been filled with ideals of religion for shining scores of centuries; for good or for evil, we have been born and brought up in the very midst of these ideals of religion, till it has entered into our very blood, and tingled with every drop in our veins, and has become one with our constitution, become the very vitality of our lives. Can you give such religion up without the rousing of the same energy in reaction, without filling the channel which that mighty river has cut out for itself in the course of thousands of years? Do you want that the Ganges should go back to its icy bed and begin a new course? Even if that were possible, it would be impossible for this country to give up her characteristic course of religious life and take up for herself a new career of politics or something else. You can only work under the law of least resistance, and this religious line is the line of least resistance in India. This is the line of life, this is the line of growth, and this is the line of well-being in India—to follow the track of religion. Aye, in other countries religion is only one of the many necessities in life. To use a common illustration which I am in the habit of using, my lady has many things in her parlour, and it is the fashion nowadays to have a Japanese vase, and she must procure it; it does not look well to be without it. So my lady, or my gentleman, has many other occupations in life, and also a little bit of religion must come in to complete it. Consequently he or she has a little religion. Politics, social improvement, in one word, this world, is the goal of mankind in the West, and God and religion come in quietly as the helpers out of the world. Their God is, so to speak, the Being who helps to cleanse and to furnish this world for them; that is apparently all the value of God for them. Do you not know how for the last hundred or two hundred years you have been hearing again and again out of the lips of men who ought to have known better, from the mouths of those who pretend, at least, to know better, that all the arguments they produce against the Indian religion is this,—that our religion does not conduce to well-being in this world, that it does not bring gold to us, that it does not make us robbers of nations, that it does not make the strong stand upon the bodies of the weak, and feed themselves with the life-blood of the weak. Certainly our religion does not do that. It cannot send cohorts, under whose feet the earth trembles, for the purpose of destruction and pillage and the ruination of races. Therefore they say—what is there in this religion? It does not bring any grist to the grinding mill, any strength to the muscles; what is there in such a religion? They little dream that that is the very argument with which we prove our religion, because it does not make for this world. Ours is the only true religion, because according to it, this little sense-world of three days' duration is not to be made the end and aim of all, is not to be our great goal. This little earthly horizon of a few feet is not that which bounds the view of our religion. Ours is away beyond, and still beyond; beyond the senses, beyond space, and beyond time, away, away beyond, till nothing of this world is left and the universe itself becomes like a drop in the transcendent ocean of the glory of the Soul. Ours is the true religion, because it teaches that God alone is true, that this world is false and fleeting, that all your gold is but as dust, that all your power is finite, and that life itself is oftentimes an evil; therefore it is, that ours is the true religion. Ours is the true religion, because, above all, it teaches renunciation, and stands up with the wisdom of ages to tell and to declare to the nations who are mere children of yesterday in comparison with us Hindus,—who own the hoary antiquity of the wisdom, discovered by our ancestors here in India—to tell them in plain words, "Children, you are slaves of the senses; there is only finiteness in the senses, there is only ruination in the senses; the three short days of luxury here bring only ruin at last. Give it all up, renounce the love of the senses and of the world; that is *the* way of religion." Through renunciation is the way to the goal and not through enjoyment. Therefore, ours is the only true religion. Aye, it is a curious fact that, while nations after nations have come upon the stage of the world, played their parts vigorously for a few moments, and died almost without leaving a mark or a ripple on the ocean of time, here, we are living as it were, an eternal life. They talk a great deal of the new theories about the survival of the fittest, and they think that it is the strength of the muscles which is the fittest to survive. If that were true, any one of the aggressively known old-world nations would have lived in glory to-day, and we, the weak Hindus, who never conquered even one other race or nation ought to have died out, yet we live here three hundred millions strong! (An young English lady once told me, what have the Hindus done? They never even conquered a single race!) And it is not at all true that all its energies are spent, that atrophy has overtaken its body; that is not true. There is vitality enough, and it comes out in torrents, and deluges the world when the time is ripe and requires it. We have, as it were, thrown a challenge to the whole world from the most ancient times. In the West, they are trying to solve the problem how much a man can possess, and we are trying here to solve the problem on how little a man can live. This struggle and this difference will still go on for some centuries. But if history has any truth in it, and if prognostications ever prove true, it must be that those who train themselves to live on the least and control themselves well, will in the end gain the battle, and that those who run after enjoyment and luxury, however vigorous they may seem for the moment, will have to die and become annihilated. There are times in the history of a man's life, nay, in the history of the lives of nations, when a sort of world-weariness becomes painfully predominant. It seems that such a tide of world-weariness has come upon the Western World. There too, they have their thinkers, great men; and they are already finding out that this race after gold and power is all vanity of vanities; many, nay most of the cultured men and women there, are already weary of this competition, this struggle, this brutality of their commercial civilisation, and they are looking forward towards something better. There is a class which still clings on to political and social changes as the only panacea for the evils in Europe, but among the great thinkers there, other ideals are growing. They have found out that no amount of political or social manipulation of human conditions can cure the evils of life. It is a change of the soul itself for the better, that alone will cure the evils of life. No amount of force, or government, or legislative cruelty will change the conditions of a race, but it is spiritual culture and ethical culture alone that can change wrong racial tendencies for the better. Thus, these races of the West are eager for some new thought, for some new philosophy; the religion they have had, Christianity, although good and glorious in many respects, has been imperfectly understood, and is, as understood hitherto, found to be insufficient. The thoughtful men of the West find in our ancient philosophy, especially in the Vedanta, the new impulse of thought they are seeking, the very spiritual food and drink for which they are hungering and thirsting. And it is no wonder that this is so.

I have become used to hear all sorts of wonderful claims put forward in favour of every religion under the sun. You have also heard, quite within recent times, the claims put forward by Dr. Barrows, a great friend of mine, that Christianity is the only universal religion. Let me consider this question awhile and lay before you my reasons why I think that it is Vedanta, and Vedanta alone, that can become the universal religion of man, and that no other is fitted for that rôle. Excepting our own, almost all the other great religions in the world are inevitably connected with the life or lives of one or more of their founders. All their theories, their teachings, their doctrines, and their ethics are built round the life of a personal founder, from whom they get their sanction, their authority, and their power; and strangely enough, upon the historicity of the founder's life is built, as it were, all the fabric of such religions. If there is one blow dealt to the historicity of that life, as has been the case is modern times with the lives of almost all the so-called founders of religion—we know that half the details of such lives is not now seriously believed in, and that the other half is seriously doubted—if this becomes the case, if that rock of historicity, as they pretend to call it, is shaken and shattered, the whole building tumbles down broken absolutely, never to regain its lost status. Everyone of the great religions in the world excepting our own, is built upon such historical characters; but ours rests upon principles. There is no man or woman who can claim to have created the Vedas. They are the embodiment of eternal principles; sages discovered them; and now and then the names of these sages are mentioned, just their names; we do not even know who or what they were. In many cases we do not know who their fathers were, and almost in every case we do not know when and where they were born. But what cared they, these sages, for their names? They were the preachers of principles, and they themselves, so far as they went, tried to become illustrations of the principles they preached. At the same time, just as our God is an impersonal and yet a personal God, so is our religion a most intensely impersonal one, a religion based upon principles; and yet it has an infinite scope for the play of persons, for what religion gives you more Incarnations, more prophets and seers, and still waits for infinitely more? The Bhagavad-Gita says that Incarnations are infinite, leaving ample scope for as many as you like, to come. Therefore if any one or more of these persons in India's religious history, any one or more of these Incarnations, and any one or more of our prophets are proved not to have been historical, it does not injure our religion at all; even then it remains firm as ever, because it is based upon principles, and not upon persons. It is in vain to try to gather all the peoples of the world around a single personality. It is difficult to make them gather together even round eternal and universal principles. If it ever becomes possible to bring the largest portion of humanity to one way of thinking in regard to religion, mark you, it must be always through principles and not through persons. Yet as I have said, our religion has ample scope for the authority and influence of persons. There is that most wonderful theory of *Ishta*, which gives you the fullest and the freest choice possible among these great religious personalities. You may take up any one of the prophets or teachers as your guide and the object of your special adoration; you are even allowed to think that He whom you have chosen is the greatest of the prophets, greatest of all the *Avatâras;* there is no harm in that, but you must keep to a firm background of eternally true principles. The strange fact here is, that the power of our Incarnations has been holding good with us only so far as they are illustrations of the principles in the Vedas. The glory of Sri Krishna is, that he has been the best preacher of our eternal religion of principles and the best commentator on the Vedanta that ever lived in India.

The second claim of the Vedanta upon the attention of the world is, that of all the scriptures in the world, it is the one scripture the teaching of which is in entire harmony with the results that have been attained by the modern scientific investigations of external nature. Two minds in the dim past of history, cognate to each other in form and kinship, and sympathy, started, being placed in different routes. The one was the ancient Hindu mind, and the other the ancient Greek mind. The former started by analysing the internal world. The latter started in search of that goal beyond, by analysing the external world. And even through the various vicissitudes of their history, it is easy to make out these two vibrations of thoughts as tending to produce similar echoes from the goal beyond. It seems clear that the conclusions of modern materialistic science can be acceptable, harmoniously with their religion, only to the Vedantins, or Hindus as they are called. It seems clear that modern materialism can hold its own and at the same time approach spirituality by taking up the conclusions of the Vedanta. It seems to us, and to all who care to know, that the conclusions of modern science are the very conclusions the Vedanta reached ages ago; only, in modern science they are written in the language of matter. This, then, is another claim of the Vedanta upon modern Western minds, its rationality, the wonderful rationalism of the Vedanta. I have myself been told by some of the best Western scientific minds of the day, how wonderfully rational the conclusions of the Vedanta were. I know one of them personally, who scarcely has time to eat his meals, or go out of his laboratory, but who yet would stand by the hour to attend my lectures on the Vedanta; for, as he expresses it, they are so scientific, they so exactly harmonise with the aspirations of the age and with the conclusions to which modern science is coming at the present time. Two such scientific conclusions drawn from Comparative Religion, I would specially like to draw your attention to; the one bears upon the idea of the universality of religions and the other, on the idea of the oneness of things. We observe in the histories of Babylon and among the Jews an interesting religious phenomenon happening. We find that each of these Babylonian and Jewish peoples was divided into so many tribes, each tribe having a god of its own, and that these little tribal Gods had often a generic name. The gods among the Babylonians were all called Baals, and among them Baal Merodac was the chief. In course of time one of these many tribes would conquer and assimilate the other racially-allied tribes, and the natural result would be, that the God of the conquering tribe would be placed at the head of all the gods of the other tribes. Thus the so-called boasted monotheism of the Semites was created. Among the Jews the gods went by the name of Moloch. Of these there was one Moloch who belonged to the tribe called Israel, and he was called the Moloch Yahva, or Moloch Yava. In time, this tribe of Israel slowly conquered some of the other tribes of the same race, destroyed their Molochs, and declared its own Moloch to be the Supreme Moloch of all the Molochs. And I am sure most of you know the amount of bloodshed, of tyranny, and of brutal savagery that this religious conquest entailed. Later on, the Babylonians tried to destroy this supremacy of Moloch Yahva, but could not succeed in doing so. It seems to me, that such an attempt at tribal self-assertion in religious matters might have taken place on the frontiers of India also. Here too, all the various tribes of the Aryans might have come into conflict with one another, for declaring the supremacy of their several tribal gods; but India's history was to be otherwise, was to be different from that of the Jews. India was alone to be the land of all lands of toleration and of spirituality, and therefore the fight between tribes and their gods did not long take place here. For one of the greatest sages that was ever born, found out here in India even at that distant time, which history cannot reach, and into whose gloom even tradition itself dares not peep —in that distant time the sage arose, and declared, "*Ekam sat viprá bahudhá vadanti.*"—He who exists is one; the sages call Him variously. This is one of the most memorable sentences that was ever uttered, one of the grandest truths that was ever discovered. And for us Hindus this truth has been the very backbone of our national existence. For throughout the vistas of the centuries of our national life, this one idea, "*Ekam sat viprá bahudhá vadanti,*" comes down, gaining in volume and in fulness till it has permeated the whole of our national existence, till it has mingled in our blood, and has become one with us. We love that grand truth in every vein, and our country has become the glorious land of religious toleration. It is here and here alone that they build temples and churches for the religions which have come with the object of condemning our own religion. This is one very great principle that the world is waiting to learn from us. Aye, you little know how much of intolerance is yet abroad. It struck me more than once, that I should have to leave my bones on foreign shores owing to the prevalence of religious intolerance. Killing a man is nothing for religion's sake; to-morrow they may do it in the very heart of the boasted civilisation of the West, if to-day they are not really doing so. Outcasting in its most horrible forms would often come down upon the head of a man in the West, if he dared to say a word against his country's accepted religion. They talk glibly and smoothly here in criticism of our caste laws. If you go to the West and live there as I have done, you will know that even some of the biggest professors you hear of, are arrant cowards and dare not say for fear of public opinion, a hundredth part of what they hold to be really true in religious matters.

Therefore the world is waiting for this grand idea of universal toleration. It will be a great acquisition to civilisation. Nay, no civilisation can long exist unless this idea enters into it. No civilisation can grow, unless fanaticism, bloodshed and brutality stop. No civilisation can begin to lift up its head until we look charitably upon one another, and the first step towards that much needed charity is to look charitably and kindly upon the religious convictions of others. Nay more, to understand, that not only should we be charitable, but positively helpful, to each other, however different our religious ideas and convictions may be. And that is exactly what we do in India, as I have just related to you. It is here in India that Hindus have built and are still building churches for Christians, and mosques for Mahommedans. That is the thing to do. In spite of their hatred, in spite of their brutality, in spite of their cruelty, in spite of their tyranny, and in spite of the vile language they are given to uttering, we will and must go on building churches for the Christians and mosques for the Mahommedans until we conquer through love, until we have demonstrated to the world that love alone is the fittest thing to survive and not hatred, that it is gentleness that has the strength to live on and to fructify, and not mere brutality and physical force.

The other great idea that the world wants from us to-day, the thinking part of Europe, nay, the whole world—more, perhaps, the lower classes than the higher, more the masses than the cultured, more the ignorant than the educated, more the weak than the strong—is that eternal grand idea of the spiritual oneness of the whole universe. I need not tell you to-day, men from the Madras University, how the modern researches of the West have demonstrated through physical means, the oneness and the solidarity of the whole universe; how, physically speaking, you and I, the sun, moon and stars, are but little waves or wavelets in the midst of an infinite ocean of matter; how Indian psychology demonstrated ages ago that, similarly, both body and mind are but mere names or little wavelets in the ocean of matter, the *Samashti;* and how, going one step further, it is also shown in the Vedanta that, behind that idea of the unity of the whole show, the real Soul is one. There is but one Soul throughout the universe, all is but One Existence. This great idea of the real and basic solidarity of the whole universe has frightened many, even in this country; it even now finds sometimes more opponents than adherents; I tell you, nevertheless, that it is the one great life-giving idea which the world wants from us to-day, and which the mute masses of India want for their uplifting, for none can regenerate this land of ours without the practical application and effective operation of this ideal of the oneness of things. The rational West is earnestly bent upon seeking out the rationality, the *raison d'être* of all its philosophy and its ethics; and you all know well that ethics cannot be derived from the mere sanction of any personage, however great and divine he may have been. Such an explanation of the authority of ethics appeals no more to the highest of the world's thinkers; they want something more than human sanction for ethical and moral codes to be binding, they want some eternal principle of truth as the sanction of ethics. And where is that eternal sanction to be found except in the only Infinite Reality, that exists in you and in me and in all, in the self, in the soul? The infinite oneness of the Soul is the eternal sanction of all morality, that you and I are not only brothers—every literature voicing man's struggle towards freedom has preached that for you—but that you and I are really one. This is the dictate of Indian philosophy. This oneness is the rationale of all ethics and all spirituality. Europe wants it to-day just as much as our down-trodden masses do, and this great principle is even now unconsciously forming the basis of all the latest political and social aspirations that are coming up in England, in Germany, in France, and in America. And mark it, my friends, that in and through all the literature voicing man's struggle towards freedom, towards universal freedom, again and again you find the Indian Vedantic ideals coming out prominently. In some cases the writers do not know the source of their inspiration, in some cases they try to appear very original, and a few there are, bold and grateful enough to mention the source and acknowledge their indebtedness to it. When I was in America, I heard once the complaint made that I was preaching too much of Advaita, and too little of dualism. Aye, I know what grandeur, what oceans of love, what infinite, ecstatic blessings and joy there are in the dualistic love-theories of worship and religion. I know it all. But this is not the time with us to weep, even in joy; we have had weeping enough; no more is this the time for us to become soft. This softness has been with us till we have become like masses of cotton, and are dead. What our country now wants, are muscles of iron and nerves of steel, gigantic wills which nothing can resist, which can penetrate into the mysteries and the secrets of the universe, and will accomplish their purpose in any fashion, even if it meant going down to the bottom of the ocean and meeting death face to face. That is what we want, and that can only be created, established and strengthened, by understanding and realising the ideal of the Advaita, that ideal of the oneness of all. Faith, faith, faith in ourselves, faith, faith in God,—this is the secret of greatness. If you have faith in all the three hundred and thirty millions of your mythological gods, and in all the gods which foreigners have now and again introduced into your midst, and still have no faith in yourselves, there is no salvation for you. Have faith in yourselves, and stand up on that faith and be strong; that is what we need. Why is it that we, three hundred and thirty millions of people, have been ruled for the last one thousand years by any and every handful of foreigners who chose to walk over our prostrate bodies? Because they had faith in themselves and we had not. What did I learn in the West, and what did I see behind those frothy sayings of the Christian sects repeating that man was a fallen and hopelessly fallen sinner? There, I saw that inside the national hearts of both Europe and America, resides the tremendous power of the men's faith in themselves. An English boy will tell you—"I am an Englishman, and I can do anything." The American boy will tell you the same thing, and so will any European boy. Can our boys say the same thing here? No, nor even the boys' fathers. We have lost faith in ourselves. Therefore, to preach the Advaita aspect of the Vedanta is necessary to rouse up the hearts of men, to show them the glory of their souls. It is therefore that I preach this Advaita, and I do so not as a sectarian, but upon universal and widely acceptable grounds.

It is easy to find out the way of reconciliation that will not hurt the dualist or the qualified monist. There is not one system in India which does not hold the doctrine that God is within, that Divinity resides within all things. Every one of our Vedantic systems admits that all purity and perfection and strength are in the soul already. According to some, this perfection sometimes becomes, as it were, contracted, and at other times it becomes expanded again. Yet it is there. According to the Advaita, it neither contracts nor expands, but becomes hidden and uncovered, now and again. Pretty much the same thing in effect. The one may be a more logical statement than the other, but as to the result, the practical conclusions, both are about the same; and this is the one central idea which the world stands in need of, and nowhere is the want more felt than in this, our own motherland. Aye, my friends, I must tell you a few harsh truths. I read in the newspapers, how, when one of our poor fellows is murdered or ill-treated by an Englishman, howls go all over the country; I read and I weep, and the next moment comes to my mind the question, who is responsible for it all. As a Vedantist I cannot but put that question to myself. The Hindu is a man of introspection, he wants to see things in and through himself, through the subjective vision. I therefore ask myself who is responsible, and the answer comes every time, not the English; no, they are not responsible; it is we who are responsible for all our misery and all our degradation, and we alone are responsible. Our aristocratic ancestors went on treading the common masses of our country under foot, till they became helpless, till under this torment the poor, poor people nearly forgot that they were human beings. They have been compelled to be merely hewers of wood and drawers of water for centuries, so much so, that they are made to believe that they are born as slaves, born as hewers of wood and drawers of water. With all our boasted education of modern times, if anybody says a kind word for them, I often find our men shrink at once from the duty of lifting them up, these poor down-trodden people. Not only so, but I also find that all sorts of most demoniacal and brutal arguments, culled from the crude ideas of hereditary transmission, and other such gibberish from the Western world, are brought forward in order to brutalise and tyrannise over the poor, all the more. At the Parliament of Religions in America, there came among others, a young man, a Negro born, a real African Negro, and he made a beautiful speech. I became interested in the young man, and now and then talked to him, but could learn nothing about him. But one day in England, I met some Americans, and this is what they told me. That this boy was the son of a Negro chief who lived in the heart of Africa, and that one day another chief became angry with the father of this boy and murdered him and murdered the mother also, and they were cooked and eaten; he ordered the child to be killed also, and cooked and eaten; but the boy fled, and after passing through great hardships and having travelled a distance of several hundreds of miles, he reached the sea-shore, and there he was taken into an American vessel and brought over to America. And this boy made that speech! After that, what was I to think of your doctrine of heredity! Aye, Brâhmans, if the Brâhman has more aptitude for learning on the ground of heredity than the Pariah, spend no more money on the Brâhman's education, but spend all on the Pariah. Give to the weak, for there all the gift is needed. If the Brâhman is born clever he can educate himself without help. If the others are not born clever, let them have all the teaching and the teachers they want. This is justice and reason as I understand it. Our poor people, these down-trodden masses of India, therefore, require to hear and to know what they really are. Aye, let every man and woman and child, without respect of caste or birth, weakness or strength, hear and learn that behind the strong and the weak, behind the high and the low, behind every one, there is that Infinite Soul, assuring the infinite possibility and the infinite capacity of all to become great and good. Let us proclaim to every soul—उत्तिष्ठत जाग्रत प्राप्य वरान्निबोधत.—Arise, awake and stop not till the goal is reached. Arise, awake! awake from this hypnotism of weakness. *None* is really weak; the soul is infinite, omnipotent, and omniscient. Stand up, assert yourself, proclaim the God within you, do not deny! Too much of inactivity, too much of weakness, too much of hypnotism, has been and is upon our race. O ye modern Hindus, de-hypnotise yourselves. The way to do that, is found in your own sacred books. Teach yourselves, teach every one his real nature, call upon the sleeping soul to see how it awakes. Power will come, glory will come, goodness will come, purity will come, and everything that is excellent will come when this sleeping soul is roused to self-conscious activity. Aye, if there is anything in the Gita that I like, it is these two verses, coming out strong as the very gist, the very essence, of Krishna's teaching—"He who sees the Supreme Lord dwelling alike in all beings, the Imperishable in things that perish, he sees indeed. For seeing the Lord as the same, everywhere present, he does not destroy the Self by the self, and thus he goes to the highest goal."

Thus there is a great opening for the Vedanta to do beneficent work both here and elsewhere. This wonderful idea of the sameness and omnipresence of the Supreme Soul has to be preached for the amelioration and elevation of the human race, here as elsewhere. Wherever there is evil and wherever there is ignorance and want of knowledge, I have found out by experience that all evil comes, as our scriptures say, by relying upon differences, and that all good comes, from faith in equality, in the underlying sameness and oneness of things. This is the great Vedantic ideal. To have the ideal is one thing, and to apply it practically to the details of daily life is quite another thing. It is very good to point out an ideal, but where is the practical way to reach it?

Here naturally comes the difficult and the vexed question of caste and of social reformation, which has been uppermost for centuries in the minds of our people. I must frankly tell you that I am neither a caste-breaker nor a mere social reformer. I have nothing to do directly with your castes or with your social reformation. Live in any caste you like, but that is no reason why you should hate another man or another caste. It is love and love alone that I preach, and I base my teaching on the great Vedantic truth of the sameness and omnipresence of the Soul of the Universe. For nearly the last one hundred years, our country has been flooded with social reformers and various social reform proposals. Personally, I have no fault to find with these reformers. Most of them are good well-meaning men, and their aims too are very laudable on certain points; but it is quite a patent fact that this one hundred years of social reform has produced no permanent and valuable result, appreciable throughout the country. Platform speeches have been made by the thousand, denunciations in volumes after volumes have been hurled upon the devoted head of the Hindu race and its civilisation, and yet no good practical result has been achieved; and where is the reason for that? The reason is not hard to find. It is in the denunciation itself. As I told you before, in the first place we must try to keep our historically acquired character as a people. I grant that we have to take a great many things from other nations, that we have to learn many lessons from outside; but I am sorry to say that most of our modern reform-movements have been inconsiderate imitations of Western means and methods of work, and that surely will not do for India; therefore it is that all our recent reform-movements have had no result. In the second place, denunciation is not at all the way to do good. That there are evils in our society even a child can see, and in what society are there no evils? And let me take this opportunity, my countrymen, of telling you that, in comparing the different races and nations of the world I have been among, I have come to the conclusion that our people are on the whole the most moral and the most godly, and our institutions are, in their plan and purpose, best suited to make mankind happy. I do not therefore want any reformation. My ideal is growth, expansion, development on national lines. As I look back upon the history of my country, I do not find in the whole world another country which has done quite so much for the improvement of the human mind. Therefore, I have no words of condemnation for my nation. I tell them, "You have done well; only try to do better." Great things have been done in the past in this land, and there is both time and room for greater things to be done yet. I am sure you know that we cannot stand still. If we stand still we die. We have either to go forward or to go backward. We have either to progress or to degenerate. Our ancestors did great things in the past, but we have to grow into a fuller life and march beyond even their great achievements. How can we now go back and degenerate ourselves? That cannot be; that must not be; going back will lead to national decay and death. Therefore, let us go forward and do yet greater things; that is what I have to tell you. I am no preacher of any momentary social reform. I am not trying to remedy evils, I only ask you to go forward and to complete the practical realisation of the scheme of human progress, that has been laid out in the most perfect order by our ancestors. I only ask you to work to realise more and more the Vedantic ideal of the solidarity of man and his inborn divine nature. Had I the time, I would gladly show you how everything we have now to do, was laid out years ago by our ancient law-givers, and how they actually anticipated all the different changes that have taken place, and are still to take place in our national institutions. They also were breakers of caste, but they were not like our modern men. They did not mean by the breaking of caste that all the people in a city should sit down together to a dinner of beefsteak and champagne, nor that all fools and lunatics in the country should marry when, where and whom they chose, and reduce the country to a lunatic asylum, nor did they believe that the prosperity of a nation, is to be gauged by the number of husbands its widows get. I have yet to see such a prosperous nation.

The ideal man of our ancestors was the Brâhman. In all our books stands out prominently this ideal of the Brâhman. In Europe, there is my Lord the Cardinal, who is struggling hard and spending thousands of pounds to prove the nobility of his ancestors, and he will not be satisfied until he has traced his ancestry to some dreadful tyrant, who lived on a hill, and watched the people passing by, and whenever he had the opportunity, sprang out on them and robbed them. That was the business of these nobility-bestowing ancestors, and my Lord Cardinal is not satisfied until he can trace his ancestry to one of these. In India, on the other hand, the greatest princes seek to trace their descent to some ancient sage, who dressed in a bit of loin-cloth, lived in a forest, eating roots, and studying the Vedas. It is there that the Indian prince goes to trace his ancestry. You are of the high caste when you can trace your ancestry to a Rishi, and not otherwise. Our ideal of high birth, therefore, is different from that of others. Our ideal is the Brâhman of spiritual culture and renunciation. By the Brâhman ideal what do I mean? I mean the ideal Brâhman-ness in which worldliness is altogether absent and true wisdom is abundantly present. That is the ideal of the Hindu race. Have you not heard how it is declared that he, the Brâhman, is not amenable to law, that he has no law, that he is not governed by kings, and that his body cannot be hurt? That is perfectly true. Do not understand it in the light thrown upon it by interested and ignorant fools, but understand it in the light of the true and original Vedantic conception. If the Brâhman is he who has killed all selfishness and who lives and works to acquire and propagate wisdom and the power of love,—if a country is altogether inhabited by such Brâhmans, by men and women who are spiritual and moral and good, is it strange to think of that country as being above and beyond all law? What police, what military are necessary to govern them? Why should any one govern them at all? Why should they live under a government? They are good and noble, and they are the men of God; these are our ideal Brâhmans, and we read that in the *Satya-Yuga* there was only one caste, and that was the Brâhman. We read in the Mahâbhârata that the whole world was in the beginning peopled with Brâhmans, and that as they began to degenerate they became divided into different castes, and that when the cycle turns round they will all go back to that Bráhmanical origin. This cycle is turning round now, and I draw your attention to this fact. Therefore our solution of the caste question is not degrading those who are already high up, is not running amuck through food and drink, is not jumping out of our own limits in order to have more enjoyment, but it comes by every one of us fulfilling the dictates of our Vedantic religion, by our attaining spirituality, and by our becoming the ideal Brâhman. There is a law laid on each one of you in this land by your ancestors, whether you are Aryans, or non-Aryans, Rishis, or Brâhmans, or the very lowest outcastes. The command is the same to you all, that you must make progress without stopping, and that, from the highest man to the lowest Pariah, every one in this country has to try and become the ideal Brâhman. This Vedantic idea is applicable not only here but over the whole world. Such is our ideal of caste, as meant for raising all humanity slowly and gently towards the realisation of that great ideal of the spiritual man, who is non-resisting, calm, steady, worshipful, pure, and meditative. In that ideal there is God.

How are these things to be brought about? I must again draw your attention to the fact that cursing and vilifying and abusing do not and cannot produce anything good. They have been tried for years and years, and no valuable result has been obtained. Good results can be produced only through love, through sympathy. It is a great subject, and it requires several lectures to elucidate all the plans that I have in view, and all the ideas that are, in this connection, coming to my mind day after day. I must therefore conclude, only reminding you of this fact, that this ship of our nation, O Hindus, has been usefully plying here for ages. To-day, perhaps, it has sprung a leak; to-day, perhaps, it has became a little worn out; and if such is the case, it behoves you and I, to try our best to stop the leak and holes. Let us tell our countrymen of the danger, let them awake and help us. I will cry at the top of my voice from one part of this country to the other, to awaken the people to the situation and their duty. Suppose they do not hear me, still, I shall not have one word of abuse for them, not one word of cursing. Great has been our nation's work in the past, and if we cannot do greater things in the future, let us have this consolation, that we can sink and die together in peace. Be patriots, love the race which has done such great things for us in the past. Aye, the more I compare notes the more I love you, my fellow-countrymen; you are good and pure and gentle. You have been always tyrânnised over, and such is the irony of this material world of Maya. Never mind that; the spirit will triumph in the long run. In the meanwhile let us work and let us not abuse our country, let us not curse and abuse the weather-beaten and work-worn institutions of our thrice-holy motherland. Have no word of condemnation, even for the most superstitious and the most irrational of its institutions, for they also must have served some good in the past. Remember always, that there is not in the world any other country whose institutions are really better in their aims and objects than the institutions of this land. I have seen castes in almost every country in the world, but nowhere is their plan and purpose so glorious as here. If caste is thus unavoidable, I would rather have a caste of purity and culture and self-sacrifice, than a caste of dollars. Therefore utter no words of condemnation. Close your lips and let your hearts open. Work out the salvation of this land and of the whole world, each of you thinking that the entire burden is on your shoulders. Carry the light and the life of the Vedanta to every door, and rouse up the divinity that is hidden within every soul. Then, whatever may be the measure of your success, you will have this satisfaction, that you have lived, worked and died for a great cause. In the success of this cause, howsoever brought about, is centred the salvation of humanity here and hereafter.

REPLY TO THE ADDRESS OF WELCOME AT MADRAS.

When Swami Vivekananda arrived at Madras, an address of welcome was presented to him by the Madras Reception Committee. It read as follows :—

REVERED SWAMIN,—

On behalf of your Hindu co-religionists in Madras, we offer you a most hearty welcome on the occasion of your return from your Religious Mission in the West. Our object in approaching you with this address is not the performance of any merely formal or ceremonial function; we come to offer you the love of our hearts and to give expression to our feeling of thankfulness for the services which you, by the grace of God, have been able to render to the great cause of Truth by proclaiming India's lofty religious ideals. When the Parliament of Religions was organised at Chicago, some of our countrymen felt naturally anxious that our noble and ancient religion should be worthily represented therein and properly expounded to the American nation, and through them to the Western World at large. It was then our privilege to meet you and to realise once again, what has so often proved true in the history of nations, that with the hour rises the man who is to help forward the cause of Truth. When you undertook to represent Hinduism at the Parliament of Religions, most of us felt, from what we had known of your great gifts, that the cause of Hinduism would be ably upheld by its representative in that memorable religious assembly. Your presentation of the doctrines of Hinduism at once clear, correct, and authoritative, not only produced a remarkable impression at the Parliament of Religions itself, but has also led a number of men and women even in foreign lands to realise, that out of the fountain of Indian spirituality refreshing draughts of immortal life and love may be taken, so as to bring about a larger, fuller and holier evolution of humanity than has yet been witnessed on this globe of ours. We are particularly thankful to you for having called the attention of the representatives of the World's Great Religions to the characteristic Hindu doctrine of the Harmony and Brotherhood of Religions. No longer is it possible for really enlightened and earnest men to insist that Truth and Holiness are the exclusive possessions of any particular locality or body of men or system of doctrine and discipline, or to hold that any faith or philosophy will survive to the exclusion and destruction of all others. In your own happy language which brings out fully the sweet harmony in the heart of the Bhagavad-Gita, "The whole world of religions is only a travelling, a coming up of different men and women through various conditions and circumstances to the same goal." Had you contented yourself with simply discharging this high and holy duty entrusted to your care, even then, your Hindu co-religionists would have been glad to recognise with joy and thankfulness the inestimable value of your work. But in making your way into Western countries you have also been the bearer of a message of light and peace to the whole of mankind, based on the old teachings of India's "Religion Eternal." In thanking you for all that you have done in the way of upholding the profound rationality of the religion of the Vedanta, it gives us great pleasure to allude to the great task you have in view, of establishing an active mission with permanent centres for the propagation of our religion and philosophy.

The undertaking to which you propose to devote your energies is worthy of the holy traditions you represent and worthy, too, of the spirit of the great Guru who has inspired your life and its aims. We hope and trust that it may be given to us also to associate ourselves with you in this noble work. We fervently pray to Him who is the all-knowing and all-merciful Lord of the Universe, to bestow on you long life and full strength and to bless your labours with that crown of glory and success, which ever deserves to shine on the brow of immortal Truth.

Next was read the following address from the Maharajah of Khetri.

YOUR HOLINESS :—

I wish to take this early opportunity of your arrival and reception at Madras to express my feelings of joy and pleasure on your safe return to India, and to offer my heartfelt congratulation on the great success which has attended your unselfish efforts in Western lands, where it is the boast of the highest intellects that, "Not an inch of ground once conquered by science has ever been reconquered by Religion"—although indeed Science has hardly ever claimed to oppose true Religion. This holy land of Aryavarta has been singularly fortunate in having been able to secure so worthy a representative of her sages at the Parliament of Religions held at Chicago, and it is entirely due to your wisdom, enterprise and enthusiasm that the Western world has come to understand what an inexhaustible store of spirituality India has, even to-day. Your labours have now proved beyond the possibility of doubt, that the contradictions of the world's numerous creeds are all reconciled in the universal light of the Vedanta, and that all the peoples of the world have need to understand and practically realise the great truth that, 'Unity in variety' is nature's plan in the evolution of the universe, and that only by harmony and brotherhood among Religions and by mutual toleration and help can the mission and destiny of humanity be accomplished. Under your high and holy auspices and the inspiring influence of your lofty teachings, we of the present generation have the privilege of witnessing the inauguration of a new era in the world's history, in which bigotry, hatred and conflict may, I hope, cease, and peace, sympathy and love reign among men. And I in common with my people pray that the blessings of God may rest on you and your labours.

When the addresses had been read, the Swami left the hall and mounted to the box seat of a carriage in waiting! Owing to the intense enthusiasm of the large crowd assembled to welcome him, the Swami was only able to make the following short reply, postponing his reply proper to a future occasion :—

Man proposes and God disposes. It was proposed that the addresses and the replies should be carried in the English fashion. But here God disposes—I am speaking to a scattered audience from the chariot, in the Gita fashion. Thankful we are, therefore, that it should have happened so. It gives a zest to the speech, and strength to what I am going to tell you. I do not know whether my voice will reach all of you, but I will try my best. I never before had an opportunity of addressing a large open-air meeting. The wonderful kindness, the fervent and enthusiastic joy with which I have been received from Colombo to Madras, and seem likely to be received with all over India, have passed even my most sanguine expectations, but that only makes me glad, for it proves the assertion which I have made again and again in the past, that as each nation has one ideal as its vitality, as each nation has one particular groove which is to become its own, so religion is the peculiarity of the growth of the Indian mind. In other parts of the world, religion is one of the many considerations, in fact it is a minor occupation. In England, for instance, religion is part of the national policy. The English Church belongs to the ruling class, and, as such, whether they believe in it or not, they all support it, thinking that it is their Church. Every gentleman and every lady is expected to belong to that Church. It is a sign of gentility. So with other countries, there is a great national power; either it is represented by politics or it is represented by some intellectual pursuits; either it is represented by militarism or by commercialism. There the heart of the nation beats; and religion is one of the many secondary ornamental things which that nation possesses. Here in India, it is religion that forms the very core of the national heart. It is the backbone, the bed-rock, the foundation upon which the national edifice has been built. Politics, power, and even intellect form a secondary consideration here. Religion, therefore, is the one consideration in India. I have been told a hundred times of the want of information there is among the masses of the Indian people; and that is true. Landing in Colombo I found not one of them had heard of the political upheavals going on in Europe, the changes, the downfall of ministries, and so forth. Not one of them had heard of what is meant by socialism, and anarchism, and of this and that change in the political atmosphere of Europe. But that there was a Sannyasin from India sent over to the Parliament of Religions, and that he had achieved some sort of success, had become known to every man, woman, and child in Ceylon. It proves that there is no lack of information, nor lack of desire for information where it is of the character that suits them, when it falls in line with the necessities of their life. Politics and all these things never formed a necessity of Indian life, but Religion and spirituality have been the one condition upon which it lived and thrived, and has got to live in the future. Two great problems are being decided by the nations of the world. India has taken up one side, and the rest of the world has taken the other side. And the problem is this; who is to survive? What makes one nation survive and the others die? Should love survive or hatred, should enjoyment survive or renunciation; should matter survive or the spirit, in the struggle of life? We think as our ancestors did, away back in pre-historic ages. Where even tradition cannot pierce the gloom of that past, there, our glorious ancestors have taken up their side of the problem and have thrown the challenge to the world. Our solution is renunciation, giving up, fearlessness and love, these are the fittest to survive. Giving up the senses makes a nation survive. As a proof of this, here is history to-day telling us of mushroom nations rising and falling almost every century—starting up from nothingness, making vicious play for a few days and then melting. This big, gigantic race, which had to grapple with some of the greatest problems of misfortunes, dangers, and vicissitudes, such as never fell upon the head of any other nation of the world, survives, because it has taken the side of renunciation; for without renunciation how can there be Religion. Europe is trying to solve the other side of the problem as to how much a man can have; how much more power a man can possess, by hook or by crook, by some means or other. Competition, cruel, cold and heartless, is the law of Europe. Our law is caste, the breaking of competition, checking its forces, mitigating its cruelties, smoothening the passage of the human soul through this mystery of life.

At this stage the crowd became so unmanageable that the Swami could not make himself heard to advantage. He therefore ended his address with these words:—

Friends, I am very much pleased with your enthusiasm. It is marvellous. Do not think that I am displeased with you at all; I am, on the other hand, intensely pleased at the show of enthusiasm. That is what is required—tremendous enthusiasm. Only make it permanent; keep it up. Let not the fire die out. We want to work out great things in India. For that I require your help; such enthusiasm is necessary. It is impossible to hold this meeting any longer. I thank you very much for your kindness and enthusiastic welcome. In calm moments we shall have better thoughts and ideas to exchange; now for the time, my friends, good-bye.

It is impossible to address you on all sides, therefore you must content yourselves this evening with merely seeing me. I will reserve my speech for some other occasion. I thank you very much for your enthusiastic welcome.

MY PLAN OF CAMPAIGN.

(*Delivered at the Victoria Hall, Madras.*)

As the other day we could not proceed, owing to the crowd, I shall take this opportunity of thanking the people of Madras for the uniform kindness that I have received at their hands. I do not know how better to express my gratitude for the beautiful words that have been expressed in the addresses, than by praying to the Lord to make me worthy of the kind and generous expressions, and by working all my life for the cause of our religion, and to serve our Motherland, and may the Lord make me worthy of them.

With all my faults, I think I have a little bit of boldness. I had a message from India to the West, and boldly I gave it to the American and the English peoples. I want, before going into the subject of the day, to speak a few bold words to you all. There have been certain circumstances growing around me, tending to thwart me, oppose my progress, and crush me out of existence, if they could. Thank God they have failed, as such attempts will always fail. But there has been, for the last three years, a certain amount of misunderstanding, and so long as I was in foreign lands, I held my peace and did not even speak one word; but now, standing upon the soil of my motherland, I want to give a few words of explanation. Not that I care what the result will be of these words—not that I care what feeling I shall evoke from you by these words; I care very little, for I am the same Sannyasin that entered your city about four years ago with his staff and *kamandalu;* the same broad world is before me. Without further preface let me begin.

First of all, I have to say a few words about the Theosophical Society; it goes without saying that a certain amount of good work has been done to India by the Society; as such, every Hindu is grateful to it, and especially to Mrs. Besant, for, though I know very little of her, yet what little I know, has impressed me with the idea that she is a sincere well-wisher of this motherland of ours, and that she is doing the best in her power to raise our country. For that, the eternal gratitude of every true-born Indian is hers, and all blessings be on her and hers for ever. But that is one thing—and joining the Society of the Theosophists is another. Regard and estimation and love are one thing, and swallowing everything any one has to say, without reasoning, without criticising, without analysing, is quite another. There is a report going round, that the Theosophists helped the little achievements of mine in America and in England. I have to tell you plainly that every word of it is wrong, every word of it is untrue. We hear so much tall talk in this world, of liberal ideas and sympathy with differences of opinion. That is very good, but as a fact, we find that one sympathises with another only so long as the other believes in everything he has to say, but as soon as he dares to differ, that sympathy is gone, that love vanishes. There are others, again, who have their own axes to grind, and if anything arises in a country which prevents the grinding of them, their hearts burn, any amount of hatred comes out, and they do not know what to do. What harm does it do to the Christian missionary that the Hindus are trying to cleanse their own houses? What injury will it do to the Brahmo Samaj and other reform bodies that the Hindus are trying their best to reform themselves? Why should they stand in opposition? Why should they be the greatest enemies of these movements? Why? I ask. It seems to me that their hatred and jealousy are so bitter that no why or how can be asked there.

Four years ago, when I, a poor, unknown, friendless Sannyasin, was going to America, going beyond the waters to America without any introductions or friends there, I called on the leader of the Theosophical Society. Naturally I thought he being an American and a lover of India, perhaps he would give me a letter of introduction to somebody there. He asked me, "Will you join my Society?" "No," I replied, "how can I? For I do not believe in most of your doctrines." "Then, I am sorry, I cannot do anything for you," he answered. That was not paving the way for me. I reached America, as you know, through the help of a few friends of Madras. Most of them are present here; only one is absent, Mr. Justice Subramania Iyer, to whom my deepest gratitude is due. He has the insight of genius, and is one of the staunchest friends I have in this life, a true friend indeed, a true child of India. I arrived in America several months before the Parliament of Religions began. The money I had with me was little, and it was soon spent. Winter approached and I had only thin summer clothes. I did not know what to do in that cold, dreary climate, for, if I went to beg in the streets, the result would have been that I should have been sent to jail. There I was with the last few dollars in my pocket. I sent a wire to my friends in Madras. This came to be known to the Theosophists, and one of them wrote,—"Now the devil is going to die; God bless us all." Was that paving the way for me? I would not have mentioned this now, but, as my countrymen wanted to know, it must come out. For three years I have not opened my lips about these things; silence has been my motto, but to-day the thing has come out. That was not all. I saw some Theosophists in the Parliament of Religions, and I wanted to talk and mix with them. I remember the looks of scorn which were on their faces, as much as to say—"What business has the worm to be here in the midst of the gods?" After I had got name and fame at the Parliament of Religions, then came tremendous work for me, but at every turn the Theosophists tried to cry me down. Theosophists were advised not to come and hear my lectures, for thereby they would lose all sympathy of the Society, because the laws of the esoteric section declare that any man who joins that esoteric section should receive instruction from Kuthumi and Moria, of course through their visible representatives—Mr. Judge and Mrs. Besant. So that, to join the esoteric section means to surrender one's independence. Certainly, I could not do any such thing, nor could I call any man a Hindu who did any such thing. I had a great respect for Mr. Judge. He was a worthy man, open, fair, simple, and he was the best representative the Theosophists ever had. I have no right to criticise the dispute between him and Mrs. Besant, when each claims that his or her Mahatma is right. And the strange part of it is, that the same Mahatma is claimed by both. Lord knows the truth: He is the Judge, and no one has the right to pass judgment when the balance is equal.

Thus they prepared the way for me all over America! They joined the other opposition—the Christian missionaries. There is not one black lie imaginable that these latter did not invent against me. They blackened my character from city to city, poor and friendless though I was in a foreign country. They tried to oust me from every house, and to make every man who became my friend my enemy.

They tried to starve me out, and I am sorry to say that one of my own countrymen took part against me in this. He is the leader of the reform party in India. This gentleman is declaring every day, "Christ has come to India." Is this the way Christ is to come to India? Is this the way to reform India? And this gentleman I knew from my childhood; he was one of my best friends; when I saw him—I had not met for a long time one of my countrymen—I was so glad, and this was the treatment I received from him. The day the Parliament cheered me, the day I became popular in Chicago, from that day his tone changed, and in an underhand way, he tried to do everything he could to injure me. Is that the way that Christ will come to India? Is that the lesson that he had learnt after sitting twenty years at the feet of Christ? Our great reformers declare, that Christianity and Christian power are going to uplift the Indian people. Is that the way to do it? Surely, if that gentleman is an illustration, it does not look very hopeful.

One word more; I read in the organ of the social reformers that I am called a Sudra, and am challenged as to what right a Sudra has to become a Sannyasin. To which I reply—I trace my descent to one at whose feet every Brâhman lays flowers when he utters the words—*Yamâya Dharmarâjâya Chitraguptaya vai namah*—and whose descendants are the purest of Kshattriyas. If you believe in your mythology, or your Pouranic scriptures, let these so-called reformers know that my caste, apart from other services in the past, ruled half of India for centuries. If my caste is left out of consideration, what will there be left of the present-day civilisation of India? In Bengal alone, my blood has furnished them with their greatest philosopher, the greatest poet, the greatest historian, the greatest archæologist, the greatest religious preachers; my blood has furnished India with the greatest of her modern scientists. These detractors ought to have known a little of our own history, and to have studied our three castes, and learnt that the Brâhman, the Kshattriya, and the Vaisya have equal right to be Sannyasins; the Traivarnika have equal rights to the Vedas. This is only by the way. I have just quoted this, but I am not at all hurt if they call me a Sudra. It will be a little reparation for the tyranny of my ancestors over the poor. If I am a Pariah I will be all the more glad, for I am the disciple of a man, who—the Brâhman of Brâhmans—wanted to cleanse the house of a Pariah. Of course the Pariah would not allow him; how could he let this Brâhman Sannyasin come and cleanse his house! And this man woke up in the dead of night, entered surreptitiously the house of this Pariah, cleansed his latrine, and with his long hair wiped the place, and that he did day after day in order that he might make himself the servant of all. I bear the feet of that man on my head; he is my hero; that hero's life I will try to imitate. By being the servant of all a Hindu seeks to uplift himself, that is how the Hindus should uplift the masses, and not by looking for any foreign influence. Twenty years of occidental civilisation brings to my mind the illustration of the man who wants to starve his own friend in a foreign land, simply because this friend is popular, simply because he thinks that this man stands in the way of his making money. And the other, is the illustration of what genuine, orthodox Hinduism itself will do at home. Let any one of our reformers bring out that life, ready to serve even a Pariah, and then I will sit at his feet and learn, and not before that. One ounce of practice is worth twenty-thousand tons of big talk.

Now I come to the reform societies in Madras. They have been very kind to me. They have given me very kind words, and they have pointed out, and I heartily agree with them, that there is a difference between the reformers of Bengal and those of Madras. Many of you will remember what I have very often told you, that Madras is in a very beautiful state just now. It has not got into the play of action and reaction as Bengal has done. Here, there is steady and slow progress all through; here is growth, and not reaction. In many cases, and to a certain extent, there is a revival in Bengal, but in Madras it is not a revival, it is a growth, a natural growth. As such, I entirely agree with what the reformers point out as the difference between the two races; but there is one difference which they do not understand. Some of these societies, I am afraid, try to intimidate me to join them. That is a strange thing for them to attempt. A man who has met starvation face to face for fourteen years of his life, who has not known where he will get a meal the next day, and where to sleep, cannot be intimidated so easily. A man almost without clothes, who dared to live where the thermometer registered thirty degrees below zero, without knowing where the next meal was to come from, cannot be so easily intimidated, in India. This is the first thing I will tell them—I have a little will of my own. I have my little experience too, and I have a message for the world which I will deliver without fear, and without care for the future. To the reformers I will point out, that I am a greater reformer than any one of them. They want to reform only little bits. I want root-and-branch reform. Where we differ is in the method. Theirs is the method of destruction, mine is that of construction. I do not believe in reform; I believe in growth. I do not dare to put myself in the position of God and dictate to our society 'This way thou shouldst move and not that.' I simply want to be like the squirrel in the building of Rama's bridge, who was quite content to put on the bridge his little quota of sand-dust. That is my position. This wonderful national machine has worked through ages, this wonderful river of national life is flowing before us. Who knows, and who dares to say whether it is good, and how it shall move? Thousands of circumstances are crowding round it, giving it a special impulse, making it dull at one time, and quicker at another. Who dares command its motion? Ours is only to work, as the Gita says, without looking for results. Feed the national life with the fuel it wants, but the growth is its own; none can dictate its growth to it. Evils are plentiful in our society, but so are there evils in every other society. Here, the earth is soaked sometimes with widows' tears; there, in the West, the air is rent with the sighs of the unmarried. Here, poverty is the great bane of life; there, the life-weariness of luxury is the great bane that is upon the race. Here, men want to commit suicide because they have nothing to eat; there, they commit suicide because they have so much to eat. Evil is everywhere; it is like chronic rheumatism. Drive it from the foot, it goes to the head; drive it from there, it goes somewhere else. It is a question of chasing it from place to place; that is all. Aye, children, to remedy evil is the true way. Our philosophy teaches that evil and good are eternally conjoined, the obverse and the reverse of the same coin. If you have one, you must have the other; a wave in the ocean must be at the cost of a hollow elsewhere. Nay, all life is evil. No breath can be breathed without killing some one else; not a morsel of food can be eaten without depriving some one of it. This is the law; this is philosophy. Therefore the only thing we can do, is to understand that all this work against evil is more subjective than objective. The work against evil is more educational than actual, however big we may talk. This, first of all, is the idea of work against evil, and it ought to make us calmer, it ought to take fanaticism out of our blood. The history of the world teaches us that wherever there have been fanatical reforms, the only result has been that they have defeated their own ends. No greater upheaval for the establishment of right and liberty can be imagined than the war for the abolition of slavery in America. You all know about it. And what has been its results? The slaves are a hundred times worse off to-day than they were before the abolition. Before the abolition, these poor negroes were the property of somebody, and, as properties, they had to be looked after, so that they might not deteriorate. To-day they are the property of nobody. Their lives are of no value; they are burnt alive on mere pretences. They are shot down without any law for their murderers; for they are niggers, they are not human beings, they are not even animals; and that is the effect of such violent taking away of evil by law, or by fanaticism. Such is the testimony of history against every fanatical movement, even for doing good. I have seen that. My own experience has taught me that. Therefore I cannot join any one of these condemning societies. Why condemn? There are evils in every society; everybody knows it; every child of to-day knows it; he can stand upon a platform and give us a harangue on the awful evils in Hindu Society. Every uneducated foreigner who comes here globe-trotting, takes a vanishing railway view of India, and lectures most learnedly on the awful evils in India. We admit that there are evils. Everybody can show what evil is, but he is the friend of mankind who finds a way out of the difficulty. Like the drowning boy and the philosopher, when the philosopher was lecturing him the boy cried—"Take me out of the water first"; so our people cry "We have had lectures enough, societies enough, papers enough, where is the man who will lend us a hand to drag us out? Where is the man who really loves us? Where is the man who has sympathy with us?" Aye, that man is wanted. That is where I differ entirely from these reform movements. For a hundred years they have been here. What good has been done, except the creation of a most vituperative, a most condemnatory literature? Would to God it was not here! They have criticised, condemned, abused the orthodox, until the orthodox have caught their tone, and paid them back in their own coin, and the result is the creation of a literature in every vernacular which is the shame of the race, the shame of the country. Is this reform? Is this leading the nation to glory? Whose fault is this?

There is, then, another great consideration. Here in India, we have always been governed by kings; kings have made all our laws. Now the kings are gone, and there is no one left to make a move. The Government dare not; it has to fashion its ways according to the growth of public opinion. It takes time, quite a long time, to make a healthy, strong, public opinion which will solve its own problems; and in the interim we shall have to wait. The whole problem of social reform, therefore, resolves itself into this: where are those who want reform? Make them first. Where are the people? The tyranny of a minority is the worst tyranny that the world ever sees. A few men who think that certain things are evil will not make a nation move. Why does not the nation move? First educate the nation, create your legislative body, and then the law will be forthcoming. First create the power, the sanction from which the law will spring. The kings are gone; where is the new sanction, the new power of the people? Bring it up. Therefore, even for social reform, the first duty is to educate the people, and you will have to wait till that time comes. Most of the reforms that have been agitated for during the last century have been ornamental. Every one of these reforms only touches the first two castes, and no other. The question of widow marriage would not touch seventy per cent. of the Indian women, and all such questions only reach the higher castes of Indian people who are educated, mark you, at the expense of the masses. Every effort has been spent in cleaning their own houses. But that is no reformation. You must go down to the basis of the thing, to the very root of the matter. That is what I call radical reform. Put the fire there and let it burn upwards and make an Indian nation. And the solution of the problem is not so easy, as it is a big and a vast one. Be not in a hurry, this problem has been known several hundred years. To-day it is the fashion to talk of Buddhism, and Buddhistic agnosticism, especially in the South. Little do they dream that this degradation which is with us to-day has been left by Buddhism.

This is the legacy which Buddhism has left to us. You read in books written by men who had never studied the rise and fall of Buddhism, that the spread of Buddhism was owing to the wonderful ethics and the wonderful personality of Gautama Buddha. I have every respect and veneration for Lord Buddha, but mark my words, the spread of Buddhism was less owing to the doctrines and the personality of the great preacher, than to the temples that were built, the idols that were erected, and the gorgeous ceremonials that were put before the nation. Thus Buddhism progressed. The little fireplaces in the houses, in which the people poured their libations were not strong enough to hold their own against these gorgeous temples and ceremonies, but later on the whole thing degenerated. It became a mass of corruption of which I cannot speak before this audience, but those who want to know about it may see a little of it in those big temples, full of sculptures, in Southern India, and this is all the inheritance we have from the Buddhists. Then arose the great reformer Sankaracharya and his followers, and during these hundreds of years, since his time to the present day, there has been the slow bringing back of the Indian masses to the pristine purity of the Vedantic religion. These reformers knew full well the evils which existed, yet they did not condemn. They did not say, "All that you have is wrong, and you must throw it away." It can never be so. To-day I read that my friend, Dr. Barrows says, that in three hundred years Christianity overthrew the Roman and Greek religious influences. That is not the word of a man who has seen Europe, and Greece, and Rome. The influence of Roman and Greek religion is all there, even in Protestant countries, only with changed names, old gods re-christened in a new fashion. They change their names; the goddesses become Marys and the gods become saints, and the ceremonials become new; even the old title of Pontifex Maximus is there. So, sudden changes cannot be, and Sankaracharya knew it. So did Ramanuja. The only way left them was slowly to bring up to the highest ideal, the existing religion. If they had sought to apply the other method they would have been hypocrites, for the very fundamental doctrine of their religion is evolution, the soul going towards the highest goal, through all these various stages and phases, which are therefore necessary and helpful. And who dares condemn them?

It has become a trite saying, that idolatry is wrong, and every man swallows it at the present time without questioning. I once thought so, and to pay the penalty of that I had to learn my lesson sitting at the feet of a man who realised everything through idols; I allude to Ramakrishna Paramahamsa. If such Ramakrishna Paramahamsas are produced by idol worship, what will you have—the reformer's creed or any number of idols? I want an answer. Take a thousand idols more if you can produce Ramakrishna Paramahamsas through idol worship, and may God speed you! Produce such noble natures by any means you can. Yet idolatry is condemned! Why? Nobody knows. Because some hundreds of years ago some man of Jewish blood happened to condemn it? That is, he happened to condemn everybody else's idols except his own. If God is represented in any beautiful form, or any symbolic form, said the Jew, it is awfully bad; it is sin. But if he is represented in the form of a chest, with two angels sitting on each side, and a cloud hanging over it, it is the holy of holies. If God comes in the form of a dove, it is holy. But if He comes in the form of a cow, it is heathen superstition; condemn it! That is how the world goes. That is why the poet says, "What fools we mortals be!" How difficult it is to look through each other's eyes, and that is the bane of humanity. That is the basis of hatred and jealousy, of quarrel and of fight. Boys, moustached babies, who never went out of Madras, standing up and wanting to dictate laws to three hundred millions of people, with thousands of traditions at their back! Are you not ashamed? Stand back from such blasphemy, and learn first your lessons! Irreverent boys, simply because you can scrawl a few lines upon paper and get some fool to publish them for you, you think you are the educators of the world, you think you are the public opinion of India! Is it so? This I have to tell to the social reformers of Madras, that I have the greatest respect and love for them. I love them for their great hearts and their love for their country, for the poor, for the oppressed. But what I would tell them with a brother's love is, that their method is not right; it has been tried a hundred years and failed. Let us try some new method. Did India ever stand in want of reformers? Do you read the history of India? Who was Ramanuja? Who was Sankara? Who was Nanaka? Who was Chaitanya? Who was Kabira? Who was Dadu? Who were all these great preachers, one following the other, a galaxy of stars of the first magnitude? Did not Ramanuja feel for the lower classes? Did he not try all his life to admit even the Pariah to his community? Did he not try to admit even Mahommedans to his own fold? Did not Nanaka confer with Hindus and Mahommedans, and try to bring about a new state of things? They all tried, and their work is still going on. The difference is this. They had not the fanfaronade of the reformers of to-day; they had no curses on their lips as modern reformers have; their lips pronounced only blessings. They never condemned. They said to the people that the race must always grow. They looked back and they said, "O Hindus, what you have done is good, but, my brothers, let us do better." They did not say, "You have been wicked, now let us be good." They said, "You have been good, but let us now be better." That makes a whole world of difference. We must grow according to our nature. Vain is it to attempt the lines of action that foreign societies have engrafted upon us; it is impossible. Glory unto God, that it is impossible, that we cannot be twisted and tortured into the shape of other nations. I do not condemn the institutions of other races; they are good for them, but not for us. What is meat for them may be poison for us. This is the first lesson to learn. With other sciences, other institutions, and other traditions behind them, they have got their present system. We, with our traditions, with thousands of years of Karma behind us, naturally can only follow our own bent, run in our own grooves, and that we shall have to do.

What is my plan then? My plan is to follow the ideas of the great ancient Masters. I have studied their work, and it has been given unto me to discover the line of action they took. They were the great originators of Society. They were the great givers of strength, and of purity, and of life. They did most marvellous work. We have to do most marvellous work also. Circumstances have become a little different, and in consequence the lines of action have to be changed a little, and that is all. I see that each nation, like each individual, has one theme in this life, which is its centre, the principal note round which every other note comes to form the harmony. In one nation political power is its vitality, as in England. Artistic life in another, and so on. In India, religious life forms the centre, the keynote of the whole music of national life; and if any nation attempts to throw off its national vitality, the direction which has become its own through the transmission of centuries,—that nation dies, if it succeeds in the attempt. And, therefore, if you succeed in the attempt to throw off your religion and take up either politics or society, or any other thing as your centre, as the vitality of your national life, the result will be, that you will become extinct. To prevent this you must make all and everything work through that vitality of your religion. Let all your nerves vibrate through the backbone of your religion. I have seen that I cannot preach even religion to Americans without showing them its practical effect on social life. I could not preach religion in England without showing the wonderful political changes the Vedanta would bring. So, in India, social reform has to be preached by showing how much more spiritual a life the new system will bring; and politics has to be preached by showing how much it will improve the one thing that the nation wants,—its spirituality. Every man has to make his own choice; so has every nation. We made our choice ages ago and we must abide by it. And, after all, it is not such a bad choice. Is it such a bad choice in this world to think, not of matter but of spirit, not of man but of God? That intense faith in another world, that intense hatred for this world, the intense power of renunciation, the intense faith in God, the intense faith in the immortal soul, is in you. I challenge anyone to give it up. You cannot. You may try to impose upon me by becoming materialists, by talking materialism for a few months, but I know what you are; if I take you by the hand, back you come as good theists as ever were born. How can you change your nature?

So every improvement in India requires first of all an upheaval in religion. Before flooding India with socialistic or political ideas, first deluge the land with spiritual ideas. The first work that demands our attention is, that the most wonderful truths confined in our Upanishads, in our Scriptures, in our Puranas—must be brought out from the books, brought out from the monasteries, brought out from the forests, brought out from the possession of selected bodies of people, and scattered broadcast all over the land, so that these truths may run like fire all over the country, from north to south, and east to west, from the Himalayas to Comorin, from Sindh to the Brahmaputra. Everyone must know of them, because it is said,—"This has first to be heard, then thought upon, and then meditated upon." Let the people hear first, and whoever helps in making the people hear about the great truths in their own scriptures, cannot make for himself a better Karma to-day. Says our Vyasa, "In this *kaliyuga* there is one Karma left. Sacrifices and tremendous Tapasyas are of no avail now. Of Karma one remains, and that is the Karma of giving. And of these gifts, the gift of spirituality and spiritual knowledge is the highest; the next gift, is the gift of secular knowledge; the next is the gift of life; and the fourth is the gift of food. Look at this wonderfully charitable race; look at the amount of gifts that are made in this poor, poor country; look at the hospitality, where a man can travel from the north to the south, having the best in the land, being treated always by everyone as if he was a friend, and where no beggar starves so long as there is a piece of bread anywhere!

In this land of charity, let us take up the energy of the first charity, the diffusion of spiritual knowledge. And that diffusion should not be confined within the bounds of India; it must go out all over the world. This has been the custom. Those that tell you that Indian thought never went outside of India, those that tell you that I am the first Sannyasin who went to foreign lands to preach, do not know the history of their own race. Again and again this phenomenon has happened. Whenever the world has required it, this perennial flood of spirituality has overflowed and deluged the world. Gifts of political knowledge can be made with the blast of trumpets, and the march of cohorts. Gifts of secular knowledge and social knowledge can be made with fire and sword; but spiritual knowledge can only be given in silence, like the dew that falls unseen and unheard, yet bringing into bloom masses of roses. This has been the gift of India to the world again and again. Whenever there has been a great conquering race, bringing the nations of the world together, making roads and transit possible, immediately India arose and gave her quota of spiritual power to the sum-total of the progress of the world. This happened ages before Buddha was born, and remnants of it are still left in China, in Asia Minor, and in the heart of the Malayan Archipelago. This was the case when the great Greek conqueror united the four corners of the then known world; then rushed out Indian spirituality, and the boasted civilisation of the West is but the remnant of that deluge. Now the same opportunity has again come; the power of England has linked the nations of the world together as was never done before. English roads and channels of communication rush from one end of the world to the other. Owing to English genius, the world to-day has been linked in such a fashion, as has never before been done. To-day trade centres have been formed such as have never been before in the history of mankind, and immediately, consciously or unconsciously, India rises up and pours forth her gifts of spirituality, and they will rush through these roads till they have reached the very ends of the world. That I went to America was not my doing, or your doing, but the God of India, who is guiding her destiny sent me, and will send hundreds of such to all the nations of the world. No power on earth can resist it. This also has to be done. You must go out to preach your religion, preach it to every nation under the sun, preach it to every people. This is the first thing to do. And after preaching spiritual knowledge, along with it will come that secular knowledge and every other knowledge that you want; but if you attempt to get the secular knowledge without religion, I tell you plainly, vain is your attempt in India, it will never have a hold on the people. Even the great Buddhistic movement was a failure, partially on account of that.

Therefore, my friends, my plan is to start institutions in India, to train our young men as preachers of the truths of our scriptures, in India and outside India. Men, men, these are wanted: everything else will be ready, but strong, vigorous, believing young men sincere to the backbone, are wanted. A hundred such and the world becomes revolutionised. The will is stronger than anything else. Everything must go down before the will, for that comes from God and God Himself; a pure and a strong will is omnipotent. Do you not believe in it? Preach, preach unto the world the great truths of your religion; the world waits for them. For centuries people have been taught theories of degradation. They have been told that they are nothing. The masses have been told all over the world that they are not human beings. They have been so frightened for centuries, till they have nearly become animals. Never were they allowed to hear of the Atman. Let them hear of the Atman—that even the lowest of the low have the Atman within, which never dies and never is born—Him whom the sword cannot pierce, nor the fire burn, nor the air dry, immortal, without beginning or end, the all-pure, omnipotent and omnipresent Atman! Let them have faith in themselves, for what makes the difference between the Englishman and you? Let them talk their religion and duty and so forth. I have found the difference. The difference is here, that the Englishman believes in himself, and you do not. He believes in his being an Englishman, and he believes he can do anything. That brings out the God within him, and he can do anything he likes. You have been told and taught that you can do nothing, and non-entities you are becoming every day. What we want is strength, so believe in yourselves. We have become weak, and that is why occultisms and mysticisms come to us, these creepy things; there may be great truths in them, but they have nearly destroyed us. Make your nerves strong. What we want is, muscles of iron and nerves of steel. We have wept long enough. No more weeping, but stand on your feet and be men. It is a man-making religion that we want. It is man-making theories that we want. It is man-making education all round that we want. And here is the test of truth—anything that makes you weak physically, intellectually and spiritually, reject as poison, there is no life in it, it cannot be true. Truth is strengthening. Truth is purity, truth is all knowledge; truth must be strengthening, must be enlightening, must be invigorating. These mysticisms, in spite of some grains of truth in them, are generally weakening. Believe me, I have a life-long experience of it, and the one conclusion that I draw is that it is weakening. I have travelled all over India, searched almost every cave here, and lived in the Himalayas. I know people who lived there all their lives. I love my nation, I cannot see you degraded, weakened any more than you are now. Therefore I am bound for your sake and for truth's sake to cry, "Hold!" and to raise my voice against this degradation of my race. Give up these weakening mysticisms, and be strong. Go back to your Upanishads, the shining, the strengthening, the bright philosophy, and part from all these mysterious things, all these weakening things. Take up this philosophy; the greatest truths are the simplest things in the world, simple as your own existence. The truths of the Upanishads are before you. Take them up, live up to them, and the salvation of India will be at hand.

One word more and I have finished. They talk of patriotism. I believe in patriotism, and I also have my own ideal of patriotism. Three things are necessary for great achievements. First, feel from the heart. What is in the intellect or reason? It goes a few steps and there it stops. But through the heart comes inspiration. Love opens the most impossible gates; love is the gate to all the secrets of the universe. Feel, therefore, my would-be reformers, my would-be patriots! Do you feel? Do you feel that millions and millions of the descendants of gods and of sages, have become next-door neighbours to brutes? Do you feel that millions are starving to-day, and millions have been starving for ages? Do you feel that ignorance has come over the land as a dark cloud? Does it make you restless? Does it make you sleepless? Has it gone into your blood, coursing through your veins, becoming consonant with your heart beats? Has it made you almost mad? Are you seized with that one idea of the misery of ruin, and have you forgotten all about your name, your fame, your wives, your children, your property, even your own bodies? Have you done that? That is the first step to become a patriot, the very first step. I did not go to America, as most of you know, for the Parliament of Religions, but this demon of a feeling was in me and within my soul. I travelled twelve years all over India, finding no way to work for my countrymen, and that is why I went to America. Most of you know that, who knew me then. Who cared about this Parliament of Religions? Here was my own flesh and blood sinking every day, and who cared for them? This was my first step.

You may feel, then; but instead of spending your energies in frothy talk, have you found any way out, any practical solution, some help instead of condemnation, some sweet words to soothe their miseries, to bring them out of this living death? Yet that is not all. Have you got the will to surmount mountain-high obstructions? If the whole world stands against you sword in hand, would you still dare to do what you think is right? If your wives and children are against you, if all your money goes, your name dies, your wealth vanishes, would you still stick to it? Would you still pursue it and go on steadily towards your own goal? As the great King Bhartrihari says—"Let the sages blame or let them praise; let the goddess of fortune come or let her go wherever she likes; let death come to-day, or let it come in hundreds of years; he indeed is the steady man who does not move one inch from the way of truth." Have you got that steadfastness? If you have these three things, each one of you will work miracles. You need not write in the newspapers, you need not go about lecturing, your very face will shine. If you live in a cave, your thoughts will permeate even through the rock walls, will go vibrating all over the world for hundreds of years, maybe, until they will fasten on to some brain, and work out there. Such is the power of thought, of sincerity, and of purity of purpose.

I am afraid I am delaying you, but one word more. This national ship, my countrymen, my friends, my children—this national ship has been ferrying millions and millions of souls across the waters of life. For scores of shining centuries it has been plying across this water, and through its agency, millions of souls have been taken to the other shore, to blessedness. But to-day, perhaps through your own fault, this boat has become a little damaged, has sprung a leak, and would you therefore curse it? Is it fit that you stand up and pronounce malediction upon it, one that has done more work than any other thing in the world? If there are holes in this national ship, this society of ours, we are its children. Let us go and stop the holes. Let us gladly do it with our hearts' blood, and if we cannot, then let us die. We will make a plug of our brains and put them into the ship, but condemn it, never. Say not one harsh word against this society. I love it for its past greatness. I love you all because you are the children of gods, and because you are the children of the glorious forefathers. How then can I curse you! Never. All blessings be upon you! I have come to you, my children, to tell you all my plans. If you hear them I am ready to work with you. But if you will not listen to them, and even kick me out of India, I will come back and tell you that we are all sinking! I am come now to sit in your midst, and, if we are to sink, let us all sink together, but never let curses rise to our lips.

VEDANTA IN ITS APPLICATION TO INDIAN LIFE.

There is a word which has become very common as an appellation of our race and our Religion. The word "Hindu," requires a little explanation in connection with what I mean by Vedantism. This word "Hindu" was the name that the ancient Persians used to apply to the river Sindhu. Whenever in Sanskrit there is an "S" in ancient Persian it changes into "H," so that "Sindhu" became "Hindu"; and you are all aware how the Greeks found it hard to pronounce "H" and dropped it altogether, so that we became known as Indians. Now this word, "Hindu" as applied to the inhabitants of the other side of the Indus, whatever might have been its meaning in ancient times, has lost all its force in modern times; for all the people that live on this side of the Indus no longer belong to one religion. There are the Hindus proper, the Mahommedans, the Parsees, the Christians, the Buddhists and Jains. The word "Hindu" in its literal sense ought to include all these; but as signifying the Religion, it would not be proper to call all these Hindus. It is very hard, therefore, to find any common name for our Religion, seeing that this Religion is a collection, so to speak, of various religions, of various ideas, of various ceremonials, and forms, all gathered together almost without a name, and without a church, and without an organisation. The only point where, perhaps, all our sects agree is, that we all believe in the Scriptures—the Vedas. This perhaps is certain, that no man can have a right to be called a Hindu who does not admit the supreme authority of the Vedas. All these Vedas, as you are aware, are divided into two portions—the Karma Kanda and the Jnana Kanda. The Karma Kanda, includes various sacrifices and ceremonials, of which the larger part has become disused in the present age. The Jnana Kanda, as embodying the spiritual teachings of the Vedas known as the Upanishads and the Vedanta, have always been cited as the hightest authority by all our teachers, philosophers, and writers, whether Dualist, or Qualified Monist, or Monist. Whatever be his philosophy or sect, every one in India has to find his authority in the Upanishads. If he cannot, his sect would be heterodox. Therefore perhaps the one name in modern times which would designate every Hindu throughout the land would be "Vedantist" or "Vaidik" as you may put it; and in that sense I always use the words "Vedantism" and "Vedanta." I want to make it a little clearer, for of late it has become the custom of most people to identify the word Vedanta with the Advaitic system of the Vedanta Philosophy. We all know that Advaitism is only one branch of the various philosophic systems that have been founded on the Upanishads. The followers of the Visishtadvaitic system have as much reverence for the Upanishads as the followers of the Advaita, and the Visishtadvaitists claim as much authority for the Vedanta as the Advaitist. So do the Dualists; so does every other sect in India; but the word Vedantist has become somewhat identified in the popular mind with the word Advaitist, and perhaps with some reason, because, although we have the Vedas for our Scriptures, we have Smritis and Puranas, —subsequent writings—to illustrate the doctrines of the Vedas; these of course have not the same weight as the Vedas. And the law is, that wherever these Puranas and Smritis differ from any part of the Sruti, the Sruti must be followed and the Smriti rejected. Now in the expositions of the great Advaitic philosopher Sankara, and the school founded by him, we find most of the authorities cited are of the Upanishads, very rarely is an authority cited from the Smritis, except, perhaps, to elucidate a point which could hardly be found in the Srutis. On the other hand, other schools take refuge more and more in the Smritis and less and less in the Srutis, and as we go to the more and more Dualistic sects we find a proportionate quantity of the Smritis quoted, which is out of all proportion to what we should expect from a Vedantist. It is perhaps because these gave such predominance to the Pauranic authorities, that the Advaitist came to be considered as the Vedantist *par excellence*, if I may say so.

However it might have been, the word Vedanta must cover the whole ground of Indian religious life, and it being the Vedas, by all acceptance it is the most ancient literature that we have; for whatever might be the idea of modern scholars, the Hindus are not ready to admit that parts of the Vedas were written at one time and parts were written at another time. They of course still hold on to their belief that the whole of the Vedas were produced at the same time, rather if I may say so, that they were never produced, but that they always existed in the mind of the Lord. This is what I mean by the word Vedanta, that it covers the ground of Dualism, of Qualified Monism and Advaitism in India. Perhaps we may even take in parts of Buddhism, and of Jainism too, if they would come in,—for our hearts are sufficiently large. But it is they that will not come in; we are ready; for upon severe analysis you will always find that the essence of Buddhism was all borrowed from the same Upanishads; even the ethics, the so-called great and wonderful ethics of Buddhism, were there word for word, in some or other of the Upanishads, and so all the good doctrines of the Jains were there, minus their vagaries. In the Upanishads, also, we find the germs of all the subsequent development of Indian religious thought. Sometimes it has been urged without any ground whatsoever, that there is no ideal of Bhakti in the Upanishads. Those that have been students of the Upanishads know that that is not true at all. There is enough of Bhakti in every Upanishad, if you will only seek for it; but many other ideas which are found so fully developed in later times in the Puranas and other Smritis are only in the germ in the Upanishads. The sketch, the skeleton, was there, as it were. It was filled in in some of the Puranas. But there is not one full-grown Indian ideal that cannot be traced back to the same source—the Upanishads. Certain ludicrous attempts have been made by persons without much Upanishadic scholarship to trace Bhakti to some foreign source; but as you know, these have all been proved to be failures, and all that you want of Bhakti is there, even in the Samhitas, not to speak of the Upanishads—it is there, worship and love and all the rest of it; only the ideals of Bhakti are becoming higher and higher. In the Samhita portions, now and then, you find traces of a religion of fear and tribulation; in the Samhitas now and then you find a worshipper quaking before a Varuna, or some other god. Now and then you will find they are very much tortured by the idea of sin, but the Upanishads have no place for the delineation of these things. There is no religion of fear in the Upanishads; it is one of Love, and one of Knowledge.

These Upanishads are our Scriptures. They have been differently explained, and, as I have told you already, whenever there is a difference between subsequent Pauranic literature and the Vedas, the Puranas must give way. But it is at the same time true that as a practical result we find ourselves ninety per cent. Pauranic and ten per cent. Vaidik, even if so much as that. And we all find the most contradictory usages prevailing in our midst, and also religious opinions prevailing in societies, which scarcely have any authority in the Scriptures of the Hindus; and in many cases, we read in books and see with astonishment, customs of the country that neither have their authority in the Vedas, nor in the Smritis or Puranas, but are simply local; and yet each ignorant villager thinks that if that little local custom dies out, he will no more remain a Hindu. In his mind Vedantism and these little local customs have been indissolubly identified. In reading the Scriptures it is hard for him to understand, that what he was doing has not the sanction of the Scriptures, and that the giving up of them will not hurt him at all, but on the other hand will make him a better man. Secondly, there is the other difficulty. These Scriptures of ours have been very vast. We read in the Mahabhashya of Patanjali, that great philological work, that the Sama Veda had one thousand branches. Where are they all? Nobody knows. So with each of the Vedas; the major portion of these books has disappeared, and it is only the minor portion that remains to us. They were all taken charge of by particular families; and either these families died out, or were killed under foreign persecution, or somehow became extinct; and with them, that branch of the learning of the Vedas they took charge of, became extinct also. This fact we ought to remember, as it always forms the sheet-anchor in the hands of those who want to preach anything new, or to defend anything, even against the Vedas. Wherever in India there is a discussion between local custom and the Srutis, and whenever it is pointed out that the local custom is against the Scriptures, the argument that is forwarded is, that it is not, that the custom existed in the branch of the Srutis which has become extinct; this has also been a custom. In the midst of all these varying methods of reading and commenting on our Scriptures, it is very difficult indeed to find the thread that runs through all of them; for we become convinced at once that there must be some common ground underlying all these varying divisions and sub-divisions; there must be harmony, a common plan, upon which all these little bits of buildings have been constructed, some basis common to this apparently hopeless mass of confusion which we call our religion. Otherwise it could not have stood so long, it could not have endured so long.

Coming to our commentators again, we find another difficulty. The Advaitic commentator, whenever an Advaitic text comes, preserves it just as it is; but the same commentator, as soon as a Dualistic text presents itself, tortures it if he can, and brings the most queer meaning out of it. Sometimes the "Unborn" becomes a "goat," such are the wonderful changes effected. To suit the commentator, "*Ajá*" the "Unborn" is explained as "*Ajá*" a she-goat. In the same way, if not in a still worse fashion, the texts are handled by the Dualistic commentator. Every Dualistic text is preserved, and every text that speaks of non-dualistic philosophy, is tortured in any fashion he likes. This Sanskrit language is so intricate, the Sanskrit of the Vedas is so ancient, and the Sanskrit philology so perfect that any amount of discussion can be carried on for ages in regard to the meaning of one word. If a Pandit takes it into his head, he can render anybody's prattle into correct Sanskrit by force of argument and quotation of texts and rules. These are the difficulties in our way of understanding the Upanishads. It was given to me to live with a man who was as ardent a Dualist, as ardent an Advaitist, as ardent a Bhakta, as a Jnani. And living with this man, first put it into my head to understand the Upanishads and the texts of the Scriptures from an independent and better basis than by blindly following the commentators; and in my opinion, and in my researches,

I came to the conclusion, that these texts are not at all contradictory. So we need have no fear of text-torturing at all! The texts are beautiful, aye, they are most wonderful, and they are not contradictory, but wonderfully harmonious, one idea leading up to the other. But the one fact I found is, that in all the Upanishads, they begin with Dualistic ideas, with worship and all that, and end with a grand flourish of Advaitic ideas.

Therefore, I now find, in the light of this man's life, that the Dualist and the Advaitist need not fight each other; each has a place, and a great place in the national life; the Dualist must remain, for he is as much part and parcel of the national religious life as the Advaitist; one cannot exist without the other; one is the fulfilment of the other; one is the building, the other is the top; the one the root, the other the fruit, and so on. Therefore, any attempt to torture the texts of the Upanishads appears to me very ridiculous. I begin to find out that the language is wonderful; apart from all its merits as the greatest philosophy, apart from its wonderful merit as theology, as showing the path of salvation of mankind, the Upanishadic literature is the most wonderful painting of sublimity that the world has. Here, comes out in full force that individuality of the human mind, that introspective intuitive Hindu mind. We have paintings of sublimity elsewhere in all nations, but almost without exception, you will find that their ideal is to grasp the sublime in the muscles. Take for instance, Milton, Dante, Homer or any of the Western poets. There are wonderfully sublime passages in them; but there, it is always grasping for the senses, the muscles getting the ideal of infinite expansion, the infinite of space. We find the same attempts made in the Samhita portion. You know some of those wonderful *Riks*, where creation is described; the very heights of expression of the sublime in expansion, and the infinite in space are attained; but they found out very soon that the Infinite cannot be reached in that way, that even infinite space and expansion, and infinite external nature could not express the ideas that were struggling to find expression in their minds, and so they fell back upon other explanations. The language became new in the Upanishads; it is almost negative, it is sometimes chaotic, sometimes taking you beyond the senses, pointing out to you something which you cannot grasp, which you cannot sense, and at the same time you feel certain that it is there. What passage in the world can compare with this?—**न तत्र सूर्यो भाति न चन्द्रतारकं नेमा विद्युतो भान्ति कुतोऽयमग्निः।** "There the sun cannot illumine, nor the moon, nor the stars, the flash of lightning cannot illumine the place, what to speak of this mortal fire." Again, where can you find a more perfect expression of the whole philosophy of the world, the gist of what the Hindus ever thought, the whole dream of human salvation, painted in language more wonderful, in figure more marvellous than this?

द्वा सुपर्णा सयुजा सखाया समानं वृक्षं परिषस्वजाते ।
तयोरन्यः पिप्पलं स्वाद्वत्त्यनश्नन्नन्यो अभिचाकशीति ॥
समाने वृक्षे पुरुषो निमग्नोऽनीशया शोचति मुह्यमानः ।
जुष्टं यदा पश्यत्यन्यमीशमस्य महिमानमिति वीतशोकः ॥

Upon the same tree there are two birds of beautiful plumage, most friendly to each other, one eating the fruits, the other sitting there calm and silent without eating; the one on the lower branch eating sweet and bitter fruits in turn and becoming happy and unhappy, but the other one on the top, calm and majestic; he eats neither sweet nor bitter fruits, cares neither for happiness nor misery, immersed in his own glory. This is the picture of the human soul. Man is eating the sweet and bitter fruits of this life, pursuing gold, pursuing his senses, pursuing the vanities of life, hopelessly, madly careering he goes. In other places the Upanishads have compared the human soul to the charioteer, and the senses to the mad horses unrestrained. Such is the career of men pursuing the vanities of life, children dreaming golden dreams only to find that they are but vain, and old men chewing the cud of their past deeds, and yet not knowing how to get out of this net-work. This is the world. Yet in the life of every one there come golden moments; in the midst of the deepest sorrows, nay, of the deepest joys there come moments when, a part of the cloud that hides the sun-light moves away as it were, and we catch a glimpse, in spite of ourselves, of something beyond,—away, away beyond the life of the senses; away, away beyond its vanities, its joys and its sorrows; away, away beyond nature, in our imaginations of happiness here or hereafter; away beyond all thirst for gold, or for fame, or for name, or for posterity. Man stops for a moment at this glimpse, and sees the other bird calm and majestic, eating neither sweet nor bitter fruits, but immersed in his own glory, self-content, self-satisfied. As the Gita says, यस्त्वात्मरतिरेव स्यादात्मतृप्तश्च मानवः । आत्मन्येव च संतुष्टस्तस्य कार्यं न विद्यते ॥ "He whose devotion is to the Atman, he who does not want anything beyond Atman, he who has become satisfied in the Atman, what work is there for him to do?" Why should he drudge? Man catches a glimpse, then again he forgets, and goes on eating the sweet and bitter fruits of life, and again he forgets; perhaps after a time, he catches another glimpse, and the lower bird goes nearer and nearer to the higher bird as blows after blows are received; if he be fortunate to receive hard knocks, then he comes nearer and nearer to his companion the other bird, his life, his friend, and as he approaches him he finds that the light from the higher bird is playing round his own plumage, and as he comes nearer and nearer, lo! the transformation is going on. The nearer and nearer he comes, he finds himself melting away, as it were, until he has entirely disappeared. He did not really exist; it was but the reflection of the other bird, who was there calm and majestic amidst the moving leaves. It was all his glory, that upper bird's. He remains without fear; perfectly satisfied, calmly serene. In this figure, the Upanishads take you from the Dualistic to the utmost Advaitic conception.

Endless examples can be cited, but we have no time in this lecture to do that, or to show the marvellous poetry of the Upanishads, the painting of the sublime, the grand conceptions. But one other idea I must note, that the language and the thought and everything come direct, they fall upon you like a sword-blade, strong as the blows of a hammer they come. There is no mistaking their meanings. Every tone of that music is firm and produces its full effect; no gyrations, no mad words, no intricacies in which the brain is lost. No signs of degradation are there;—no attempts at too much allegorising, too much piling of adjectives after adjectives, making it more and more intricate, till the whole of the sense is lost, and the brain becomes giddy, and man does not know his way out from the maze of that literature. There was none of that yet. If it be human literature, it must be the production of a race which has not yet lost any of its national vigour.

Strength, strength is what the Upanishads speak to me from every page. This is the one great thing to remember; it has been the one great lesson I have been taught in my life; strength, it says, strength, oh man, be not weak. Are there no human weaknesses, says man? There are, say the Upanishads, but will more weakness heal them, would you try to wash dirt with dirt? Will sin cure sin, weakness cure weakness? Strength, oh man, strength, say the

Upanishads, stand up and be strong; aye, it is the only literature in the world where you find the word, "*Abhih*," "fearless," used again and again; in no other scripture in the world is this adjective applied either to God or to man. "*Abhih*" "fearless!" And in my mind rises from the past, the vision of the great Emperor of the West, Alexander the Great, and I see, as it were in a picture, the great monarch standing on the banks of the Indus, talking to one of our Sannyasins in the forest; the old man he was talking to, perhaps naked, stark naked, sitting upon a block of stone, and the Emperor astonished at his wisdom tempting him with gold and honor, to come over to Greece. And this man smiles at his gold, and smiles at his temptations, and refuses, and then the Emperor standing on his authority as an Emperor, says, "I will kill you, if you do not come," and the man bursts into a laugh, and says, "You never told such a falsehood in your life, as you tell just now. Who can kill me? Me you kill, Emperor of the material world! Never! For I am Spirit unborn and undecaying, never was I born and never do I die, I am the Infinite, the Omnipresent, the Omniscient; and you kill me, child that you are!" That is strength, that is strength! And the more I read the Upanishads, my friends, my countrymen, the more I weep for you, for therein is the great practical application. Strength, strength for us. What we need is strength, who will give us strength? There are thousands to weaken us, and of stories we have had enough. Every one of our Puranas if you press it, gives out stories enough to fill three-fourths of the libraries of the world. Everything that can weaken us as a race we have had for the last thousand years. It seems as if during that period the national life had this one end in view, *viz.*, how to make us weaker and weaker, till we have become real earth-worms, crawling at the feet of every one who dares to put his foot on us. Therefore my friends, as one of your blood, as one that lives and dies with you, let me tell you that we want strength, strength, and every time strength. And the Upanishads are the great mine of strength. Therein lies strength enough to invigorate the whole world; the whole world can be vivified, made strong, energised through them. They will call with trumpet voice upon the weak, the miserable, and the down-trodden of all races, all creeds, and all sects, to stand on their feet and be free; freedom, physical freedom, mental freedom, and spiritual freedom are the watchwords of the Upanishads.

Aye, this is the one Scripture in the world, of all others, that does not talk of salvation, but of freedom. Be free from the bonds of nature, be free from weakness! And it shows to you that you have this freedom already in you. That is another peculiarity of its teachings. You are a Dvaitist; never mind, you have got to admit that by its very nature the soul is perfect; only by certain actions of the soul has it become contracted. Indeed Ramanuja's theory of contraction and expansion is exactly what the modern evolutionists call Evolution and Atavism. The soul goes back, becomes contracted as it were, its powers become potential, and by good deeds and good thoughts it expands again and reveals its natural perfection. With the Advaitist the one difference is, that he admits evolution in nature and not in the soul. Suppose there is a screen, and there is a small hole in the screen. I am a man standing behind the screen and looking at this grand assembly. I can only see very few faces here. Suppose the hole increases; as it increases more and more, all this assembly is revealed to me, until the hole has become identified with the screen. There is nothing between you and me in this case; neither you changed nor I changed; all the change was in the screen. You were the same from first to last; only the screen changed. This is the Advaitist's position with regard to Evolution—evolution of nature and manifestation of the Self within. Not that the Self can by any means be made to contract. It is unchangeable, the Infinite One. It was covered, as it were, with a veil, the veil of Maya, and as this Maya veil becomes thinner and thinner, the inborn, natural glory of the Soul comes out and becomes more manifest. This is the one great doctrine which the world is waiting to learn from India. Whatever they may talk, however they may try to boast, they will find out day after day, that no society can stand without admitting this. Do you not find how everything is being revolutionised? Do you not see how it was the custom to take for granted, that everything is wicked until it proves itself good? In education, in punishing criminals, in treating lunatics, in the treatment of common diseases even, that was the old law. What is the modern law? The modern law says, the body itself is healthy; it cures diseases of its own nature. Medicine can at the best but help the storing up of the best in the body. What says it of criminals? It takes for granted that however low a criminal may be, there is still the divinity within, which does not change, and we must treat criminals accordingly. All these things are now changing, and reformatories and penitentiaries are established. So with everything; consciously or unconsciously, that Indian idea of the divinity within every one is expressing itself even in other countries. And in your books is the explanation, which other nations have to accept. The treatment of one man to another will be entirely revolutionised, and these old old ideas of pointing to the weakness of mankind will have to go. They will have received their death-blow within this century. Now people may stand up and criticise us. I have been criticised from one end of the world to the other, as one who preaches the diabolical idea that there is no sin! Very good. The descendants of these very men will bless me as the preacher of virtue, and not of sin. I am the teacher of virtue, not of sin. I glory in being the preacher of light, and not of darkness.

The second great idea which the world is waiting to receive from our Upanishads is the solidarity of this universe. The old lines of demarcation and differentiation are vanishing rapidly. Electricity and steam-power are placing the different parts of the world in intercommunication with each other, and, as a result, we Hindus no longer say that every country beyond our own land is peopled with demons and hobgoblins; nor do the people of Christian countries say that India is only peopled by cannibals and savages. When we go out of our country, we find the same brother-man, with the same strong hand to help, with the same lips to say god-speed, and sometimes they are better than in the country in which we are born. When they come here, they find the same brotherhood, the same cheer, the same god-speed. Our Upanishads say that the cause of all misery is ignorance; and that is perfectly true when applied to every state of life, either social or spiritual. It is ignorance that makes us hate each other, it is through ignorance that we do not know, and do not love each other. As soon as we come to know each other love comes, must come, for, are we not one? Thus we find solidarity coming in spite of itself. Even in Politics and Sociology, problems that were only national twenty years ago can no more be solved on national grounds only. They are assuming huge proportions, gigantic shapes. They can only be solved when looked at in the broader light of international grounds. International organisations, international combinations, international laws are the cry of the day. That shows the solidarity. In science, every day they are coming to a similar broad view of matter. You speak of matter, the whole universe as one mass, one ocean of matter, in which you and I, the sun and the moon, and everything, else, are but the names of different little whirlpools and nothing more. Mentally speaking it is one universal ocean of thought, in which you and I are similar little whirlpools, and as spirit it moveth not, it changeth not. It is the One Unchangeable, Unbroken, Homogeneous Atman. The cry for morality is coming also, and that is to be found in our books. The explanation of morality, the fountain of ethics, that also the world wants; and that it will get here. What do we want in India? If foreigners want these things, we want them twenty times more. Because, in spite of the greatness of the Upanishads, in spite of our boasted ancestry of sages, compared to many other races, I must tell you that we are weak, very weak. First of all, is our physical weakness. That physical weakness is the cause at least of one-third of our miseries. We are lazy; we cannot work; we cannot combine; we do not love each other; we are intensely selfish; not three of us can come together without hating each other, without being jealous of each other. That is the state in which we are,—hopelessly disorganised mobs, immensely selfish, fighting each other for centuries as to whether a certain mark is to be put on our forehead this way or that way; writing volumes and volumes upon such momentous questions as to whether the look of a man spoils my food or not! This we have been doing for the last few centuries. We cannot expect anything high from a race whose whole brain energy has been occupied in such wonderfully beautiful problems and researches! And are we not ashamed of ourselves? Aye, sometimes we are, but though we think these things frivolous, we cannot give them up. We think many things and never do them; parrot-like, thinking has become a habit with us, and never doing. What is the cause of that? Physical weakness. This sort of weak brain is not able to do anything; we must strengthen it. First of all, our young men must be strong. Religion will come afterwards. Be strong my young friends; that is my advice to you. You will be nearer to Heaven through foot-ball than through the study of the Gita. These are bold words, but I have to say them, for I love you. I know where the shoe pinches. I have gained a little experience. You will understand Gita better with your biceps, your muscles a little stronger. You will understand the mighty genius and the mighty strength of Krishna better with a little of strong blood in you. You will understand the Upanishads better and the glory of the Atman, when your body stands firm upon your feet, and you feel yourselves as men. Thus we have to apply these to our needs.

People get disgusted many times at my preaching Advaitism. I do not mean to preach Advaitism, or Dvaitism, or any *ism* in the world. The only *ism* that we require now is this wonderful idea of the soul—its eternal might, its eternal strength, its eternal purity, and its eternal perfection. If I had a child I would from its very birth begin to tell it, "Thou art the Pure One." You have read in one of the Puranas that beautiful story of Queen Madalasa, how as soon as she has a child she puts her baby with her own hands in the cradle, and how as the cradle rocks to and fro, she begins to sing, "Thou art the Pure One, the Stainless, Sinless, the Mighty One, the Great One." Aye, there is much in that. Feel that you are great and you become great. What did I get as my experience all over the world, is the question. They may talk about sinners; and if all Englishmen really believed that they were sinners, Englishmen would be no better than the Negroes in central Africa. God bless them that they do not believe it! On the other hand, the Englishman believes he is born the lord of the world. He believes he is great and can do anything in the world; if he wants to go to the sun or the moon, he believes he can, and that makes him great. If he had believed his priests that he was a poor miserable sinner, going to be barbecued through all eternity, he would not be the same Englishman that he is to-day. So I find in every nation that, in spite of priests and superstition, the divine within lives and asserts itself. We have lost faith. Would you believe me, we have less faith than the Englishman and woman, a thousand times less faith! These are plain words, but I say it, I cannot help it. Don't you see how Englishmen and women, when they catch our ideals, become mad as it were, and although they are the ruling class, they come to India to preach our own religion notwithstanding the jeers and ridicule of their own countrymen? How many of you could do that? And why cannot you do that? Do you not know it? You know more than they do; you are more wise than is good for you, that is your difficulty! Simply because your blood is only like water, your brain is sloughing, your body is weak! You must change the body. Physical weakness is the cause and nothing else. You have talked of reforms, of ideals, and all these things, for the last hundred years, and when it comes to practice, you are not to be found anywhere;—till you have disgusted the whole world, and the very name of Reform is a thing of ridicule! And what is the cause? Do you not know? You know too well. The only cause is that you are weak, weak, weak, your body is weak, your mind is weak, you have no faith in yourselves! Centuries and centuries, a thousand years of crushing tyranny of castes, and kings, and foreigners, and your own people, have taken out all your strength, my brethren! Your backbone is broken, you are like down-trodden worms! Who will give you strength? Let me tell you, strength, strength, is what we want. And the first step in getting strength is to uphold the Upanishads, and believe that "I am the Soul." "Me the sword cannot cut; no weapons pierce; me the fire cannot burn; me the air cannot dry; I am the Omnipotent, I am the Omniscient." So repeat these blessed saving words. Do not say we are weak; we can do anything and everything. What can we not do, everything can be done by us; we all have the same glorious soul, let us believe in it. Have faith, as Nachiketa. At the time of his father's sacrifice, faith came unto Nachiketa; aye, I wish that faith would come to each of you; and every one of you would stand up a giant, a world-mover with a gigantic intellect, an infinite God in every respect; that is what I want you to become. This is the strength that you get from the Upanishads, this is the faith that you get from there.

Aye, but it was only for the Sannyasin! *Rahasya!* The Upanishads were in the hands of the Sannyasin; he went into the forest! Sankara was a little kind, and says even *Grihasthas* may study the Upanishads, it will do them good; it will not hurt them. But still the idea is that the Upanishads talked only of the forest life of the recluse. As I told you the other day, the only commentary, the authoritative commentary on the Vedas, has been made once and for all by Him who inspired the Vedas, by Krishna in the Gita. It is there for every one in every occupation of life. These conceptions of the Vedanta must come out, must remain not only in the forest, not only in the cave, but they must come to work out at the Bar and the Bench, in the Pulpit, and in the cottage of the poor man, with the fishermen that are catching fish, and with the students that are studying. They call to every man, woman, and child, whatever be their occupation, wherever they may be; and what is there to fear! How can the fishermen and all these carry out the ideals of the Upanishads? The way has been shown. It is infinite; religion is infinite, none can go beyond it; and whatever you do sincerely, is good for you.

Even the least thing well done brings marvellous results; therefore let every one do what little he can. If the fisherman thinks that he is the spirit, he will be a better fisherman; if the student thinks he is spirit, he will be a better student. If the lawyer thinks that he is spirit, he will be a better lawyer, and so on, and the result will be that the castes will remain for ever. It is in the nature of society to form itself into groups; and what will go will be these privileges! Caste is a natural order. I can perform one duty in social life, and you another; you can govern a country, and I can mend a pair of old shoes, but that is no reason why you are greater than I, for can you mend my shoes? Can I govern the country? I am clever in mending shoes, you are clever in reading Vedas, but that is no reason why you should trample on my head; why if one commits murder should he be praised, and if another steals an apple why should he be hanged! This will have to go. Caste is good. That is the only natural way of solving life. Men must form themselves into groups, and you cannot get rid of that. Wherever you go there will be caste. But that does not mean that there should be these privileges. They should be knocked on the head. If you teach Vedanta to the fisherman, he will say, I am as good a man as you, I am a fisherman, you are a philosopher, but I have the same God in me, as you have in you. And that is what we want, no privilege for any one, equal chances for all; let every one be taught that the Divine is within, and every one will work out his own salvation.

Liberty is the first condition of growth. It is wrong, a thousand times wrong, if any of you dares to say 'I will work out the salvation of this woman or child.' I am asked again and again, what I think of the widow problem and what I think of the woman question. Let me answer once for all,—am I a widow that you ask me that nonsense. Am I a woman, that you ask me that question again and again? Who are you to solve women's problems? Are you the Lord God that you should rule over every widow and every woman? Hands off! They will solve their own problems. Oh tyrants, attempting to think that you can do anything for any one! Hands off! The Divine will look after all. Who are you to assume that you know everything? How dare you think, oh blasphemers, that you have the right over God? For don't you know that every soul is the soul of God? Mind your own Karma, a load of Karma is there in you to work out. Your nation may put you upon a pedestal, your society may cheer you up to the skies, and fools may praise you; but He sleeps not, and retribution will be sure to follow, here or hereafter.

Look upon every man, woman and every one as God. You cannot help anyone; you can only serve; serve the children of the Lord, serve the Lord Himself, if you have the privilege. If the Lord grants that you can help any one of His children, blessed you are; do not think too much of yourselves. Blessed you are that that privilege was given to you, when others had it not. Do it only as a worship. I should see God in the poor, and it is for my salvation that I go and worship them. The poor and the miserable are for our salvation, so that we may serve the Lord, coming in the shape of the diseased, coming in the shape of the lunatic, the leper, and the sinner! Bold are my words, and let me repeat that it is the greatest privilege in our life that we are allowed to serve the Lord in all these shapes. Give up the idea that by ruling over others, you can do any good to them. But you can do just the same as in the case of the plant; you can supply the growing seed with the materials for the making up of its body, bringing to it the earth, the water, the air, that it wants. It will take all that it wants by its own nature, it will assimilate and grow by its own nature.

Bring all light into the world; light, bring light! Let light come unto every one; the task will not be finished till every one has reached the Lord. Bring light to the poor, and bring more light to the rich, for they require it more than the poor; bring light to the ignorant, and more light to the educated, for the vanities of the education of our time are tremendous! Thus bring light to all and leave the rest unto the Lord, for in the words of the same Lord, "To work you have the right and not to the fruits thereof." Let not your work produce results for *you*, and at the same time may you never be without work.

May He who taught such grand ideas to our forefathers ages ago, help us to get strength to carry into practice His commands.

THE SAGES OF INDIA.

In speaking of the sages of India, my mind goes back to those periods of which history has no record, and tradition tries in vain to bring the secrets out of the gloom of the past. The sages of India have been almost innumerable, for what has the Hindu nation been doing for thousands of years except producing sages? I will take, therefore, the lives of a few of the most brilliant ones, the epoch-makers, and present them before you, that is to say, my study of them. In the first place, we have to understand a little about our scriptures. Two ideals of truth are in our scriptures, the one is, what we call the eternal, and the other is not so authoritative, yet binding under particular circumstances, times, and places. The eternal relations which deal with the nature of the soul, and of God, and the relations between souls and God, are embodied in what we call the Srutis, the Vedas. The next set of truths is what we call the Smritis, as embodied in the works of Manu, Yajnavalkya, and other writers, and also in the Puranas, down to the Tantras. This second class of books and teachings is subordinate to the Srutis, inasmuch as whenever anyone of these contradicts anything in the Srutis, the Srutis must prevail. This is the law. The idea is that the framework of the destiny and goal of man has been all delineated in the Vedas, the details have been left to be worked out in the Smritis and Puranas. As for general directions, the Srutis are enough; for spiritual life, nothing more can be said, nothing more can be known. All that is necessary has been known, all the advice that is necessary to lead the soul to perfection has been completed in the Srutis; the details alone were left out, and these the Smritis have supplied from time to time. Another peculiarity is that these Srutis have many sages as the recorders of the truths in them, mostly men, even, some women. Very little is known of their personalities, the dates of their birth, and so forth, but their best thoughts, their best discoveries, I should say, are preserved there, embodied in the sacred literature of our country, the Vedas. In the Smritis, on the other hand, personalities are more in evidence. Startling, gigantic, impressive, world-moving persons stand before us, as it were, for the first time, sometimes of more magnitude, even, than their teachings.

This is a peculiarity which we have to understand,—that our religion preaches an Impersonal Personal God. It preaches any amount of impersonal laws *plus* any amount of personality, but the very fountain-head of our religion is in the Srutis, the Vedas, which are perfectly impersonal; the persons all come in the Smritis and Puranas, the great Avatars, Incarnations of God, Prophets, and so forth. And this ought also to be observed, that except our religion, every other religion in the world, depends upon the life or lives of some personal founder or founders. Christianity is built upon the life of Jesus Christ, Mahommedanism, upon Mahommed, Buddhism, upon Buddha, Jainism, upon the Jinas, and so on. It naturally follows that there must be in all these religions a good deal of fight about what they call the historical evidences of these great personalities. If at any time the historical evidences about the existence of these personages in ancient times become weak, the whole building of the religion tumbles down and is broken to pieces. We escaped this fate because our religion is not based upon persons but on principles. That you obey your religion is not because it came through the authority of a sage, no, not even of an Incarnation. Krishna is not the authority of the Vedas, but the Vedas are the authority of Krishna himself. His glory is that he is the greatest preacher of the Vedas that ever existed. So as to the other Incarnations; so with all our sages. Our first principle is that all that is necessary for the perfection of man and for attaining unto freedom is there, in the Vedas. You cannot find anything new. You cannot go beyond a perfect unity, which is the goal of all knowledge; this has been already reached there, and it is impossible to go beyond the unity. Religious knowledge became complete when *Tat twam asi* was discovered, and that was in the Vedas. What remained, was the guidance of people from time to time, according to different times and places, according to different circumstances and environments; people had to be guided along the old, old path, and for this these great teachers came, these great sages. Nothing can bear out more clearly this position than the celebrated saying of Sri Krishna in the Gita—"Whenever virtue subsides and irreligion prevails, I create Myself for the protection of the good; for the destruction of all immorality I am coming from time to time." This is the idea in India.

What follows? That on the one hand, there are these eternal principles which stand upon their own foundations, without depending on any reasoning even, much less on the authority of sages however great, of Incarnations however brilliant they may have been. We may remark that as this is the unique position in India, our claim is that the Vedanta only can be the universal religion, that it is already the existing universal religion in the world, because it teaches principles and not persons. No religion built upon a person can be taken up as a type by all the races of mankind. In our own country we find that there have been so many grand characters; in even a small city many persons are taken up as types by the different minds in that one city. How is it possible that one person, as Mahommed or Buddha or Christ, can be taken up as the one type for the whole world? nay, that the whole of morality, ethics, spirituality and religion can be true only from the sanction of that one person, and one person alone? Now, the Vedantic religion does not require any such personal authority; its sanction is the eternal nature of man, its ethics are based upon the eternal spiritual solidarity of man, already existing, already attained and not to be attained. On the other hand, from the very earliest times, our sages have been feeling conscious of this fact that the vast majority of mankind require a personality. They must have a Personal God, in some form or other. The very Buddha who declared against the existence of a Personal God had not died fifty years before his disciples manufactured a Personal God, out of him. This Personal God is necessary, and at the same time we know that instead of and better than vain imaginations of a Personal God, which in ninety-nine cases out of a hundred are unworthy of human worship, we have in this world, living and walking in our midst, living Gods, now and then. These are more worthy of worship than any imaginary God, any creation of our imaginations, that is to say any idea of God which we can make. Sri Krishna is much greater than any idea of God you or I can make. Buddha is a much higher idea, a more living and idolised idea, than they ideal you or I can conceive of in our minds, and therefore it is that they always command the worship of mankind, even to the exclusion of all imaginary deities. This our sages knew, and therefore left it open to all Indian people to worship such great personages, such Incarnations. Nay, the greatest of these Incarnations goes further.—"Wherever there is an extraordinary spiritual power manifested by external man, know that I am there; it is from Me that that manifestation comes." That leaves the door open for the Hindu to worship the Incarnations of all the countries in the world. The Hindu can worship any sage and any saint from any country whatsoever, and as a fact we know that we go and worship many times in the churches of the Christians, and many, many times in the Mahommedan mosques, and that is good. Why not? Ours, as I have said, is the universal religion. It is inclusive enough, it is broad enough to include all the ideals. All the ideals of religion that already exist in the world can be immediately included, and we can patiently wait for all the ideals that are to come in the future, to be taken in the same fashion, embraced in the infinite arms of the religion of the Vedanta.

This, more or less, is our position with regard to the great sages, the Incarnations of God. There are also secondary characters. We find the word Rishi again and again mentioned in the Vedas, and it has become a common word at the present time. The Rishi is the great authority. We have to understand that idea. The definition is that the Rishi is the *Mantra drashtâ*, the seer of thought. What is the proof of religion?—this was asked in very ancient times. There is no proof in the senses, was the declaration. यतो वाचो निवर्तन्ते अप्राप्य मनसा सह। "From whence words reflect back with thought without reaching the goal," न तत्र चक्षुर्गच्छति न वाग् गच्छति नो मनो। "There the eyes cannot reach, neither can the mind, nor any of the organs,"—that has been the declaration for ages and ages. Nature outside cannot give us any answer as to the existence of the soul, the existence of God, the eternal life, the goal of man, and all that. This mind is continually changing, always in a state of flux; it is finite, it is broken into pieces. How can Nature tell of the Infinite, the Unchangeable, the Unbroken, the Indivisible, the Eternal? It never can. And whenever mankind has striven to get an answer from dull dead matter, history shows how disastrous the results have been. How comes, then, the knowledge which the Vedas declared? It comes through being a Rishi. This knowledge is not in the senses; but are the senses the be-all and the end-all of the human being? Who dares say that the senses are the all-in-all of man? Even in our lives, in the life of everyone of us here, there come moments of calmness, perhaps, when we see before us the death of one we loved, when some shock comes to us, or when extreme blessedness comes to us; many other occasions there are when the mind, as it were, becomes calm, feels for the moment its real nature, and a glimpse of the Infinite beyond, where words cannot reach nor the mind go, is revealed to us. This happens in ordinary life, but it has to be heightened, practised, perfected. Men found out ages ago that the soul is not bound or limited by the senses, no, not even by consciousness. We have to understand that this consciousness is only the name of one link in the infinite chain. Being is not identical with consciousness, but consciousness is only one part of Being. Beyond consciousness is where the bold search. Consciousness is bound by the senses. Beyond that, beyond the senses, men must go, in order to arrive at truths of the spiritual world; and there are even now persons who succeed in going beyond the bounds of the senses. These are called Rishis, because they come face to face with spiritual truths.

The proof, therefore, of the Vedas is just the same as the proof of this table before me, *pratyaksham*, direct perception. This I see with the senses, and the truths of spirituality we also see in a superconscious state of the human soul. This Rishi state is not limited by time or place, by sex or race. Vâtsâyana boldly declares that this Rishihood is the common property of the descendant of the sage, of the Aryan, of the non-Aryan, of even the Mlechcha. This is the sageship of the Vedas, and constantly we ought to remember this ideal of religion in India, which I wish other nations of the world would also remember and learn, so that there may be less fight and less quarrel. Religion is not in books, nor in theories, nor in dogmas, nor in talking, not even in reasoning. It is—being and becoming. Aye, my friends, until each one of you has become a Rishi and come face to face with spiritual facts, religious life has not begun for you. Until the superconscious opens for you, religion is mere talk, it is nothing but preparation. You are talking second-hand, third-hand, and here applies that beautiful saying of Buddha when he had a discussion with some Brâhmanas! They came discussing about the nature of Brahman, and the great sage asked, "Have you seen Brahman?" "No," said the Brâhmana; "Or your father?" "No, neither has he;" "Or your grandfather?" "I don't think even he saw Him." "My friend, how can you discuss about a person, whom your father and grandfather never saw, and try to put each other down?" That is what the whole world is doing. Let us say in the language of the Vedanta, "This Atman is not to be reached by too much talk, no, not even by the highest intellect, no, not even by the study of the Vedas themselves." Let us speak to all the nations of the world in the language of the Vedas:—Vain are your fights and your quarrels; have you seen God whom you want to preach? If you have not seen, vain is your preaching; you do not know what you say, and if you have seen God you will not quarrel, your very face will shine. An ancient sage of the Upanishads, sent his son out to learn about Brahman, and the child came back, and the father asked, "What have you learnt?" The child replied he had learnt so many sciences. But the father said, "That is nothing, go back." And the son went back, and when he returned again the father asked the same question, and the same number of sciences was the answer from the child. Once more he had to go back, and the next time he came, his whole face was shining, and his father stood up and declared, "Aye, to-day, my child, your face shines like a knower of Brahman." When you have known God your very face will be changed, your voice will be changed, your whole appearance will be changed. You will be a blessing to mankind; none will be able to resist the Rishi. This is the Rishihood, the ideal in our religion. The rest, all these talks, and reasonings, and philosophies, and dualisms, and monisms, and even the Vedas themselves, are but preparations, secondary things. The other is primary. The Vedas, Grammar, Astronomy, &c., all these are secondary; that is supreme knowledge which makes us realise the Unchangeable One. Those who realised are the sages whom we find in the Vedas, and we understand how this Rishi is the name of a type, of a class, which every one of us, as true Hindus, is expected to become at some period of our life, and becoming which, to the Hindu, means salvation. Not belief in doctrines, nor going to thousands of temples, nor bathing in all the rivers in the world, but becoming the Rishi, the *Mantra drashtá*, that is freedom, that is salvation.

Coming down to later times, there have been great world-moving sages, great Incarnations, of whom there have been many, and according to the Bhâgavatam they also are infinite in number, and those that are worshipped most in India are Rama and Krishna. Rama, the ancient idol of the Heroic ages, the embodiment of truth, of morality, the ideal son, the ideal husband, the ideal father, and above all, the ideal King, this Rama has been presented before us by the great sage Valmiki. No language can be purer, none chaster, none more beautiful, and at the same time simpler, than the language in which the great poet has depicted the life of Rama. And what to speak of Sita? You may exhaust the literature of the world that is past, and I may assure you, that you will have to exhaust the literature of the world of the future, before finding another Sita. Sita is unique; that character was depicted once and for all. There may have been several Ramas, perhaps, but never more than one Sita! She is the very type of the true Indian woman, for, all the Indian ideals of a perfected woman have grown out of that one life of Sita; and here she stands these thousands of years, commanding the worship of every man, woman, and child, throughout the length and breadth of the land of Aryavartha. There she will always be, this glorious Sita, purer than purity itself, all patience, and all suffering. She who suffered that life of suffering without a murmur, she is the ever-chaste and ever-pure wife, she the ideal of the people, the ideal of the gods, the great Sita, our national God she must always remain. And every one of us knows her too well to require much delineation. All our mythology may vanish, even our Vedas may depart, and our Sanskrit language may vanish for ever, but so long as there will be five Hindus living here, even if only speaking the most vulgar *patois*, there will be the story of Sita present, mark my words. Sita has gone into the very vitals of our race. She is there in the blood of every Hindu man and woman; we are all children of Sita. Any attempt to modernise our women, if it tries to take our women apart from that ideal of Sita, is immediately a failure, as we see every day. The women of India must grow and develop in the foot-prints of Sita, and that is the only way.

The next is He who is worshipped in various forms, the favourite ideal of men as well as of women, the ideal of children, as well as of grown-up men. I mean He whom the writer of the Bhagavad-Gita was not content to call an Incarnation but says, "The other Incarnations were but parts of the Lord. He, Krishna was the Lord Himself." And it is not strange that such adjectives are applied to him when we marvel at the many-sidedness of his character. He was the most wonderful Sannyasin, and the most wonderful householder in one; he had the most wonderful amount of *Rajas*, power, and was at the same time living in the midst of the most wonderful renunciation. Krishna can never be understood until you have studied the Gita, for he was the embodiment of his own teaching. Every one of these Incarnations came as a living illustration of what they came to preach. Krishna, the preacher of the Gita, was all his life the embodiment of that Song Celestial; he was the great illustration of non-attachment. He gives up his throne and never cares for it. He, the leader of India, at whose word kings come down from their thrones, never wants to be a king. He is the simple Krishna, ever the same Krishna who played with the Gopis. Ah, that most marvellous passage of his life, the most difficult to understand, and which none ought to attempt to understand until he has become perfectly chaste and pure, that most marvellous expansion of love, allegorised and expressed in that beautiful play at Brindavan, which none can understand but he who has become mad with, and drunk deep of, the cup of love! Who can understand the throes of the love of the Gopis—the very ideal of love, love that wants nothing, love that even does not care for heaven, love that does not care for anything in this world, or the world to come? And here, my friends, through this love of the Gopis has been found the only solution of the conflict between the Personal and the Impersonal God. We know how the Personal God is the highest point of human life; we know that it is philosophical to believe in an Impersonal God, immanent in the universe, of whom everything is but a manifestation. At the same time our souls hanker after something concrete, something which we want to grasp, at whose feet we can pour out our soul, and so on. The Personal God is therefore the highest conception of human nature. Yet reason stands aghast at such an idea. It is the same old, old question which you find discussed in the Brahma Sutras, which you find Draupadi discussing with Yudhisthira in the forest,—if there is a Personal God, all-merciful, all-powerful, why is this hell of an earth here, why did He create this; He must be a partial God. There was no solution, and the only solution that can be found is what you read about the love of the Gopis. They hated every adjective that was applied to Krishna; they did not care to know that he was the Lord of creation, they did not care to know that he was almighty, they did not care to know that he was omnipotent, and so forth. The only thing they understood was, that he was infinite Love, that was all. The Gopis understood Krishna only as the Krishna of Brindavan. He, the leader of the hosts, the king of kings, to them was the shepherd, and the shepherd for ever. "I do not want wealth, nor many people, nor do I want learning; no, not even do I want to go to heaven. Let me be born again and again, but Lord, grant me this, that I may have love for Thee, and that for love's sake." A great landmark in the history of religion is here, the ideal of love for love's sake, work for work's sake, duty for duty's sake, and it for the first time fell from the lips of the greatest of Incarnations, Krishna, and for the first time in the history of humanity, upon the soil of India. The religions of fear and of temptations were gone for ever, and in spite of the fear of hell, and temptation to enjoyment in heaven, came the grandest of ideals, love for love's sake, duty for duty's sake, work for work's sake.

And what a love! I have told you just now that it is very difficult to understand the love of the Gopis. There are not wanting fools, even in the midst of us, who cannot understand the marvellous significance of that most marvellous of all episodes. There are, let me repeat, impure fools, even born of our blood, who try to shrink from that as if from something impure. To them I have only to say, first make yourselves pure; and you must remember that he who tells the history of the love of the Gopis is none else but Suka Deva. The historian who records this marvellous love of the Gopis is one who was born pure, the eternally pure Suka, the son of Vyasa. So long as there is selfishness in the heart, so long is love of God impossible; it is nothing but shopkeeping. I give you something, Oh Lord, you give me something in return. And says the Lord, if you do not do this I will take good care of you when you die. I will roast you all the rest of your lives, perhaps, and so on. So long as such ideas are in the brain how can one understand the mad throes of the Gopis' love? "Oh for one, one kiss of those lips, one who has been kissed by Thee, his thirst for Thee increases for ever, all sorrows vanish, and we forget love for everything else but for Thee and Thee alone." Aye! forget first the love for gold, and name and fame, and for this little trumpery world of ours. Then, only then, you will understand the love of the Gopis, too holy to be attempted without giving up everything, too sacred to be understood until the soul has become perfectly pure. People with ideas of sex, and of money, and of fame, bubbling up every minute in the heart, daring to criticise and understand the love of the Gopis! That is the very essence of the Krishna incarnation. Even the Gita, the great philosophy itself, does not compare with that madness, for in the Gita the disciple is taught slowly how to walk towards the goal, but here is the madness of enjoyment, the drunkenness of love, where disciples and teachers and teachings and books, and all these things have become one, even the ideas of fear and God, and heaven. Everything has been thrown away. What remains is the madness of love. It is forgetfulness of everything, and the lover sees nothing in the world except that Krishna, and Krishna alone, when the face of every being becomes a Krishna, when his own face looks like Krishna, when his own soul has become tinged with the Krishna colour. That was the great Krishna!

Do not waste your time upon little details. Take up the framework, the essence of the life. There may be many historial discrepancies, there many be interpolations in the life of Krishna. All these things may be true, but, at the same time, there must have been a basis, a foundation for this new and tremendous departure. Taking the life of any other sage or prophet, we find that that prophet is only the evolution of what had gone before him, we find that that prophet is only preaching the ideas that had been scattered about his own country even in his own times. Great doubts may exist even as to whether that prophet existed or not. But here, I challenge any one to show whether these things, these ideals—work for work's sake, love for love's sake, duty for duty's sake, were not original ideas with Krishna, and as such, there must have been someone with whom these ideas originated. They could not have been borrowed from anybody else. They were not floating about in the atmosphere when Krishna was born. But the Lord Krishna was the first preacher of this; his disciple Vyasa took it up and preached it unto mankind. This is the highest idea to picture. The highest thing we can get out of him is Gopijanavallava, the Beloved of the Gopis of Brindavan. When that madness comes in your brain, when you understand the blessed Gopis, then you will understand what love is. When the whole world will vanish, when all other considerations will have died out, when you will become pure-hearted with no other aim, not even the search after truth, then and then alone will rush before you the madness of that love, the strength and the power of that infinite love which the Gopis had, that love for love's sake. That is the goal. When you have got that you have got everything.

To come down to the lower stratum,—Krishna, the preacher of the Gita. Aye, there is an attempt in India now which is like putting the cart before the horse. Many of our people think that Krishna as the lover of the Gopis is something rather uncanny, and the Europeans do not like it much. Dr. So-and-so does not like it. Certainly then, the Gopis have to go! Without the sanction of Europeans how can Krishna live? He cannot! In the Mahabharata there is no mention of the Gopis except in one or two places, and those not very remarkable places. In the prayer of Draupadi there is mention of a Brindavan life, and in the speech of Sisupal there is again mention of this Brindavan. All these are interpolations! What the Europeans do not want must be thrown off! They are interpolations, the mention of the Gopis and of Krishna too! Well, with these men, steeped in commercialism, where even the ideal of religion has become commercial, they are all trying to go to heaven by doing something here; the Bunya wants compound interest, wants to lay by some thing here and enjoy it there. Certainly the Gopis have no place in such a system of thought. From that ideal lover we come down to the lower stratum of Krishna, the preacher of the Gita. Than the Gita no better commentary on the Vedas has been written or can be written. The essence of the Srutis, or of the Upanishads, is hard to be understood, seeing that there are so many commentators, each one trying to interpret in his own way. Then the Lord Himself comes, He who is the inspirer of the Srutis, to show us the meaning of them, as the preacher of the Gita, and to-day

India wants nothing better, the world wants nothing better than that method of interpretation. It is a wonder that subsequent interpreters of the Scriptures, even commenting upon the Gita, many times could not catch the meaning, many times could not catch the drift. For what do you find in the Gita, and what even in modern commentators? One non-dualistic commentator takes up an Upanishad, there are so many dualistic passages, and he twists and tortures them into some meaning, and wants to bring them all into a meaning of his own. If a dualistic commentator comes, there are so many dualistic texts which he begins to torture, to bring them all round to dualistic meaning. But you find in the Gita there is no attempt at torturing any one of them. They are all right, says the Lord; for slowly and gradually the human soul rises up and up, step after step, from the gross to the fine, from the fine to the finer, until it reaches the Absolute, the goal. That is what is in the Gita. Even the Karma Kanda is taken up, and it is shown that although it cannot give salvation direct, but only indirectly, yet that is also valid; images are valid indirectly; ceremonies, forms, everything is valid only with one condition, purity of the heart. For worship is valid, and leads to the goal, if the heart is pure and the heart is sincere; and all these various modes of worship are necessary, else, why should they be here? Religions and sects are not the work of hypocrites and wicked people, who invented all these to get a little money, as some of our modern men want to think. However reasonable that explanation may seem, it is not true, and they were not invented that way at all. They are the outcome of the necessity of the human soul. They are all here to satisfy the hankering and thirst of different classes of human minds, and you need not preach against them. The day when that necessity will cease they will vanish along with the cessation of that necessity, and so long as that necessity remains they must be there, in spite of your preaching, in spite of your criticisms. You may bring the sword or the gun into play, you may deluge the world with human blood, but so long as there is a necessity for idols, they must remain. These forms, and all the various steps in religion will remain, and we understand from the Lord Sri Krishna why they should.

A rather sadder chapter of India's history comes now. In the Gita we already hear the distant sound of the conflicts of sects, and the Lord comes in the middle to harmonise them all; He the great preacher of harmony, the greatest teacher of harmony, Lord Krishna Himself. He says, "In Me they are all strung like pearls upon a thread." We already hear the distant sounds, the murmurs of the conflict, and possibly there was a period of harmony and calmness, when it broke out anew, not only on religious grounds, but most possibly on caste grounds,—the fight between the two powerful factors in our community, the kings and the priests. And from the topmost crest of the wave that deluged India for nearly a thousand years, we see another glorious figure, and that was our Gautama Sakyamuni. You all know about his teachings and preachings. We worship Him as God incarnate, the greatest, the boldest preacher of morality that the world ever saw, the greatest Karma Yogi; as a disciple of himself, as it were, the same Krishna came to show how to make his theories practical. There came once again the same voice that in the Gita preached, "Even the least bit done of this religion saves from great fear." "Women, or Vaisyas, or even Sudras, all reach the highest goal." Breaking the bondages of all, the chains of all, declaring liberty to all to reach the highest goal, come the words of the Gita, rolls like thunder the mighty voice of Krishna—"Even in this life they have conquered heaven whose minds are firmly fixed upon the sameness, for God is pure and the same to all, therefore such are said to be living in God." "Thus seeing the same Lord equally present everywhere, the sage does not injure the Self by the self, and thus reaches the highest goal." As it were to give a living example of this preaching, as it were to make at least one part of it practical, the preacher himself came in another form, and this was Sakyamuni, the preacher to the poor and the miserable, he who rejected even the language of the gods to speak in the language of the people, so that he might reach the hearts of the people; he who gave up a throne to live with beggars, and the poor, and the downcast; he who pressed the Pariah to his breast like a second Râma.

You all know about his great work, his grand character. But the work had one great defect, and for that we are suffering even to-day. No blame attaches to the Lord. He is pure and glorious, but unfortunately such high ideals could not be well assimilated by the different uncivilised and uncultured races of mankind who flocked within the fold of the Aryans. These races, with varieties of superstition and hideous worship, rushed within the fold of the Aryan, and for a time appeared as if they had become civilised, but before a century had passed they brought out their snakes, their ghosts, and all the other things their ancestors used to worship, and thus the whole of India became one degraded mass of superstition. The earlier Buddhists in their rage against the killing of animals, had denounced the sacrifices of the Vedas; and these sacrifices used to be held in every house. There was a fire burning, and that was all the paraphernalia of worship. These sacrifices were obliterated, and in their place came gorgeous temples, gorgeous ceremonies, and gorgeous priests, and all that you see in India in modern times. I smile when I read books written by some modern people who ought to have known better, that the Buddha was the destroyer of Brahmanical idolatry. Little do they know that Buddhism created Brahmanism and idolatry in India. There was a book written a year or two ago by a Russian gentleman, who claimed to have found out a very curious life of Jesus Christ, and in one part of the book he says, that Christ went to the Temple of Jagannath to study with the Brâhmans, but became disgusted with their exclusiveness and their idols, and so he went to the Lamas of Thibet instead, became perfect, and went home. To any man who knows anything about Indian history, that very statement proves that the whole thing was a fraud, because the Temple of Jagannath is an old Buddhistic Temple. We took this and others over and re-Hinduised them. We shall have to do many things like that yet. That is Jagannath, and there was not one Brâhman there then, and yet we are told that Jesus Christ came to study with the Brâhmans there. So says our great Russian archæologist. Thus, in spite of the preaching of mercy to animals, in spite of the sublime ethical religion, in spite of the hair-splitting discussions about the existence, or non-existence of a permanent soul, the whole building of Buddhism tumbled down piecemeal; and the ruin was simply hideous. I have neither the time nor the inclination to describe to you the hideousness that came in the wake of Buddhism. The most hideous ceremonies, the most horrible, the most obscene books that human hands ever wrote, or the human brain ever conceived, the most bestial forms that ever passed under the name of religion, have all been the creation of degraded Buddhism.

But India has to live, and the spirit of the Lord descended again. He who declared that "I will come whenever virtue subsides" came again, and this time the manifestation was in the South, and up rose that young Brâhman of whom it has been declared that at the age of sixteen he had completed all his writings; the marvellous boy Sankaracharya arose. The writings of this boy of sixteen are the wonders of the modern world, and so was the boy. He wanted to bring back the Indian world to its pristine purity, but think of the amount of the task before him. I have told you a few points about the state of things that existed in India. All these horrors that you are trying to reform are the outcome of that reign of degradation. The Tartars and the Belluchis and all the hideous races of mankind came to India and became Buddhists, and assimilated with us, and brought their national customs, and the whole of our national life became a huge page of the most horrible and the most bestial customs. That was the inheritance which that boy got from the Buddhists, and from that time to this, the whole world in India is a re-conquest of this Buddhistic degradation, by the Vedanta. It is still going on, it is not yet finished. Sankara came, a great philosopher, and showed that the real essence of Buddhism and that of the Vedanta are not very different, but that the disciples did not understand the Master, and have degraded themselves, denied the existence of the soul and of God, and have become Atheists. That was what Sankara showed, and all the Buddhists began to come back to the old religion. But then they had become accustomed to all these forms; what could be done?

Then came the brilliant Ramanuja. Sankara, with his great intellect, I am afraid, had not as great a heart. Ramanuja's heart was greater. He felt for the down-trodden, he sympathised with them. He took up the ceremonies, the accretions that had gathered, made them pure so far as they could be, and instituted new ceremonies, new methods of worship, for the people who absolutely required them. At the same time he opened the door to the highest spiritual worship, from the Brâhman to the Pariah. That was Ramanuja's work. That work rolled on, invaded the North, was taken up by some great leaders there, but that was much later, during the Mahommedan rule, and the brightest of these prophets of comparatively modern times in the North was Chaitanya. You may mark one characteristic since the time of Ramanuja,—the opening of the door of spirituality to everyone. That has been the watchword of all prophets succeeding Ramanuja, as it had been the watchword of all the prophets before Sankara. I do not know why Sankara should be represented as rather exclusive; I do not find anything in his writings which is exclusive. As in the case of the declarations of the Lord Buddha, this exclusiveness that has been attributed to Sankara's teachings is most possibly not due to his teachings, but to the incapacity of his disciples. This one great northern sage, Chaitanya, represented the mad love of the Gopis. Himself a Brâhman, born of one of the most rationalistic families of the day, himself a professor of logic, fighting and gaining a word-victory,—for, this he had learnt from his childhood as the highest ideal of life,—and yet through the mercy of some sage the whole life of that man became changed, he gave up his fight, his quarrels, his professorship of logic, and became one of the greatest teachers of Bhakti the world has ever known,—mad Chaitanya. His Bhakti rolled over the whole land of Bengal, bringing solace to every one. His love knew no bounds. The saint or the sinner, the Hindu or the Mahommedan, the pure or the impure, the prostitute, the street-walker—all had a share in his love, all had a share in his mercy, and even to the present day, although greatly degenerated, as everything does become in time, yet his sect is the refuge of the poor, of the down-trodden, of the outcast, of the weak, of those who have been rejected by all society. But at the same time I must remark for truth's sake that we find this. In the philosophic sects we find wonderful liberalism. There is not a man who follows Sankara who will say that all the different sects of India are really different. At the same time he was a tremendous upholder of exclusiveness as regards caste. But with every Vaishnavite preacher we find a wonderful liberalism as to the teaching of caste questions, but exclusiveness as regards religious questions.

The one had a great head, the other a large heart, and the time was ripe for one to be born, the embodiment of both this head and heart; the time was ripe for one to be born, who in one body would have the brilliant intellect of Sankara and the wonderfully expansive, infinite heart of Chaitanya; one who would see in every sect the same spirit working, the same God; one who would see God in every being, one whose heart would weep for the poor, for the weak, for the outcast, for the down-trodden, for every one in this world, inside India or outside India; and at the same time whose grand brilliant intellect would conceive of such noble thoughts as would harmonise all conflicting sects, not only in India but outside of India, and bring a marvellous harmony, the universal religion of head and heart into existence; such a man was born, and I had the good fortune to sit at his feet for years. The time was ripe, it was necessary that such a man should be born, and he came; and the most wonderful part of it was, that his life's work was just near a city which was full of Western thought, a city which had run mad after these occidental ideas, a city which had become more Europeanised than any other city in India. There he lived, without any book-learning whatsoever; this great intellect never learnt even to write his own name, but the most brilliant graduates of our university found in him an intellectual giant. He was a strange man, this Sri Ramakrishna Paramahamsa. It is a long, long story, and I have no time to tell anything about him to-night. Let me now only mention the great Sri Ramakrishna, the fulfilment of the Indian sages, the sage for the time, one whose teaching is just now, in the present time, most beneficial. And mark the Divine power working behind the man. The son of a poor priest, born in an out-of-the-way village, unknown and unthought of, to-day is worshipped literally by thousands in Europe and America, and to-morrow will be worshipped by thousands more. Who knows the plans of the Lord! Now, my brothers, if you do not see the hand, the finger of Providence, it is because you are blind, born blind indeed. If time comes, and another opportunity, I will speak to you more fully about him. Only let me say now, that if I have told you one word of truth it was his and his alone, and if I have told you many things which were not true, which were not correct, which were not beneficial to the human race, they were all mine, and on me is the responsibility.

THE WORK BEFORE US.

(Delivered at the Triplicane Literary Society, Madras).

The problem of life is becoming deeper and broader every day as the world moves on. The watchword and the essence have been preached in the days of yore, when the Vedantic truth was first discovered, the solidarity of all life. One atom in this universe cannot move without dragging the whole world along with it. There cannot be any progress without the whole world following in the wake, and it is becoming every day clearer that the solution of any problem can never be attained on racial, or national, or narrow grounds. Every idea has to become broad till it covers the whole of this world, every aspiration must go on increasing till it has engulfed the whole of humanity, nay, the whole of life, within its scope. This will explain why our country for the last few centuries has not been what she was in the past. We find that one of the causes which led to this degeneration was the narrowing of our view, narrowing the scope of our actions.

Two curious nations there have been,—sprung of the same race, but placed in different circumstances and environments, working out the problems of life each in its own particular way. I mean the ancient Hindu and the ancient Greek. The Indian Aryan bounded on the north, by the snow-caps of the Himalayas, with fresh-water rivers like rolling oceans surrounding him in the plains, with eternal forests which, to him, seemed to be the end of the world,—turned his vision inward; and given the natural instinct, the superfine brain of the Aryan, with this sublime scenery surrounding him, the natural result was—that he became introspective. The analysis of his own mind was the great theme of the Indo-Aryan. With the Greek, on the other hand, who arrived at a part of the earth which was more beautiful than sublime, the beautiful islands of the Grecian Archipelago, nature all around him generous yet simple,—his mind naturally went outside. It wanted to analyse the external world. And, as a result we find, that from India have sprung all the analytical sciences, and from Greece all the sciences, of generalisation. The Hindu mind went on in its own direction and produced the most marvellous results. Even at the present day, the logical capacity of the Hindus, and the tremendous power which the Indian brain still possesses is beyond compare. We all know that our boys pitched against the boys of any other country triumph always. At the same time when the national vigour went, perhaps one or two centuries before the Mahommedan conquest of India, this national faculty became so much exaggerated that it degraded itself, and we find some of this degradation in everything in India, in art, in music, in sciences, in everything. In art no more was there a broad conception, no more the symmetry of form and sublimity of conception, but the tremendous attempt at the ornate and florid style had arisen. The originality of the race seemed to have been lost. In music no more were there the soul-stirring ideas of the ancient Sanskrit music, no more did each note stand, as it were, on its own feet, and produce the marvellous harmony, but each note had lost its individuality. The whole of modern music is a jumble of notes, a confused mass of curves. That is a sign of degradation in music. So, if you analyse your idealistic conceptions, you will find the same attempt at ornate figures, and loss of originality.

And even in religion, your special field, there came the most horrible degradations. What can you expect of a race which for hundreds of years has been busy in discussing such momentous problems as whether we should drink a glass of water with the right hand or the left? What more degradation can there be than that the greatest minds of a country have been discussing about the kitchen for several hundreds of years, discussing whether I may touch you or you touch me, and what is the penance for this touching! The themes of the Vedanta, the sublimest and the most glorious conceptions of God and soul ever preached on earth, were half-lost, buried in the forests, preserved by a few Sannyasins, while the rest of the nation discussed the momentous questions of touching each other, and dress and food. The Mahommedan conquest gave us many good things, no doubt; even the lowest man in the world can teach something to the highest; at the same time it could not bring vigour into the race. Then for good or bad, the English conquest of India took place. Of course every conquest is bad, for conquest is an evil, foreign Government is an evil, no doubt, but even through evil comes good sometimes, and the great good of the English conquest is this: England, nay the whole of Europe, has to thank Greece for its civilisation. It is Greece that speaks through everything in Europe. Every building, every piece of furniture has the impress of Greece upon it; European science and art are nothing but Grecian. To-day the ancient Greek is meeting the ancient Hindu on the soil of India. Thus, slowly and silently, the leaven has come, the broadening out, the life-giving, and the revivalist movement, that we see all around us, has been worked out by all these forces together. A broader and more generous conception of life is before us, and, although at first we have been deluded a little and wanted to narrow things down, we are finding out to-day that these generous impulses which are at work, these broader conceptions of life, are the logical interpretation of what is in our ancient books. They are the carrying out, to the rigorously logical effect, of the primary conceptions of our own ancestors. To become broad, to go out, to amalgamate, to universalise, is the end of our aims. And all the time we have been making ourselves smaller and smaller, and dissociating ourselves, contrary to the plans laid down in our scriptures.

Several dangers are in the way, and one is that of the extreme conception that we are *the* people in the world. With all my love for India, and with all my patriotism, and veneration for the ancients, I cannot but think that we have to learn many things from other nations. We must be always ready to sit at the feet of all, for, mark you, every one can teach us great lessons. Says our great law-giver, Manu: "Receive some good knowledge even from the low-born and even from the man of lowest birth, learn by service the road to heaven." We, therefore, as true children of Manu, must obey his commands, and be ready to learn the lessons of this life, or the life hereafter from any one who can teach us. At the same time we must not forget, that we have also to teach a great lesson to the world. We cannot do without the world outside India; it was our foolishness that we thought we could, and we have paid the penalty by about a thousand years of slavery. That we did not go out to compare things with other nations, did not mark the workings that have been all around us, has been the one great cause of this degradation of the Indian mind. We have paid the penalty; let us do it no more. All such foolish ideas, that Indians must not go out of India, are childish. They must be knocked on the head; the more you go out and travel among the nations of the world, the better for you and for your country. If you had done that for hundreds of years past you would not be here to-day, at the feet of every nation that wants to rule India. The first manifest effect of life is expansion. You must expand if you want to live. The moment you have ceased to expand, death is upon you, danger is ahead. I went to America and Europe, to which you so kindly allude; I had to, because that is the first sign of the revival of national life, expansion. This national reviving life, expanding inside, threw me off and thousands will be thrown off in that way. Mark my words, it has got to come if this nation lives at all. This expansion, therefore, is the greatest of the signs of the revival of national life, and through this expansion our quota of offering to the general mass of human knowledge, our part of the general upheaval of the world, is going out to the external world. Again, this is not a new thing. Those of you who think that the Hindus have been always confined within the four walls of their country through all ages, are entirely mistaken; you have not studied the whole books, you have not studied the history of the race aright if you think so. Each nation must give in order to live. When you give life you will have life; when you receive you must pay it by giving to all others, and that we have been living for so many thousands of years is a fact that stares us in the face, and the solution that remains is that we have been always giving to the outside world, whatever the ignorant may think.

But the gift of India is the gift of religion and philosophy, and wisdom, and spirituality, and religion does not want cohorts to march before its path and clear its way. Wisdom and philosophy do not want to be carried on floods of blood. Wisdom and philosophy do not march upon bleeding human bodies, do not march with violence but come on the wings of peace and love, and that has always been so. Therefore we had to give. I was asked by a young lady in London, "What have you Hindus done? You have never even conquered a single nation." That is true from the point of view of the Englishman, the brave, the heroic, the Kshatriya—conquest is the greatest glory that one man can have over another. That is true from his point of view, but from ours it is quite the opposite. If I ask myself what has been the cause of India's greatness, I answer, because we have never conquered. That is our glory. You are hearing every day, and sometimes I am sorry to say from men who ought to know better, denunciations of our religion, because it is not at all a conquering religion. To my mind that is the argument why our religion is truer than any other religion, because it never conquered, because it never shed blood, because its mouth always shed on all, words of blessing, of peace, words of love and sympathy. It is here and here alone that the ideals of toleration were first preached; and it is here and here alone that toleration and sympathy have become practical; it is theoretical in every other country; it is here and here alone, that the Hindu builds mosques for the Mahommedans and churches for the Christians. So, you see, our message has gone out to the world many a time, but slowly, silently, unperceived. It is on a par with everything in India. The one characteristic of Indian thought is its silence, its calmness. At the same time the tremendous power that is behind it is never expressed by violence. It is always the silent mesmerism of Indian thought. If a foreigner takes up our literature to study, at first it is disgusting to him; there is not the same stir, perhaps, the same amount of go that rouses him instantly. Compare the tragedies of Europe with our tragedies. The one is full of action, that rouses you for the moment, but when it is over there comes the reaction, and everything is gone, washed off as it were from your brains. Indian tragedies are like the mesmerist's power, quiet, silent, but as you go on studying them they fascinate you; you cannot move; you are bound; and whoever has dared to touch our literature has felt the bondage, and is there bound for ever.

Like the gentle dew that falls unseen and unheard, and yet brings into blossom the fairest of roses, so has been the contribution of India to the thought of the world. Silent, unperceived, yet omnipotent in its effect, it has revolutionised the thought of the world, yet nobody knows when it did so. It was once remarked to me, "How difficult it is to ascertain the name of any writer in India," to which I replied, 'That is the Indian idea.' Indian writers are not like modern writers, who steal ninety per cent. of their ideas from other authors, while only ten per cent. is their own, and they take care to write a preface in which they say, 'For these ideas I am responsible.' Those great master-minds producing momentous results in the hearts of mankind, were content to write their books without even putting their names, and to die quietly, leaving the books to posterity. Who knows the writers of our philosophy, who knows the writers of our Puranas? They all pass under the generic name of Vyasa, and Kapila, and so on. They have been true children of Sri Krishna. They have been true followers of the Gita; they practically carried out the great mandate, "To work you have the right, but not to the fruits thereof."

Thus, India is working upon the world, but one condition is necessary. Thoughts, like merchandise, can only run through channels made by somebody. Roads have to be made before even thought can travel from one place to another, and whenever in the history of the world a great conquering nation has arisen, linking the different parts of the world together, then has poured through these channels the thought of India, and thus entered into the veins of every race. Before even the Buddhists were born, there are evidences accumulating every day that Indian thought penetrated the world. Before Buddhism, Vedanta had penetrated into China, into Persia, and the Islands of the Eastern Archipelago. Again, when the mighty mind of the Greek had linked the different parts of the eastern world together, there came Indian thought; and Christianity with all its boasted civilisation is but a collection of little bits of Indian thought. Ours is the religion of which Buddhism, with all its greatness, is a rebel child, and of which Christianity is a very patchy imitation. One of these cycles has again arrived. There is the tremendous power of England which has linked the different parts of the world together. English roads no more are content like Roman roads to run over lands, but they have also ploughed the deep in all directions. From ocean to ocean run the roads of England. Every part of the world has been linked to every other part, and electricity plays a most marvellous part as the new messenger. Under all these circumstances we find again India reviving, and ready to give her own quota to the progress and civilisation of the world. And that I have been forced, as it were, by nature, to go over and preach to America and England, is the result. Every one of us ought to have seen that the time had arrived. Everything looked propitious, and Indian thought, philosophical and spiritual, must once more go over and conquer the world. The problem before us, therefore, is assuming larger proportions every day. It is not only that we must revive our own country,—that is a small matter; I am an imaginative man,—and my idea is the conquest of the whole world by the Hindu race.

There have been great conquering races in the world. We also have been great conquerors. The story of our conquest has been described by that noble Emperor of India, Asoka, as the conquest of religion and of spirituality. Once more the world must be conquered by India. This is the dream of my life, and I wish that each one of you who hear me to-day will have the same dream in your minds, and stop not till you have realised the dream. They will tell you every day that we had better look to our own homes first, and then go to work outside. But I will tell you in plain language that you work best when you work for others. The best work that you ever did for yourselves was when you worked for others, trying to disseminate your ideas in foreign languages beyond the seas, and this very meeting is proof how the attempt to enlighten other countries with your thoughts is helping your own country. One fourth of the effect that has been produced in this country by my going to England and America would not have been brought about had I confined my ideas only to India. This is the great ideal before us, and every one must be ready for it—the conquest of the whole world by India—nothing less than that, and we must all get ready for it, strain every nerve for it. Let foreigners come and flood the land with their armies, never mind. Up, India, and conquer the world with your spirituality! Aye, as has been declared on this soil first, love must conquer hatred, hatred cannot conquer itself. Materialism and all its miseries can never be conquered by materialism. Armies when they attempt to conquer armies only multiply and make brutes of humanity. Spirituality must conquer the West. Slowly they are finding out that what they want is spirituality to preserve them as nations. They are waiting for it, they are eager for it. Where is the supply to come from? Where are the men ready to go out to every country in the world with the messages of the great sages of India? Where are the men who are ready to sacrifice everything, so that this message shall reach every corner of the world? Such heroic souls are wanted to help the spread of truth. Such heroic workers are wanted to go abroad and help to disseminate the great truths of the Vedanta. The world wants it; without it the world will be destroyed. The whole of the Western world is on a volcano which may burst to-morrow, go to pieces to-morrow. They have searched every corner of the world and have found no respite. They have drunk deep of the cup of pleasure and found it vanity. Now is the time to work so that India's spiritual ideas may penetrate deep into the West. Therefore, young men of Madras, I specially ask you to remember this. We must go out, we must conquer the world through our spirituality and philosophy. There is no other alternative, we must do it or die. The only condition of national life, of awakened and vigorous national life, is the conquest of the world by Indian thought.

At the same time we must not forget that what I mean by the conquest of the world by spiritual thought, is the sending out the life-giving principles, not the hundreds of superstitions that we have been hugging to our breasts for centuries. These have to be weeded out even on this soil, and thrown aside, so that they may die for ever. These are the causes of the degradation of the race and will lead to softening of the brain. That brain which cannot think high and noble thoughts, which has lost all power of originality, which has lost all vigour, that brain which is always poisoning itself with all sorts of little superstitions passing under the name of religion, we must beware of. In our sight, here in India, there are several dangers. Of these, the two, Scylla and Charybdis, rank materialism and its rebound, arrant superstition, must be avoided. There is the man to-day who after drinking the cup of western wisdom, thinks that he knows everything. He laughs at the ancient sages. All Hindu thought to him is arrant trash, philosophy, mere child's prattle, and religion, the superstition of fools. On the other hand, there is the man educated, but a sort of monomaniac, who runs to the other extreme, and wants to explain the omen of this and that. He has philosophical and metaphysical, and Lord knows what other puerile explanations for every superstition that belongs to his peculiar race, or his peculiar gods, or his peculiar village. Every little village superstition is to him a mandate of the Vedas, and upon the carrying out of it, according to him, depends the national life. You must beware of this. I would rather see everyone of you rank atheists than superstitious fools, for the atheist is alive, and you can make something out of him. But if superstition enters, the brain is gone, the brain is softening, degradation has seized upon the life. Avoid these two. Brave, bold men, these are what we want. What we want is vigour in the blood, strength in the nerves, iron muscles and nerves of steel, not softening namby-pamby ideas. Avoid all these. Avoid all mystery. There is no mystery in religion. Is there any mystery in the Vedanta, or in the Vedas, or in the Samhitas, or in the Puranas? What secret societies did the sages of yore establish to preach their religion? What sleight-of-hand tricks are there recorded, as used by them to bring their grand truths to humanity? Mystery-mongering and superstition are always signs of weakness. These are always signs of degradation and of death. Therefore beware of them; be strong, and stand on your own feet. Great things are there, most marvellous things. We may call them supernatural things so far as our ideas of nature go, but not one of these things is a mystery. It was never preached on this soil that the truths of religion were mysteries or that they were the property of secret societies sitting on the snow-caps of the Himalayas. I have been in the Himalayas. You have not been there; it is several hundreds of miles from your homes. I am a Sannyasin, and I have been for the last fourteen years on my feet. These mysterious societies do not exist anywhere. Do not run after these superstitions. Better for you and for the race that you become rank atheists, because you would have strength, but these are degradation and death. Shame on humanity that strong men should spend their time on these superstitions, spend all their time in inventing allegories, to explain the most rotten superstitions of the world. Be bold; do not try to explain everything that way. The fact is that we have many superstitions, many bad spots and sores on our body—these have to be excised, cut off, and destroyed—but these do not destroy our religion, our national life, our spirituality. Every principle of religion is safe, and the sooner these black spots are purged away, the better the principles will shine, the more gloriously. Stick to them.

You hear claims made by every religion as being the universal religion of the world. Let me tell you in the first place that perhaps there never will be such a thing, but if there is a religion which can lay claim to that, it is only ours and none else, because every other religion depends on some person or persons. All the other religions have been built round the life of what they think an historical man, and what they think the strength of religion is really the weakness, for disprove the historicality of the man and the whole fabric tumbles to the ground. Half the lives of these great founders of religions have been broken into pieces, and the other half doubted very seriously. As such, every truth that had its sanction only in their words vanishes into air. But the truths of our religion, although we have persons by the score, do not depend upon them. The glory of Krishna is not that he was Krishna, but that he was the great teacher of Vedanta. If he had not been so, his name would have died out of India in the same way as the name of Buddha has done. Thus our allegiance is to the principles always, and not to the persons. Persons are but the embodiments, the illustrations of the principles. If the principles are there, the persons will come by the thousands and millions. If the principle is safe, persons like Buddha will be born by the hundreds and thousands. But if the principle is lost and forgotten and the whole of national life tries to cling round a so-called historical person, woe unto that religion, danger unto that religion! Ours is the only religion, that does not depend on a person or persons; it is based upon principles. At the same time there is room for millions of persons. There is ample ground for introducing persons, but each one of them must be an illustration of the principles. We must not forget that. These principles of our religion are all safe, and it should be the life-work of every one of us to keep them safe, and to keep them free from the accumulating dirt and dust of ages. It is strange that in spite of the degradation that seized upon the race again and again, these principles of the Vedanta were never tarnished. No one, however wicked, ever dared to throw dirt upon them. Our scriptures are the best preserved scriptures in the world. Compared to other books there have been no interpolations, no text-torturing, no destroying of the essence of the thought in them. It is there just as it was at first, directing the human mind towards the ideal, the goal.

You find that these texts have been commented upon by different commentators, preached by great teachers, and sects founded upon them, and you find that in these books of the Vedas there are various apparently contradictory ideas. There are certain texts which are entirely Dualistic, others are entirely Monistic. The Dualistic commentator, knowing no better, wishes to knock the Monistic texts on the head. Preachers and priests want to explain them in the Dualistic meaning. The Monistic commentator serves the Dualistic texts in a similar fashion. Now this is not the fault of the Vedas. It is foolish to attempt to prove that the whole of the Vedas is Dualistic. It is equally foolish to attempt to prove that the whole of the Vedas is non-Dualistic. They are Dualistic and non-Dualistic both. We understand them better to-day in the light of newer ideas. These are but different conceptions leading to the final conclusion that both Dualistic and Monistic conceptions are necessary for the evolution of the mind, and therefore the Vedas preach them. In mercy to the human race the Vedas show the various steps to the higher goal. Not that they are contradictory vain words used by the Vedas to delude children; they are necessary, not only for children but for many a grown-up man. So long as we have a body and so long as we are deluded by the idea of the identity of the body, so long as we have five senses and see the external world, we must have a Personal God. For if we have all these ideas, we must take, as the great Ramanuja has proved, all the ideas about God and Nature and the individualised soul; when you take the one you have to take the whole triangle—we cannot avoid it. Therefore as long as you see the external world, to avoid a Personal God and a personal soul is arrant lunacy. But there may be times in the lives of sages when the human mind transcends as it were its own limitations, when man goes even beyond Nature, and even beyond where the Sruti declares—"From whence words fall back with the mind without reaching It. There the eyes cannot reach nor the ears, we cannot say that we know It, we cannot say that we will know It." Even there the human soul transcends all limitations, and then and then alone flashes into the human soul the conception of Monism—I and the whole universe are one, I and Brahman are one. And this conclusion you will find has not only been reached through knowledge and philosophy, but parts of it through the power of love. You read in the Bhâgavata when Krishna disappeared and the Gopis bewailed his disappearance, that at last the thought of Krishna became so prominent in their minds that each one forgot her own body and thought she was Krishna, and began to decorate herself and to play as he did. We understand therefore that this identity comes even through love. There was an ancient Persian Sufi poet, and one of his poems says—"I came to the Beloved and beheld the door was closed; I knocked at the door and from inside a voice came, 'Who is there?' I replied 'I am.' A second time I came and knocked at the door and the same voice asked, 'Who is there?' 'I am so-and-so.' The door did not open. A third time I came and the same voice asked 'Who is there?' 'I am Thyself, my Love,' and the door opened."

There are therefore many stages and we need not quarrel about them, even if there have been quarrels among the ancient commentators, whom all of us ought to revere, for there is no limitation to knowledge, there is no omniscience exclusively the property of any one in ancient or modern times. If there have been sages and Rishis in the past, be sure that there will be many now. If there have been Vyasas and Valmikis and Sankaracharyas in ancient times, why may not each one of you become a Sankaracharya? This is another point of our religion that you must always remember, that in all other scriptures inspiration is quoted as their authority, but this inspiration is limited to a very few persons, and through them the truth came to the masses, and we have all to obey them. Truth came to Jesus of Nazareth and we must all obey him. And the truth came to the Rishis of India—the *mantra-drashtâs*, the seers of thought—and will come to all Rishis in the future, not to talkers, not to book-swallowers, not to scholars, not to philologists, but to seers of thought. The self is not to be reached by too much talking, not even by the highest intellects, not even by the study of the Scriptures. The Scriptures themselves say so. Do you find in any other Scriptures such a bold assertion as that—not even by the study of the Vedas will you reach the Atman? You must open your heart. Religion is not going to church, or putting marks on the forehead, or dressing in a peculiar fashion; you may paint yourselves in all the colours of the rainbow, but if the heart has not been opened, if you have not realised God, it is all vain. If one has the colour of the heart he does not want any external colour. That is the true religious realisation. We must not forget that colours and all these things are good so far as they help; so far they are all welcome, but they are apt to degenerate and instead of helping they retard; and a man identifies religion with externalities. Going to the temple becomes tantamount to spiritual life. Giving something to a priest becomes tantamount to religious life. These are dangerous, and pernicious, and should be at once checked. Our scriptures declare again and again that even the knowledge of the external senses, is not religion. That is religion which makes us realise the unchangeable One, and that is the religion for every one. He who realises transcendental truths, he who realises the Atman in his own nature, he who comes face to face with God, sees God alone in everything, has become a Rishi. And there is no religious life for you until you have become a Rishi. Then alone religion begins for you, now is only the preparation. Then religion dawns upon you, now you are only undergoing intellectual gymnastics and physical tortures.

We must therefore remember that our religion lays down distinctly and clearly, that every one who wants salvation must pass through the stage of Rishihood

THE FUTURE OF INDIA.

This is the ancient land, where widsom made its home before it went into any other country, the same India whose influx of spirituality is represented, as it were, on the material plane, by rolling rivers like oceans, where the eternal Himalayas, rising tier above tier with their snow-caps looking as it were, into the very mysteries of heaven. Here is the same India whose soil has been trodden by the feet of the greatest sages that ever lived. Here first sprang up inquiries into the nature of man, and into the internal world. Here first arose the doctrines of the immortality of the Soul, the existence of a supervising God, an immanent God in Nature and in man, and here the highest ideals of religion and philosophy have attained their culminating points. This is the land from whence, like the tidal waves, spirituality and philosophy have again and again rushed out and deluged the world, and this is the land from whence once more such tides must proceed in order to bring life and vigour into the decaying races of mankind. It is the same India which has withstood the shocks of centuries, of hundreds of foreign invasions, of hundreds of upheavals of manners and customs. It is the same land which stands firmer than any rock in the world, with its undying vigour, indestructible life. Its life is of the same nature as the Soul, without beginning and without end, immortal, and we are the children of such a country.

Children of India, I am here to speak to you to-day about some practical things, and my object in reminding you about the glories of the past is simply this. Many times have I been told that looking into the past only degenerates and leads to nothing, and that we should look to the future. That is true. But out of the past is built the future. Look back, therefore, as far as you can, drink deep of the eternal fountains that are behind, and after that, look forward, march forward and make India brighter, greater, much higher than she ever was. Our ancestors were great. We must first recall that. We must learn the elements of our being, the blood that courses in our veins; we must have faith in that blood, and what it did in the past; and out of that faith, and consciousness of past greatness, we must build an India yet greater than what she has been. There have been periods of decay and degradation. I do not attach much importance to them; we all know that. Such periods have been necessary. A mighty tree produces beautiful ripe fruit. That fruit falls on the ground, it decays and rots, and out of that decay springs the root and the future tree, perhaps mightier than the first one. This period of decay through which we have passed was all the more necessary. Out of this decay is coming the India of the future; it is sprouting, its first leaves are already out, and a mighty gigantic tree, the *Urdhwamulam* is here, already beginning to appear, and it is about that, that I am going to speak to you.

The problems in India are more complicated, more momentous, than the problems in any other country. Race, religion, language, Government—all these together make a nation. The elements which compose the nations of the world are indeed very few taking race after race, compared to this country. Here have been the Aryan, the Dravidian, the Tartar, the Turk, the Mogul, the European,—all the nations of the world as it were, pouring their blood into this land. Of languages the most wonderful conglomeration is here; of manners and customs there is more [illegible] produce a disease [illegible] everyone's [illegible] It is only when [illegible] and produce disease. Just [illegible] is weak that all sorts of disease germs in the political state of the races or in its social state, or in its educational, intellectual state, crowd into the system and produce disease. To remedy it, therefore, we must go to the root of this disease and cleanse the blood of all impurities. The one tendency will be to strengthen the man, to make the blood pure, the body vigorous, so that it will be able to resist and throw off all external poisons. We have seen that our vigour, our strength, nay, our national life is in our religion. I am not going to discuss now whether it is right or not, whether it is correct or not, whether it is beneficial or not in the long run, to have this vitality in religion, but for good or evil it is there; you cannot get out of it, you have it now and for ever, and you have to stand by it, even if you have not the same faith, that I have, in our religion. You are bound by it, and if you give it up you are smashed to pieces. That is the life of our race and that must be strengthened. You have withstood the shocks of centuries simply because you took great care of it, you sacrificed everything else for it. Your forefathers underwent everything boldly, even death itself, but preserved their religion. Temple after temple was broken down by the foreign conqueror, but no sooner had the wave passed than the spire of the temple rose up again. Some of these old temples of Southern India, and those like Somenath of Gujerat, will teach you volumes of wisdom, will give you a keener insight into the history of the race than any amount of books. Mark how these temples bear the marks of a hundred attacks and a hundred regenerations, continually destroyed and continually springing up out of the ruins, rejuvenated and strong as ever! That is the national mind, that is the national life-current. Follow it and it leads to glory. Give it up and you die; death will be the only result, annihilation the only effect, the moment you step beyond that life-current. I do not mean to say that other things are not necessary. I do not mean to say that political or social improvements are not necessary, but what I mean is this, and I want you to bear it in mind, that they are secondary here, and that religion is primary. The Indian mind is first religious, then anything else. So this is to be strengthened, and how to do it? I will lay before you my ideas. They have been in my mind for a long time, even years before I left the shores of Madras for America, and that I went to America and England was simply for propagating those ideas. I did not care at all for the Parliament of Religions or anything else; it was simply an opportunity; for it was really those ideas of mine that took me all over the world.

My idea is, first of all to bring out the gems of spirituality that are stored up in our books, and in the possession of a few only, hidden, as it were, in monasteries and in forests—to bring them out; to bring the knowledge out of them, not only from the hands where it is hidden, but from the still more inaccessible chest, the language in which it is preserved, the incrustation of centuries of Sanskrit words. In one word, I want to make them popular. I want to bring out these ideas and let them be the common property of all, of every man in India, whether he knows the Sanskrit language or not. The great difficulty in the way is the Sanskrit language, this glorious language of ours, and this difficulty cannot be removed until, if it is possible, the whole of our nation are good Sanskrit scholars. You will understand the difficulty when I tell you, that I have been studying this language all my life, and yet every new book is new to me. How much more difficult would it then be for people who never had time to study the language thoroughly! Therefore the ideas must be taught in the language of the people; at the same time, Sanskrit education must go on along with it, because the very sound of Sanskrit words gives a prestige and a power and a strength to the race. The attempts of the great Ramanuja, and of Chaitanya and of Kabir to raise the lower classes of India, show that marvellous results were attained during the lifetimes of those great prophets; yet the later failures have to be explained, and cause shown why the effect of their teachings stopped almost within a century of the passing away of these great Masters. The secret is here. They raised the lower classes; they had all the wish that these should come up, but they did not apply their energies to the spreading of the Sanskrit language among the masses. Even the great Buddha made one false step when he stopped the Sanskrit language from being studied by the masses. He wanted rapid and immediate results, and translated and preached in the language of the day, Pâli. That was grand, he spoke in the language of the people, and the people understood him. That was great; it spread the ideas quickly and made them reach far and wide, but along with that, Sanskrit ought to have spread. Knowledge came but the prestige was not there, culture was not there. It is culture that withstands shocks, not a simple mass of knowledge. You can put a mass of knowledge into the world, but that will not do it much good. There must come culture into the blood. We all know in modern times, of nations which have masses of knowledge, but what of them? They are like tigers, they are like savages, because culture is not there. Knowledge is only skin-deep, as civilisation is, and a little scratch brings out the old savage; such things happen; this is the danger. Teach the masses in the vernaculars, give them ideas; they will get information, but something more is necessary; give them culture. Until you give them that, there can be no permanence in the raised condition of the masses. There will be another caste created, having the advantage of the Sanskrit language, which will quickly get above the rest and rule them all the same. The only safety, I tell you men who belong to the lower castes, the only way to raise your condition is to study Sanskrit, and this fighting and writing and frothing against the higher castes is in vain, it does no good, and it creates fight and quarrel, and this race, unfortunately already divided, is going to be divided more and more. The only way to bring about the levelling of caste is to appropriate the culture, the education which is the strength of the higher castes. That done, you have what you want.

In connection with this I want to discuss one question which has a particular bearing with regard to Madras. There is a theory that there was a race of mankind in Southern India called Dravidians, entirely differing from another race in Northern India called the Aryans, and that the Southern India Brâhmans are the only Aryans that came from the North, the other men of Southern India belong to an entirely different caste and race to those of Southern India Brâhmans. Now I beg your pardon, Mr. Philologist, this is entirely unfounded. The only proof of it is, that there is a difference of language between the North and the South. I do not see any other difference. We are so many Northern men here, and I ask my European friends to pick out the Northern and Southern men from this assembly. Where is the difference? A little difference of language. But the Brâhmans are a race that came here speaking the Sanskrit language! Well then, they took up the Dravidian language and forgot their Sanskrit. Why should not the other castes have done the same? Why should not all the other castes have come one after the other from Northern India, taken up the Dravidian language, and so forgotten their own? That is an argument working both ways. Do not believe in such silly things. There may have been a Dravidian people who vanished from here, and the few who remained lived in forests and other places. It is quite possible that the language may have been taken up, but all these are Aryans who came from the North. The whole of India is Aryan, nothing else. Then there is the other idea that the Sudra caste are surely the aborigines. What are they? They are slaves. They say history repeats itself. The Americans, English, Dutch, and the Portuguese got hold of the poor Africans, and made them work hard while they lived, and their children of mixed birth were born in slavery and kept in that condition for a long period. From that wonderful example, the mind jumps back several thousand years and fancies that the same thing happened here, and our archæologist dreams of India being full of dark-eyed aborigines, and the bright Aryan came from—the Lord knows where. According to some, they came from Central Thibet, others will have it that they came from Central Asia. There are patriotic Englishmen who think that the Aryans were all red-haired. Others, according to their idea, think that they were all black-haired. If the writer happens to be a black-haired man, the Aryans were all black. Of late, there was an attempt made to prove that the Aryans lived on the Swiss lakes. I should not be sorry if they had been all drowned there, theory and all. Some say now that they lived at the North Pole. Lord bless the Aryans and their habitations! As for the truth of these theories, there is not one word in our scriptures, not one, to prove that the Aryan ever came from anywhere outside of India, and in ancient India was included Afghanistan. There it ends. And the theory that the Sudra caste were all non-Aryans and they were a multitude, is equally illogical and equally irrational. It could not have been possible in those days that a few Aryans settled and lived there with a hundred thousand slaves at their command. These slaves would have eaten them up, made 'chutney' of them in five minutes. The only explanation is to be found in the Mahabharata, which says, that in the beginning of the Satya Yuga there was one caste, the Bráhmans, and then by difference of occupations they went on dividing themselves into different castes, and that is the only true and rational explanation that has been given. And in the coming Satya Yuga all the other castes will have to go back to the same condition. The solution of the caste problem in India, therefore, assumes this form, not to degrade the higher castes, not to crush out the Brâhman.

The Brâhmanhood is the ideal of humanity in India, as wonderfully put forward by Sankaracharya at the beginning of his commentary on the Gita, where he speaks about the reason for Krishna's coming as a preacher for the preservation of Brâhmanhood, of Brâhmanness. That was the great end. This Brâhman, the man of God, he who has known Brahman, the ideal man, the perfect man, must remain; he must not go. And with all the defects of the caste now, we know that we must all be ready to give to the Brâhmans this credit, that from them have come more men with real Brâhmanness in them than from all the other castes. That is true. That is the credit due to them from all the other castes. We must be bold enough, must be brave enough to speak of their defects, but at the same time we must give the credit that is due to them. Remember the old English proverb, 'Give every man his due.' Therefore, my friends, it is no use fighting among the castes. What good will it do? It will divide us all the more, weaken us all the more, degrade us all the more. The days of exclusive privileges and exclusive claims are gone, gone for ever from the soil of India, and it is one of the great blessings of the British Rule of India. Even to the Mahommedan Rule we owe that great blessing, the destruction of exclusive privilege. That Rule was, after all, not all bad; nothing is all bad, and nothing is all good. The Mahommedan conquest of India came as salvation to the down-trodden, to the poor. That is why one-fifth of our people have become Mahommedans. It was not the sword that did it all. It would be the height of madness to think it was all the work of sword and fire. And one-fifth—one-half—of your Madras people will become Christians if you do not take care. Was there ever a sillier thing before in the world than what I saw in Malabar country? The poor Pariah is not allowed to pass through the same street as the high-caste man, but if he changes his name to a hodge-podge English name, it is all right; or to a Mahommedan name, it is all right. What inference would you draw except that these Malabaris are all lunatics, their homes so many lunatic asylums, and that they are to be treated with derision by every race in India until they mend their manners and know better. Shame upon them that such wicked and diabolical customs are allowed; their own children are allowed to die of starvation, but as soon as they take up some other religion they are well fed. There ought to be no more fight between the castes.

The solution is not by bringing down the higher, but by raising the lower up to the level of the higher. And that is the line of work that is found in all our books, in spite of what you may hear from some people whose knowledge of their own scriptures and whose capacity to understand the mighty plans of the ancients are only zero. They do not understand, but those do that have brains, that have the intellect to grasp the whole scope of the work. They stand aside and follow the wonderful procession of national life through the ages. They can trace it step by step through all the books, ancient and modern. What is the plan? The ideal at one end is the Brâhman and the ideal at the other end is the Chandâla, and the whole work is to raise the Chandâla up to the Brâhman. Slowly and slowly you find more and more privileges granted to them. There are books where you read such fierce words as these: "If the Sudra hears the Vedas, fill his ears with molten lead, and if he remembers a line, cut his tongue out. If he says to the Brâhman, 'You Brâhman,' cut his tongue out." This is diabolical old barbarism, no doubt, that goes without saying; but do not blame the law-givers, who simply record the customs of some section of the community. Such devils sometimes arose among the ancients. There have been devils everywhere more or less in all ages. Accordingly, you will find that later on, this tone is modified a little; as for instance—"Do not disturb the Sudras but do not teach them higher things." Then gradually we find in other Smritis, especially in those that have full power now, that if the Sudras imitate the manners and customs of the Brâhmans they do well, they ought to be encouraged. Thus it is going on. I have no time to place before you all these workings, nor how they can be traced in detail; but coming to plain facts, we find that all the castes are to rise slowly and slowly; however, there are thousands of castes and some are even getting admission into Brâhmanhood, for what prevents any caste from declaring they are Brâhmans? Thus caste, with all its rigour has been created in that manner. Let us suppose that there are castes here with ten thousand people in each. If these put their heads together and say, we will call ourselves Brâhmans, nothing can stop them; I have seen it in my own life. Some castes become strong, and as soon as they all agree, who is to say nay? Because whatever it was, each caste was exclusive of the other. It did not meddle with others' affairs; even the several divisions of one caste did not meddle with the other divisions, and those powerful epoch-makers, Sankaracharya and others, were the great caste-makers. I cannot tell you all the wonderful things they fabricated, and some of you may resent what I have to say. But in my travels and experiences I have traced them out, and have arrived at most wonderful results. They would sometimes get hordes of Beluchees and at once make them Kshatriyas, also get hold of hordes of fishermen and make them Brâhmans forthwith. They were all Rishis and sages and we have to bow down to their memory. So, be you all Rishis and sages; that is the secret. More or less we shall all be Rishis. What is meant by a Rishi?—the pure one. Be pure first, and you will have power. Simply saying "I am a Rishi," will not do, but when you are a Rishi you will find that others obey you instinctively. Something mysterious emanates from you, which makes them follow you, makes them hear you, makes them unconsciously, even against their will, carry out your plans. That is Rishihood.

Now, as to the details, they, of course, have to be worked out through generations. But this is merely a suggestion in order to show you that these quarrels should cease. Especially do I regret that in modern times there should be so much discussion between the castes. This must stop. It is useless on both sides, especially on the side of the higher caste, the Brâhman, because, the day for these privileges and exclusive claims is gone. The duty of every aristocracy is to dig its own grave, and the sooner it does so, the better. The more it delays, the more it will fester and the worse death it will die. It is the duty of the Brâhman, therefore, to work for the salvation of the rest of mankind, in India. If he does that and so long as he does that, he is a Brâhman, but he is no Brâhman, when he goes about making money. You on the other hand should give help only to the rightful Brâhman, who deserves it; that leads to heaven, but sometimes a gift to another person who does not deserve it, leads to the other place, says our scripture. You must be on your guard about that. He only is the Brâhman who has no secular employment. Secular employment is not for the Brâhman but for the other castes. To the Brâhmans I appeal, that they must work hard to raise the Indian people by teaching them what they know, by giving out the culture that they have accumulated for centuries. It is clearly the duty of the Brâhmans of India to remember what real Brâhmanhood is. As Manu says, all these privileges and honours are given to the Brâhman because, "with him is the treasury of virtue." He must open that treasury and distribute its valuables to the world. It is true that he was the earliest preacher to the Indian races, he was the first to renounce everything in order to attain to the higher realisation of life, before others could reach to the idea. It was not his fault that he marched ahead of the other castes. Why did not the other castes so understand and do as they did? Why did they sit down and be lazy, and let the Bârhmans win the race? But it is one thing to gain an advantage, and another thing to preserve it for evil use. Whenever power is used for evil it becomes diabolical; it must be used for good only. So this accumulated culture of ages of which the Bráhman has been the trustee, he must now give to the people at large, and it was because he did not give it to the people, that the Mahommedan invasion was possible. It was because he did not open this treasury to the people from the beginning, that for a thousand years we have been trodden under the heels of every one who chose to come to India; it was through that we have become degraded, and the first task must be to break open the cells that hide the wonderful treasures which our common ancestors accumulated; bring them out, and give them to everybody, and the Bráhman must be the first to do it.

There [illegible] his own power from the [illegible]. Then the Brahmin must work out his own power. To the non-Brahmin castes I say, wait, be not in a hurry. Do not seize every opportunity of fighting the Brahman, because as I have shown you are suffering from your own fault. Who told you to neglect spirituality and Sanskrit learning? What have you been doing all this time? Why have you been indifferent? Why do you now fret and fume because somebody else had more brains, more energy, more pluck and go, than you? Instead of wasting your energies in vain discussions and quarrels in the newspapers, instead of fighting and quarrelling in your own homes, which is sinful,—use all your energies in acquiring the culture which the Brâhman has, and the thing is done. Why do you not become Sanskrit scholars? Why do you not spend millions to bring Sanskrit education to all the castes of India? That is the question. The moment you do these things, you are equal to the Brâhman. That is the secret of power in India.

Sanskrit and prestige go together in India. As soon as you have that, none dares say anything against you. That is the one secret; take that up. The whole universe, to use the ancient Advaitist's simile, is in a state of self-hypnotism. It is will that is the power. It is the man of strong will that throws, as it were, a halo round him and brings all other people to the same state of vibration as he has in his own mind. Such gigantic men do appear. And what is the idea? When a powerful individual appears, his personality infuses his thoughts into us, and many of us come to have the same thoughts and thus we become powerful. Why is it that organisations are so powerful? Do not say organisation is material. Why is it, to take a case in point, that forty millions of Englishmen rule three hundred millions of people here? What is the psychological explanation? These forty millions put their wills together and that means infinite power, and you three hundred millions have a will each separate from the other. Therefore to make a great future India, the whole secret lies in organisation, accumulation of power, co-ordination of wills. Already before my mind rises one of the marvellous verses of the Atharva Veda Samhita which says, "Be thou all of one mind, be thou all of one thought, for in the days of yore, the gods being of one mind were enabled to receive oblations. That the gods can be worshipped by men is because they are of one mind." Being of one mind is the secret of society. And the more you go on fighting and quarrelling about all trivialities such as "Dravidian" and "Aryan," and the question of Brâhmans and non-Brâhmans and all that, the further you are off from that accumulation of energy and power which is going to make the future India. For mark you, the future India depends entirely upon that. This is the secret, accumulation of will-power, co-ordination, bringing them all, as it were, into one focus. Each Chinaman thinks in his own way, and a handful of Japanese all think in the same way, and you know the result. That is how it goes throughout the history of the world. You find in every case, compact little nations always governing and ruling huge unwieldy nations, and this is natural, because it is easier for the little compact nations to bring their ideas into the same focus, and thus they become developed. And the bigger the nation, the more unwieldy it is. Born, as it were, a disorganised mob, they cannot combine. All these dissensions must stop.

There is yet another defect in us. Ladies, excuse me, but through centuries of slavery, we have become like a nation of women. You scarcely can get three women together for five minutes in this country, or any other country but they quarrel. Women make big societies in European countries, and make tremendous declarations of women's power and so on; then they quarrel, and some man comes and rules them all. All over the world they still require some man to rule them. We are like them. Women we are. If a woman comes to lead women they all begin immediately to criticise her, tear her to pieces, and make her sit down. If a man comes and gives them a little harsh treatment, scolds them now and then, it is all right, they have been used to that sort of mesmerism. The whole world is full of such mesmerists and hypnotists. In the same way, if one of our countrymen stands up and tries to become great, we all try to hold him down, but if a foreigner comes and tries to kick us, it is all right. We have been used to it, have we not? And slaves must become great masters! So give up being a slave. For the next fifty years this alone shall be our keynote,—this, our great Mother India. Let all other vain Gods disappear for that time from our minds. This is the only God that is awake, our own race, everywhere His hands, everywhere His feet, everywhere His ears, He covers everything. All other Gods are sleeping What vain Gods shall we go after and yet cannot worship the God that we see all round us, the *Virát*. When we have worshipped this, we shall be able to worship all other Gods. Before we can crawl half a mile, we want to cross the ocean, like Hanumán! It cannot be. Everyone going to be a Yogi, everyone going to meditate! It cannot be. The whole day mixing with the world, with Karma-kanda, and in the evening sitting down and blowing through your nose! Is it so easy? Should Rishis come flying through the air, because you have blown three times through the nose? Is it a joke? It is all nonsense. What is needed is *Chittashuddhi*, purification of the heart. And how does that come? The first of all worship, is the worship of the *Virát*,—of those all around us. Worship It. Worship is the exact equivalent of the Sanskrit word, and no other English word will do. These are all our Gods,—men and animals, and the first Gods we have to worship are our own countrymen. That is what we have to worship, instead of being jealous of each other and fighting each other. It is the most terrible Karma for which we are suffering, and yet it does not open our eyes!

Well, the subject is so great that I do not know where to stop, and I must bring my lecture to a close by placing before you in a few words the plans I want to carry out in Madras. We must have a hold on the spiritual and secular education of the nation. Do you understand that? You must dream it, you must talk it, you must think it, and you must work it out. Till then there is no salvation for the race. The education that you are getting now has some good points, but it has a tremendous disadvantage which is so great that the good things are all weighed down. In the first place it is not a man-making education, it is merely and entirely a negative education. A negative education or any training that is given to negation, is worse than death. The child is taken to school, and the first thing he learns is that his father is a fool, the second thing, that his grandfather is a lunatic, the third thing that all his teachers are hypocrites, the fourth, that all the sacred books are lies! By the time he is sixteen he is a mass of negation, lifeless and boneless. And the result is, that fifty years of such education has not produced one original man in the three Presidencies. Every man of originality that has been produced has been educated elsewhere, and not in this country, or they have gone to the old universities once more to cleanse themselves of superstitions. Education is not the amount of information that is put into your brain and runs riot there, undigested, all your life. We must have life-building, man-making, character-making, assimilation of ideas.

If you have assimilated five ideas and made them your life and character, you have more education than any man who has got by heart a whole library. यथा खरश्चन्दनभारवाही भारस्य वेत्ता न तु चन्दनस्य। "The ass carrying its load of sandalwood knows only the weight and not the value of the sandalwood." If education is identical with information, the libraries are the greatest sages in the world, and encyclopædias are the Rishis. The ideal therefore is, that we must have the whole education of our country, spiritual and secular, in our own hands, and it must be on national lines, through national methods, as far as practicable. Of course this is a very big scheme, a very big plan. I do not know whether it will ever work out. But we must begin the work. But how? Take Madras, for instance. We must have a temple, for with Hindus, religion must come first. Then, you may say, all sects will quarrel about it. But we will make it a non-sectarian temple, having only "Om," as the symbol, the greatest symbol of any sect. If there is any sect here, which believes that "Om" ought not to be the symbol, it has no right to call itself Hindu. All will have the right to interpret Hinduism, each one according to his own sect ideas, but we must have a common temple. You can have your own images and symbols in other places, but do not quarrel here with those who differ from you. Here should be taught the common grounds of our different sects, and at the same time the different sects should have perfect liberty to come and teach their doctrines, with only one restriction, that is, not to quarrel with other sects. Say what you have to say, the world wants it, but the world has no time to hear what you think about other people; you can keep that to yourselves. Secondly, in connection with this temple there should be an institution to train teachers who must go about preaching religion and giving secular education to our people; they must carry both. As we have been already carrying religion from door to door, let us along with it carry secular education also. That can be easily done. Then the work will extend through these bands of teachers and preachers, and gradually we shall have similar temples in other centres, until we have covered the whole of India. That is my plan. It may appear gigantic, but it is much needed. You may ask, where is the money. Money is not needed. Money is nothing. For the last twelve years of my life, I did not know where the next meal would come from; but money and everything else I want must come, because they are my slaves, and not I theirs; money and everything else must come. Must,—that is the word. Where are the men? That is the question. Young men of Madras, my hope is in you. Will you respond to the call of your nation? Each one of you has a glorious future if you dare believe me. Have a tremendous faith in yourselves, like the faith I had when I was a child, and which I am working out now. Have that faith, each one of you, in yourself, that eternal power is lodged in every soul, and you will revive the whole of India. Aye, we will then go to every country under the sun, and our ideas will before long be a component of the many forces that are working to make up every nation in the world. We must enter into the life of every race in India and abroad; we shall have to *work* to bring this about. Now for that, I want young men. "It is the young, the strong, and healthy, of sharp intellect, that will reach the Lord," say the Vedas. This is the time to decide your future—while you possess the energy of youth, not when you are worn out and jaded, but in the freshness and vigour of youth. Work; this is the time, for the freshest, the ntouched and unsmelled flowers alone are to be laid at the feet of the Lord, and ch He receives. Rouse yourselves, therefore, for life is short. There are greater works to be done than aspiring to become lawyers, and picking quarrels, and such things. A far greater work is this sacrifice of yourselves for the benefit of your race, for the welfare of humanity. What is in this life? You are Hindus, and there is the instinctive belief in you that life is eternal. Sometimes I have young men come and talk to me about Atheism; I do not believe a Hindu can become an atheist. He may read European books, and persuade himself he is a materialist, but it is only for a time. It is not in your blood. You cannot believe what is not in your constitution; it would be a hopeless task for you. Do not attempt that sort of thing. I once attempted it when I was a boy; but it could not be. Life is short, but the Soul is immortal and eternal, and one thing being certain, death, let us therefore take up a great ideal, and give up our whole life to it. Let this be our determination, and may He, the Lord, who "comes again and again for the salvation of His own people," to quote from our scriptures,—may the great Krishna bless us, and lead us all to the fulfilment of our aims!

ON CHARITY.

During his stay in Madras the Swami presided at the annual meeting of the Chennapuri Annadána Samâjam, an institution of a charitable nature, and in the course of a brief address referred to a remark by a previous speaker deprecating special alms-giving to the Brâhman over and above the other castes. Swamiji pointed out, that this had its good as well as its bad side. All the culture practically, which the nation possessed was among the Brâhmans, and they also had been the thinkers of the nation. Take away the means of living which enabled them to be thinkers, and the nation as a whole would suffer. Speaking of the indiscriminate charity of India as compared with the legal charity of other nations, he said, the outcome of their system of relief was, that the vagabond in India was contented to receive readily what he was given readily, and lived a peaceful and contented life: while the vagabond in the West, unwilling to go to the poor-house,—for man loved liberty more than food—turned a robber, the enemy of society, and necessitated the organisation of a system of magistracy, police, jails, and other establishments. Poverty there must be, so long as the disease known as civilisation existed: and hence the need for relief. So that they had to choose between the indiscriminate charity of India, which, in the case of Sannyasins at any rate, even if they were not sincere men, at least forced them to learn some little of their scriptures before they were able to obtain food; and the discriminate charity of Western nations which necessitated a costly system of poor-law relief, and in the end succeeded only in changing mendicants into criminals.

ADDRESS OF WELCOME PRESENTED IN CALCUTTA AND SWAMIJI'S REPLY.

On his arrival in Calcutta, the Swami Vivekananda was greeted with intense enthusiasm, and the whole of his progress through the decorated streets of the City was thronged with an immense crowd waiting to have a sight of him. The official reception was held a week later, at the residence of the late Raja Radha Kanta Deb Bahadur at Sobha Bazar, when Raja Benoy Krishna Deb Bahadur took the chair. After a few brief introductory remarks from the Chairman, the following address was read and presented to him, enclosed in a silver casket:—

To Srimat Vivekananda Swami.

Dear Brother,—

We, the Hindu inhabitants of Calcutta and of several other places in Bengal, offer you on your return to the land of your birth a hearty welcome. We do so with a sense of pride as well as of gratitude, for by your noble work and example in various parts of the world you have done honour not only to our religion, but also to our country and to our province in particular.

At the great Parliament of Religions which constituted a Section of the World's Fair held in Chicago in 1893, you presented the principles of the Aryan religion. The substance of your exposition was to most of your audience a revelation, and its manner overpowering alike by its grace and its strength. Some may have received it in a questioning spirit, a few may have criticised it, but its general effect was a revolution in the religious ideas of a large section of cultivated Americans. A new light had dawned on their mind, and with their accustomed earnestness and love of truth they determined to take full advantage of it. Your opportunities widened; your work grew. You had to meet call after call from many cities in many States, answer many queries, satisfy many doubts, solve many difficulties. You did all this work with energy, ability and sincerity; and it has led to lasting results. Your teaching has deeply influenced many an enlightened circle in the American Commonwealth, has stimulated thought and research; and has in many instances definitely altered religious conceptions in the direction of an increased appreciation of Hindu ideals. The rapid growth of clubs and societies for the co-operative study of religions and the investigation of spiritual truth, is witness to your labour in the far West. You may be regarded as the founder of a College in London for the teach-[illegible] the Vedanta philosophy. Your lectures have been regularly delivered, punctu-[illegible]nded and widely appreciated. Their influence has extended beyond the [illegible] the lecture-rooms. The love and esteem which have been evoked by your [illegible] are evidenced by the warm acknowledgments, in the address presented to [illegible] the eve of your departure from London, by the students of the Vedanta [illegible]phy in that town.

[illegible]our success as a teacher has been due not only to your deep and intimate [illegible]aintance with the truths of the Aryan religion, and your skill in exposition by [illegible]eech and writing, but also, and largely, to your personality. Your lectures, your [illegible]ssays and your books have high merits, spiritual and literary, and they could not [illegible] produce their effect. But it has been heightened in a manner that defies expression, by the example of your simple, sincere, self-denying life, your modesty, devotion and earnestness.

While acknowledging your services as a teacher of the sublime truths of our religion, we feel that we must render a tribute to the memory of your revered preceptor Sri Ramakrishna Paramahamsa. To him we largely owe even you. With his rare magical insight he early discovered the heavenly spark in you, and predicted for you a career which happily is now in course of realisation. It was he who unsealed the vision and the faculty divine with which God had blessed you, gave to your thoughts and aspirations the bent that was awaiting the holy touch, and aided your pursuits in the region of the unseen. His most precious legacy to posterity was yourself.

Go on noble soul, working steadily and valiantly in the path you have chosen. You have a world to conquer. You have to interpret and vindicate the religion of the Hindus to the ignorant, the sceptical, the wilfully blind. You have begun the work in a spirit which commands our admiration, and have already achieved a success to which many lands bear witness. But a great deal yet remains to be done; and our own country, or rather we should say your own country, waits on you. The truths of the Hindu religion have to be expounded to large numbers of Hindus themselves. Brace yourself then for the grand exertion. We have confidence in you and in the righteousness of our cause. Our national religion seeks to win no material triumphs. Its purposes are spiritual; its weapon is a truth which is hidden away from material eyes and yields only to the reflective reason. Call on the world, and where necessary, on Hindus themselves, to open the inner eye, to transcend the senses, to read rightly the sacred books, to face the supreme reality, and realise their position and destiny as men. No one is better fitted than yourself to give the awakening or make the call, and we can only assure you of our hearty sympathy and loyal co-operation in that work which is apparently your mission ordained by Heaven.

We remain, dear brother,
Your loving friends & admirers.

The Swami's reply was as follows :—

One wants to lose the universal in the individual, one renounces, flies off, and tries to cut himself off from all associations of the body, of the past, one works hard to forget even that he is a man; yet, in the heart of his heart, there is a soft sound, one string vibrating, one whisper, which tells him, East or West, home is best. Citizens of the capital of this Empire, before you I stand, not as a Sannyasin, no, not even as a preacher, but I come before you the same Calcutta boy to talk to you as I used to do. Aye, I would like to sit in the dust of the streets of this city, and, with the freedom of childhood, open my mind to you, my brothers. Accept, therefore, my heart-felt thanks for this unique word that you have used, "Brother." Yes, I am your brother, and you are my brothers. I was asked by an English friend on the eve of my departure, "Swami, how do you like now your motherland after four years' experience of the luxurious, glorious, powerful West?" I could only answer, "India I loved before I came away, now the very dust of India has become holy to me, the very air is now to me holy, it is now the holy land, the place of pilgrimage, the *Tirtha.*" Citizens of Calcutta—my brothers—I cannot express my gratitude to you for the kindness you have shown, or rather I should not thank you at all, for you are my brothers, you have done only a brother's duty, aye, only a Hindu brother's duty, for such family ties, such relationships, such love, exist nowhere beyond the bonds of this motherland of ours.

The Parliament of Religions was a great affair, no doubt. From various cities of this land, we have thanked the gentlemen who organised the meeting, and they deserved all our thanks for the kindness that has been shown to us, but yet allow me to construe for you the history of the Parliament of Religions. They wanted a horse, and they wanted to ride it. There were people there who wanted to make it a heathen show, but it was ordained otherwise; it could not help being so. Most of them were kind, but we have thanked them enough.

On the other hand, my mission in America was not to the Parliament of Religions. That was only something by the way, it was only an opening, an opportunity, and for that we are very thankful to the members of the Parliament; but really, our thanks are due to the great people of the United States, the American nation, the warm-hearted, hospitable, great nation of America, where more than anywhere else the feeling of brotherhood has been developed. An American meets you for five minutes on board a train, and you are his friend, and the next moment he invites you as a guest to his home, and opens the secret of his whole living there. That is the character of the American race, and we highly appreciate it. Their kindness to me is past all narration, it would take me years yet to tell you how I have been treated by them, most kindly and most wonderfully. So are our thanks due to the other nation on the other side of the Atlantic. No one ever landed on English soil with more hatred in his heart for a race than I did for the English, and on this platform are present English friends, who can bear witness to the fact; but the more I lived among them, and saw how the machine was working,—the English national life,—and mixed with them, I found where the heart-beat of the nation was, and the more I loved them. There is none among you here present, my brothers, who loves the English people more than I do now. You have to see what is going on there, and you have to mix with them. As the philosophy, our national philosophy of the Vedanta, has summarised all misfortune, all misery, as coming from that one cause, ignorance, herein also we must understand that the difficulties that arise between us and the English people are mostly due to that ignorance; we do not know them, they do not know us. Unfortunately, to the Western mind, spirituality, nay, even morality, is eternally connected with worldly prosperity, and as soon as an Englishman or any other Western man, lands on our soil, and finds a land of poverty and of misery, he forthwith concludes, that there cannot be any religion here, there cannot be any morality even. His own experience is true. In Europe, owing to the inclemency of the climate and many other circumstances, poverty and sin go together, but not so in India. In India, on the other hand, my experience is, that the poorer the man the better he is in point of morality. Now this takes time to understand, and how many foreign people are there who will stop to understand this, the very secret of national existence in India? Few are there who will have the patience to study the nation and understand. Here and here alone, is the only race where poverty does not mean crime, poverty does not mean sin, and here is the only race where not only poverty does not mean crime, but poverty has been deified, and the beggar's garb is the garb of the highest in the land. On the other hand, we have also similarly, patiently to study the social institutions of the West, and not rush into mad judgments about them. Their intermingling of the sexes, their different customs, their manners, have all their meaning, have all their grand sides, if you have the patience to study them. Not that I mean that we are going to borrow their manners and customs, not that they are going to borrow ours, for the manners and customs of each race are the outcome of centuries of patient growth in that race and each one has a deep meaning behind it, and therefore neither are they to ridicule our manners and customs, nor we theirs.

Again, I want to make another statement before this assembly. My work in England has been more satisfactory to me than my work in America. The bold, brave and steady Englishman, if I may use the expression, with his skull a little thicker than those of other people—if he has once an idea put into his brain, it never comes out, and the immense practicality and energy of the race makes it sprout up and immediately bear fruit. It is not so in any other country. That immense practicality, that immense vitality of the race, you do not see anywhere else. There is less of imagination, but more of work, and who knows the well-spring, the main-spring of the English heart? How much of imagination and of feeling is there! They are a nation of heroes, they are the true Kshatriyas; their education is to hide their feelings and never to show them. From their childhood they have been educated up to that. Seldom will you find an Englishman manifesting feeling, nay, even an Englishwoman. I have seen Englishwomen go to work and do deeds which would stagger the bravest of Bengalees to follow. But with all this heroic superstructure, behind this covering of the fighter, there is a deep spring of feeling in the English heart. If you once know how to reach it, if you get there, if you have personal contact and mix with him, he will open his heart, he is your friend for ever, he is your servant. Therefore in my opinion, my work in England has been more satisfactory than anywhere else. I firmly believe that if I should die to-morrow, the work in England would not die, but would go on expanding all the time.

Brothers, you have touched another chord in my heart, the deepest of all, and that is the mention of my teacher, my master, my hero, my ideal, my God in life—Sri Ramakrishna Paramahamsa. If there has been anything achieved by me, by thoughts, or words, or deeds, if from my lips has ever fallen one word that has helped any one in the world, I lay no claim to it, it was his. But if there have been curses falling from my lips, if there has been hatred coming out of me, it is all mine, and not his. All that has been weak has been mine, and all that has been life-giving, strengthening, pure, and holy, has been his inspiration, his words, and he himself. Yes, my friends, the world has yet to know that man. We read in the history of the world, about prophets and their lives, and these come down to us through centuries of writings and workings by their disciples. Through thousands of years of chiselling and modelling, the lives of the great prophets of yore come down to us; and yet, in my opinion, not one stands so high in brilliance as that life which I saw with my own eyes, under whose shadow I have lived, at whose feet I have learnt everything,—the life of Ramakrishna Paramahamsa. Aye, friends, you all know the celebrated saying of the Gita:—यदा यदा हि धर्मस्य ग्लानिर्भवति भारत । अभ्युत्थानमधर्मस्य तदात्मानं सृजाम्यहम् ॥
परित्राणाय साधुनां विनाशाय च दुष्कृताम् । धर्मसंस्थापनार्थाय संभवामि युगे युगे ॥

"Whenever, O descendant of Bharata, there is decline of Dharma, and rise of Adharma, then I body Myself forth. For the protection of the good, for the destruction of the wicked, and for the establishment of Dharma, I come into being in every age."

Along with it you have to understand one thing more. Such a thing is before us to-day. Before one of these tidal waves of spirituality comes, there are whirlpools of lesser manifestation all over society. One of these comes up, at first unknown, unperceived, and unthought of, assuming proportion, swallowing, as it were, and assimilating all the other little whirlpools, becoming immense, becoming a tidal wave, and falling upon society with a power which none can resist. Such is happening before us. If you have eyes you will see it. If your heart is open you will receive it. If you are truth-seekers you will find it. Blind, blind indeed is the man who does not see the signs of the day! Aye, this boy born of poor Bráhman parents in an out-of-the-way village, of which very few of you have even heard, is literally being worshipped in lands which have been fulminating against heathen worship for centuries. Whose power is it? Is it mine, or yours? It is none else than the power which was manifested here as Ramakrishna Paramahamsa. For, you and I, and sages and prophets, nay, even Incarnations, the whole universe, are but manifestations of power more or less individualised, more or less concentrated. Here has been a manifestation of an immense power, just the very beginning of whose workings we are seeing, and before this generation passes away, you will see more wonderful workings of that power. It has come just in time for the regeneration of India, for we forget from time to time the vital power that must always work in India.

Each nation has its own peculiar method of work. Some work through politics, some through social reforms, some through other lines. With us, religion is the only ground along which we can move. The Englishman can understand religion even through politics. Perhaps, the American can understand religion even through social reforms. But the Hindu can understand even politics when it is given through religion; sociology must come through religion, everything must come through religion. For that is the theme, the rest are the variations in the national life-music. And that was in danger. It seemed that we were going to change this theme in our national life, that we were going to exchange the backbone of our existence, as it were, that we were trying to replace a spiritual by a political backbone. And if we could have succeeded, the result would have been annihilation. But it was not to be. So this power became manifest. I do not care in what light you understand this great sage, it matters not how much respect you pay to him, but I challenge you face to face with the fact, that here is a manifestation of the most marvellous power that has been for several centuries in India, and it is your duty, as Hindus, to study this power, to find what has been done for the regeneration, for the good of India, and for the good of the whole human race through it. Aye, long before ideas of universal religion and brotherly feeling between different sects had been mooted and discussed in any country in the world, here, in sight of this city, was living a man whose whole life was a Parliament of Religions, as it should be.

The highest ideal in our Scriptures is the Impersonal, and would to God every-one of us here were high enough to realise that Impersonal ideal; but, as that cannot be, it is absolutely necessary for the vast majority of human beings to have a Personal ideal; and no nation can rise, can become great, can work at all, with-out enthusiastically coming under the banner of one of these great ideals in life. Political ideals, personages representing political ideals, even social ideals, commercial ideals, would have no power in India. We want spiritual ideals before us, we want enthusiastically to gather round grand spiritual names. Our heroes must be spiritual. Such a hero has been given to us in the person of Ramakrishna Paramahamsa. If this nation wants to rise, take my word for it, it will have to rally enthusiastically round this name. It does not matter who preaches Ramakrishna Paramahamsa, whether I, or you, or anybody else. But him I place before you, and it is for you to judge, and for the good of our race, for the good of our nation, to judge now, what you shall dó with this great ideal of life. One thing we are to remember, that it was the purest of all lives that you have ever seen, or let me tell you distinctly, that you have ever read of. And before you is the fact that it is the most marvellous manifestation of Soul-power that you can read of, much less expect to see. Within ten years of his passing away, this power has encircled the globe; that fact is before you. In duty bound therefore for the good of our race, for the good of our religion, I place this great spiritual ideal before you. Judge him not through me. I am only a weak instrument. Let not his character be judged by seeing me. It was so great that if I, or any other of his disciples spent hundreds of lives, we could not do justice to a millionth part of what he really was. Judge for yourselves; in the heart of your hearts is the Eternal Witness, and may He, the same Ramakrishna Paramahamsa, for the good of our nation, for the welfare of our country, and for the good of humanity, open your hearts, make you true and steady to work for the immense change which must come, whether we exert ourselves or not. For, the work of the Lord does not wait for the likes of you or me. He can raise His workers from the dust by hundreds and by thousands. It is a glory and a privilege that we are allowed to work at all under Him.

From this the idea expands. As you have pointed out to me, we have to conquer the world. That we have to! India must conquer the world, and nothing less than that is my ideal. It may be very big, it may astonish many of you, but it is so. We must conquer the world or die. There is no other alternative. The sign of life is expansion; we must go out, expand, show life, or degrade, fester and die. There is no other alternative. Take either of these, either live or die. Now, we all know about the petty jealousies and quarrels that we have in our country. Take my word, it is the same everywhere. The other nations with their political lives have foreign policies. When they find too much quarrelling at home, they look for somebody abroad to quarrel with, and the quarrel at home stops. We have these quarrels, without any foreign policy to stop them. This must be our eternal foreign policy, preaching the truths of our Shâstras to the nations of the world. I ask you who are politically-minded, do you require any other proof that this will unite us as a race? This very assembly is a sufficient witness. Secondly, apart from these selfish considerations, there are the unselfish, the noble, the living examples behind us. One of the great causes of India's misery and downfall has been that she narrowed herself, went into her shell, as the oyster does, and refused to give her jewels and her treasures to the other races of mankind, refused to give the life-giving truths to thirsting nations outside the Aryan fold. That has been the one great cause, that we did not go out, that we did not compare notes with other nations,—that has been the one great cause of our downfall, and every one of you know that that little stir, the little life that you see in India, begins from the day when Raja Rammohan Roy broke through the walls of that exclusiveness. Since that day, history in India has taken another turn, and now it is growing with accelerated motion. If we have had little rivulets in the past, deluges are coming, and none can resist them. Therefore we must go out, and the secret of life is to give and take. Are we to take always, to sit at the feet of the Westerners to learn everything, even religion? We can learn mechanism from them. We can learn many other things. But we have to teach them something, and that is our religion, that is our spirituality. For a complete civilisation the world is waiting, waiting for the treasures to come out of India, waiting for the marvellous spiritual inheritance of the race, which, through decades of degradation and misery, the nation has still clutched to her breast. The world is waiting for that treasure; little do you know how much of hunger and of thirst there is outside of India for these wonderful treasures of our forefathers. We talk here, we quarrel with each other, we laugh at and we ridicule everything sacred, till it has become almost a national vice to ridicule everything holy. Little do we understand the heart-pangs of millions waiting outside the walls, stretching forth their hands for a little sip of that nectar which our forefathers have preserved in this land of India. Therefore we must go out, exchange our spirituality for anything they have to give us; for the marvels of the region of spirit we will exchange the marvels of the region of matter. We will not be students always, but teachers also. There cannot be friendship without equality, and there cannot be equality when one party is always the teacher and the other party sits always at his feet. If you want to become equal with the Englishman or the American, you will have to teach as well as to learn, and you have plenty yet to teach to the world for centuries to come. This has to be done. Fire and enthusiasm must be in our blood. We Bengalees have been credited with imagination, and I believe we have it. We have been ridiculed as an imaginative race, as men with a good deal of feeling. Let me tell you, my friends, intellect is great indeed, but it stops within certain bounds. It is through the heart, and the heart alone, that inspiration comes. It is through the feelings that the highest secrets are reached, and therefore, it is the Bengalee, the man of feeling, that has to do this work.

उत्तिष्ठत जाग्रत प्राप्य वरान्निबोधत । "Awake, arise, and stop not till the desired end is reached." Young men of Calcutta, arise, awake, for the time is propitious. Already everything is opening out before us. Be bold and fear not. It is only in our scriptures that this adjective is given unto the Lord—*Abhih, Abhih.* We have to become *Abhih,* fearless, and our task will be done. Arise, awake, for your country needs this tremendous sacrifice. It is the young men that will do it. "The young, the energetic, the strong, the well-built, the intellectual,"—for them is the task. And we have hundreds and thousands of such young men in Calcutta. If, as you say, I have done something, remember that I was that good-for-nothing boy playing in the streets of Calcutta. If I have done so much, how much more will you do? Arise and awake, the world is calling upon you. In other parts of India, there is intellect, there is money, but enthusiasm is only in my motherland. That must come out, and, therefore arise, young men of Calcutta, with enthusiasm in your blood. Think not that you are poor, that you have no friends. Aye, whoever saw money make the man; it is man that always makes money. The whole world has been made by the energy of man, by the power of enthusiasm, by the power of faith.

Those of you who have studied that most beautiful of all the Upanishads, the *Katha,* will remember how the king was going to make a great sacrifice, and, instead of giving away things that were of any worth, he was giving away cows and horses that were not of any use, and the book says that at that time *Shraddhà* entered into the heart of his son Nachiketa. I would not translate this word *Shraddhà* to you, it would be a mistake; it is a wonderful word to understand, and much depends on it; we will see how it works, for immediately we find Nachiketa telling himself, "I am superior to many, I am inferior to few, but nowhere am I the last, I can also do something." And this boldness increased, and the boy wanted to solve the problem which was in his mind, the problem of death. The solution could only be got by going to the house of Death, and the boy went. There he was, brave Nachiketa, waiting at the house of Death for three days, and you know how he obtained what he desired. What we want, is this *Shraddhâ*. Unfortunately, it has nearly vanished from India, and this is why we are in our present state. What makes the difference between man and man is the difference in this *shraddhâ*, and nothing else. What makes one man great and another weak and low, is this *shraddhâ*. My Master used to say, he who thinks himself weak will become weak, and that is true. This *shraddhâ* must enter into you. Whatever of material power you see manifested by the Western races is the outcome of this *shraddhâ*, because they believe in their muscles, and if you believe in your spirit, how much more will it work. Believe in that Infinite Soul, the Infinite Power, which, with consensus of opinion, your books and sages preach. That Atman which nothing can destroy, in It is Infinite Power only waiting to be called out. For here is the great difference between all other philosophies, and the Indian Philosophy. Whether Dualistic, qualified Monistic, or Monistic, they all firmly believe that everything is in the soul itself; it has only to come out and manifest itself. Therefore, this *shraddhâ* is what I want, and what all of us here want, this faith in ourselves, and before you is the great task to get that faith. Give up the awful disease that is creeping into our national blood, that idea of ridiculing everything, that loss of seriousness. Give that up. Be strong and have this *shraddhâ*, and everything else is bound to follow.

I have done nothing as yet; you have to do the task. If I die to-morrow the work will not die. I sincerely believe that there will be thousands coming up from the ranks to take up the work and carry it further and further, beyond all my most hopeful imagination ever painted. I have faith in my country, and especially in the youth of my country. The youth of Bengal have the greatest of all tasks that has ever been placed on the shoulders of young man. I have travelled for the last ten years or so over the whole of India, and my conviction is, that from the youth of Bengal will come the power which will raise India once more to her proper spiritual place. Aye, from the youth of Bengal, with this immense amount of feeling and enthusiasm in the blood, will come those heroes, who will march from one corner of the earth to the other, preaching and teaching the eternal spiritual truths of our forefathers. And this is the great work before you. Therefore, let me conclude by reminding you once more, "Arise, awake, and stop not till the desired end is reached." Be not afraid, for all great power, throughout the history of humanity, has been with the people. From out of their ranks have come all the greatest geniuses of the world, and history can only repeat itself. Be not afraid of anything. You will do marvellous work. The moment you fear, you are nobody. It is fear that is the great cause of misery in the world. It is fear that is the greatest of all superstitions. It is fear that is the cause of our woes, and it is fearlessness that brings heaven even in a moment. Therefore, "Arise, awake, and stop not till the goal is reached."

Gentlemen, allow me to thank you once more for all the kindness that I have received at your hands. It is my wish—my intense, sincere wish—to be even of the least service to the world, and above all to my own country and countrymen.

THE VEDANTA IN ALL ITS PHASES.

(Delivered in Calcutta.)

Away back, where no recorded history, nay, even the dim light of tradition, can penetrate, has been steadily shining the light, sometimes dimmed by external circumstances, at others effulgent, but undying and steady, shedding its light not only over India, but permeating the whole thought-world with its power, silent, unperceived, gentle, yet omnipotent, like the dew that falls in the morning, unseen and unnoticed, yet bringing into bloom the fairest of roses—this has been the thought of the Upanishads, the philosophy of the Vedanta. Nobody knows when it first came to flourish on the soil of India. Guess-work has been vain. The guesses, especially of Western writers, have been so conflicting that no certain date can be ascribed to them. But we Hindus, from the spiritual standpoint, do not admit that they had any origin. This Vedanta, the philosophy of the Upanishads, I would make bold to state, has been the first, as well as the final thought on the spiritual plane that has ever been vouchsafed to man. From this ocean of the Vedanta, waves of light from time to time have been going Westward and Eastward. In the days of yore it travelled Westward and gave its impetus to the mind of the Greeks, either in Athens, or in Alexandria, or in Antioch. The Sankhya system must clearly have made its mark on the minds of the ancient Greeks, and the Sankhya, and all other systems in India, had that one authority, the Upanishads, the Vedanta. In India, too, in spite of all these jarring sects that we see to-day and all those that have been in the past, the one authority, the basis of all these systems, has yet been the Upanishads, the Vedanta. Whether you are a Dualist, or a Qualified Monist, an Advaitist, or a Visishtàdvaitist, a Shuddhàdvaitist, or any other Advaitist or Dvaitist, or whatever you may call yourself, there stands behind you as authority, your Shástras, your scriptures, the Upanishads. Whatever system in India does not obey the Upanishads cannot be called orthodox, and even the systems of the Jains and the Buddhists have been rejected from the soil of India, only because they did not bear allegiance to the Upanishads. Thus the Vedanta, whether we know it or not, has penetrated all the sects in India, and what we call Hinduism, this mighty Banyan with its immense, almost infinite ramifications, has been throughout interpenetrated by the influence of the Vedanta. Whether we are conscious of it or not, we think the Vedanta, we live in the Vedanta, we breathe the Vedanta, and we die in the Vedanta, and every Hindu does that. To preach Vedanta in the land of India, and before an Indian audience, seems, therefore, to be an anomaly. But it is the one thing that has to be preached, and it is the necessity of the age that it must be preached. For, as I have just told you, all the Indian sects must bear allegiance to the Upanishads, but among these sects there are many apparent contradictions. Many times the great sages of yore themselves could not understand the underlying harmony of the Upanishads. Many times, even sages quarrelled, and so much so that at times it became a proverb, that there are no sages who do not differ. But the time requires that a better interpretation should be given to this underlying harmony of the Upanishadic texts; whether they are dualistic, or non-dualistic, quasi-dualistic, or so forth, it has to be shown before the world at large; and this work is required as much in India as outside of India, and I myself [illegible] a [illegible] for more than [illegible] I have got a [illegible] of the [illegible] Vedanta [illegible] it or not. But this is [illegible] are not contradictory [illegible] Advaita [illegible] as it were, the stepping-stone of the other [illegible] is reached. There was a time in India when the Karma-kanda had its sway. There are many grand ideals, no doubt, in that portion of the Vedas. Some of our present daily worship is still according to the precepts of the Karma-kanda. But with all that, the Karma-kanda of the Vedas has almost disappeared from India. Very little of our life to-day is bound and regulated by the orders of the Karma-kanda of the Vedas. In our ordinary lives we are mostly Pauranikas or Tantrikas, and even where some Vedic texts are used by the Brahmans of India, the adjustment of the texts is mostly not according to the Vedas but according to the Tantras or the Puranas. As such, to call ourselves Vaidikas in the sense of following the Karma-kanda of the Vedas, I do not think, would be proper. But the other fact stands, that we are all of us Vedantists. The people who call themselves Hindus had better be called Vedantists, and, as I have shown you, under that one name Vaidantika come in all our various sects, whether dualists or non-dualists.

The sects that are at the present time in India, come to be divided in general into the two great classes of dualists and monists. The little differences which some of these sects insist upon, and upon the authority of which want to take new names, as pure Advaitists, or qualified Advaitists, and so forth, do not matter much. As a classification, either they are dualists or monists, and of the sects existing at the present time, some of them are very new, and others seem to be reproductions of very ancient sects. The one class I would present by the life and philosophy of Ramanuja, and the other, by Sankaracharya. Ramanuja is the leading dualistic philosopher of later India, whom all the other dualistic sects have followed, directly or indirectly, both in substance of their teaching, and in the organisations of their sects, even down to some of the most minute points of their organisation. You will be astonished, if you compare Ramanuja and his work with the other dualistic Vaishnava sects in India, to see how much they resemble each other in organisation, teaching, and method. There have been the great Southern preacher Madhva Muni, and following him, our great Chaitanya of Bengal, who took up the philosophy of the Madhvas, and preached it in Bengal. There have been some other sects in Southern India also, as the qualified dualistic Shaivas. The Shaivas in most parts of India are Advaitists, except in some portions of Southern India, and in Ceylon. But they also only substitute Shiva for Vishnu, and are Ramanujists in every sense of the term except in the doctrine of the soul. The followers of Ramanuja hold that the soul is *Anu*, like a particle, very small, and the followers of Sankaracharya hold that it is *Vibhu*, omnipresent. There have been several non-dualistic sects. It seems that there have been sects in ancient times which Sankara's movement has entirely swallowed up and assimilated. You find sometimes a fling at Sankara himself in some of the commentaries, especially in that of Vijnana Bhikshu who, although an Advaitist, attempts to upset the *Mâyâvâda* of Sankara. It seems there were schools who did not believe in this *Mâyâvâda*, and they went so far as to call

Sankara a crypto-Buddhist, *Prachhchhanna Bauddha*, and they thought this *Mâyâvâda* was taken from the Buddhists, and brought within the Vedantic fold. However that may be, in modern times the Advaitists have all ranged themselves under Sankaracharya; and Sankaracharya and his disciples have been the great preachers of Advaita, both in Southern and in Northern India. The influence of Sankaracharya did not penetrate much into our country of Bengal, and in Cashmere and the Punjab, but in Southern India the Smarthas are all followers of Sankaracharya, and with Benares as the centre, his influence is simply immense, even in many parts of Northern India.

Now both Sankara and Ramanuja laid aside all claim to originality. Ramanuja expressly tells us he is only following the great commentary of Bodhàyana. भगवद्बोधायनकृतां विस्तीर्णां ब्रह्मसूत्रवृत्तिं पूर्वाचार्याः संचिक्षिपुः तन्मतानुसारेण सूत्राक्षराणि व्याख्यास्यन्ते । "Ancient teachers abridged that extensive commentary on the Brahma Sutras which was composed by the Bhagavân Bodhayana; in accordance with their opinion the words of the Sutra are explained." That is what Ramanuja says at the beginning of his commentary, the Sri-Bhashya. He takes it up and makes of it a *Sankshiptam*, and that is what we have to-day. I myself never had an opportunity of seeing this commentary of Bodhayana. The late Swami Dayananda Saraswati wanted to reject every other commentary of the Vyasa Sutras except that of Bodhayana, and although he never lost an opportunity of having a fling at Ramanuja, he himself could never produce the Bhodhayana. I have sought for it all over India, and never yet have been able to see it. But Ramanuja is very plain on the point, and he tells us that he is taking the ideas, and sometimes the very passages, out of Bodhayana, and condensing them into the present Ramanuja Bhashya. It seems that Sankaracharya was also doing the same. There are a few places in his Bhashya which mention older commentaries, and when we know that his Guru, and his Guru's Guru, had been Vedantists of the same school as he, sometimes even more thorough-going, bolder even than Sankara himself on certain points, it seems pretty plain that he also was not preaching anything very original, and that even in his Bhashya he himself had been doing the same work that Ramanuja did with Bodhayana, but from what Bhashya, cannot be discovered at the present time. All these Darsanas that you have ever seen or heard of are based upon Upanishadic authority. Whenever they want to quote a Sruti, they mean the Upanishads. They are always quoting the Upanishads. Following the Upanishads there come other philosophies of India, but every one of them failed in getting that hold on India which the philosophy of Vyasa got, although the philosophy of Vyasa is a development out of an older one, the Sankhya, and every philosophy and every system in India—I mean throughout the world—owes much to Kapila, perhaps the greatest name in the history of India in psychological and philosophical lines. The influence of Kapila is everywhere seen throughout the world. Wherever there is a recognised system of thought, there you can trace his influence; even if it be thousands of years back, yet he stands there, the shining, glorious, wonderful Kapila. His psychology and a good deal of his philosophy have been accepted by all the sects of India, with but very little differences. In our own country, our Naiyayik philosophers could not make much impression on the philosophical world of India. They were too busy with little species and genus, and so forth, and that most cumbersome terminology, which it is a life's work to study. As such, they were very busy with logic, and left philosophy to the Vedantists, but every one of the Indian philosophic sects in modern times has adopted the logical terminology of the Naiyayiks of Bengal. Jagadish, Gadadhar, and Siromani are as well-known at Nuddea as in some of the cities in Malabar. But the philosophy of Vyasa, the Vyasa Sutras, is firm-seated, and has attained the permanence of that which it intended to present to men, the orthodox and Vedantic side of philosophy. Reason was entirely subordinated to the Srutis, and as Sankaracharya declares, Vyasa did not care to reason at all. His idea in writing the Sutras was just to bring together, and with one thread to make a garland of the flowers of Vedantic texts. His Sutras are admitted so far as they are subordinate to the authority of the Upanishads, and no further.

And, as I have said, all the sects of India now hold these Vyasa Sutras to be the great authority, and every new sect in India starts with a fresh commentary on the Vyasa Sutras according to its light. The difference between some of these commentators is sometimes very great, sometimes the text-torturing is quite disgusting. The Vyasa Sutras have got the place of authority, and no one can expect to found a sect in India, until he can write a fresh commentary on the Vyasa Sutras.

Next in authority is the celebrated Gita. The great glory of Sankaracharya was his preaching of the Gita. It is one of the greatest works that this great man did among the many noble works of his noble life—the preaching of the Gita, and writing the most beautiful commentary upon it. And he has been followed by every founder of an orthodox sect in India, each of whom has written a commentary on the Gita.

The Upanishads are many, and said to be one hundred and eight, but some declare them to be still larger in number. Some of them are evidently of a much later date, one, for instance, called the Allopanishad, in which Allah is praised, and Mahomet is called the Rajasulla. I have been told that this was written during the reign of Akbar, to bring the Hindus and Mahommedans together, and sometimes they got hold of some word, as Allah, or Illa in the Samhitas, and made an Upanishad on it. So in this Allopanishad, Mahomet is the Rajasulla, whatever that may mean. There are other sectarian Upanishads of the same species, which you find to be entirely modern, and it has been so easy to write them, seeing that this language of the Samhita portion of the Vedas is so archaic that there is no grammar to it. Years ago I had an idea of studying the grammar of the Vedas, and I began with all earnestness to study Panini and the Mahabhashya, but to my surprise I found that the best part of the Vedic grammar consists only of exceptions to rules. A rule is made, and after that comes a statement in the Vedas,—"This rule will be an exception." So you see what an amount of liberty there is for anybody to write anything, the only safeguard being the dictionary of Yâska. Still, in this you will find, for the most part, but a large number of synonyms. Given all that, how easy it is to write any number of Upanishads you please. Just have a little knowledge of Sanskrit, enough to make words look like the old archaic words, and you have no fear of grammar. Then you bring in *Rajasulla,* or any other *Sulla* you like. In that way many Upanishads have been manufactured, and, I am told that, that is being done even now. In some parts of India, I am perfectly certain, they are trying to manufacture such Upanishads, among the different sects. But among the Upanishads are those, which, on the face of them, bear the evidence of genuineness, and these have been taken up by the great commentators and commented upon, especially those which have been taken up by Sankara, followed by Ramanuja, and all the rest.

There are one or two more ideas with regard to the Upanishads which I want to bring to your notice, for these are an ocean of knowledge, and to talk about the

Upanishads, even by an incompetent person like myself takes years, and not one lecture only. I want, therefore, to bring to your notice one or two points in the study of the Upanishads. In the first place, they are the most wonderful poems in the world. If you read the Samhita portion of the Vedas, you now and then find passages of most marvellous beauty. For instance, the famous *Sloka* which describes Chaos— तम आसीत्तमसा गूढमग्रे *&c.*, "When darkness was hidden in darkness," so on it goes. One reads and feels the wonderful sublimity of the poetry. Do you mark this, that outside of India, and inside also, there have been attempts at painting the sublime. But outside, it has always been the infinite in the muscles, the external world, the infinite of matter, or of space. When Milton or Dante, or any other great European poet, either ancient or modern, wants to paint a picture of the Infinite, he tries to soar outside, to make you feel the Infinite through the muscles. That attempt has been made here also. You find it in the Samhitas, the Infinite of extension, most marvellously painted and placed before the readers, such as has been done nowhere else. Mark that one sentence *Tama àsit tamasà gudham*, and now mark the description of darkness by three poets. Take our own Kalidasa—"Darkness which can be penetrated with the point of a needle"; then Milton—"No light but rather darkness visible," but come now to the Upanishad, "Darkness was covering darkness," "Darkness was hidden in darkness." We who live in the tropics can understand it, the sudden outburst of the monsoon, when in a moment, the horizon becomes darkened, and clouds become covered with more and more rolling black clouds. So on, the poem goes, but yet, in the Samhita portion, all these attempts are external. Like everywhere else, the attempts at finding the solution of the great problems of life have been through the external world. Just as the Greek mind, or the modern European mind wants to find the solution of life and of all the sacred problems of Being by searching into the external world, so also did our forefathers, and just as the Europeans failed, they failed also. But the Westerns never made a move more, they remained there, they failed in the search for the solution of the great problems of life and death in the external world, and there they remained, stranded; our forefathers also found it impossible, but were bolder in declaring the utter helplessness of the senses to find the solution. Nowhere else was the answer better put than in the Upanishad. यतो वाचो निवर्तन्ते अप्राप्य मनसा सह। "From whence the word comes back reflected by the mind." न तत्र चक्षुर्गच्छति न वाग्गच्छति। "There the eye cannot go, nor can speech reach." There are various sentences which declared the utter helplessness of the senses, but they did not stop there; they fell back upon the internal nature of man, they went to get the answer from their own soul, they became introspective; they gave up external nature as a failure, as nothing could be done there, as no hope, no answer, could be found; they discovered that dull, dead matter would not give them truth, and they fell back upon the shining soul of man, and there, the answer was found.

तमेवैकम् जानथ आत्मानम् अन्यावाचो विमुञ्चथ "Know this Atman alone" they declared, "give up all other vain words," and hear no other. In the Atman they found the solution—the greatest of all atmans, the God, the Lord of this Universe, His relation to the atman of man, our duty to Him, and through that our relation to each other. And herein you find the most sublime poetry in the world. No more is the attempt made to paint this Atman in the language of matter. Nay, even for it they have given up all positive language. No more is there attempt to come to the senses to give them the idea of the Infinite, no more is there an external, dull, dead, material, spacious, sensuous infinite, but instead of that comes something, which is as fine as even that mentioned in the saying,—

न तत्र सूर्यो भाति न चन्द्रतारकं नेमा विद्युतो भान्ति कुतोऽयमग्निः।
तमेव भान्तमनुभाति सर्वं तस्यभासा सर्वमिदं विभाति ॥

What poetry in the world can be more sublime than this! "There the sun cannot illumine, nor the moon, nor the stars, there this flash of lightning cannot illumine; what to speak of this mortal fire!" Such poetry you find nowhere else. Take that most marvellous Upanishad, the Katha. What a wonderful finish, what a most marvellous art displayed in that poem! How wonderfully it opens, with that little boy to whom *Shraddhà* came, who wanted to see Yama, and how that most marvellous of all teachers, Death himself, teaches him the great lessons of life and death! And what was his quest? To know the secret of death.

The second point that I want you to remember is the perfectly impersonal character of the Upanishads. Although we find many names, and many speakers, and many teachers in the Upanishads, not one of them stands as an authority of the Upanishads, not one verse is based upon the life of any one of them. These are simply figures like shadows moving in the background, unfelt, unseen, unrealised, but the real force is in the marvellous, the brilliant, the effulgent texts of the Upanishads, perfectly impersonal. If twenty Yàjnavalkyas came, and lived, and died, it does not matter; the texts are there. And yet it is against no personality; it is broad and expansive enough to embrace all the personalities that the world has yet produced, and all that are yet to come. It has nothing to say against the worship of persons, or Avatârs, or sages. On the other hand it is always upholding it. At the same time, it is perfectly impersonal. It is a most marvellous idea, like the God it preaches, the impersonal idea of the Upanishads. At the same time, for the sage, the thinker, the philosopher, for the rationalist it is as much impersonal as any modern scientist can wish. And these are our scriptures. You must remember that what the Bible is to the Christians, what the Quoran is to the Mahommedans, what the Tripitaka is to the Buddhists, what the Zend Avesta is to the Parsis, so these Upanishads are to us. These and nothing but these, are our scriptures. The Puranas, the Tantras, and all the other books, even the Vyasa Sutras, are of secondary, tertiary authority, but primary are the Vedas. Manu, and the Puranas, and all the other books are to be taken so far as they agree with the authority of the Upanishads, and when they disagree they are to be rejected without mercy. This we ought to remember always, but unfortunately for India, at the present time we have forgotten it. A petty village custom seems now the real authority for the teaching of the Upanishads. A petty idea current in a wayside village in Bengal seems to have the authority of the Vedas, and even something better. And that word "orthodox," how wonderful its influence! To the villager, the following of every little bit of the Karma-kanda is the very height of "orthodoxy," and one who does not do it is told,—"Go away, you are no more a Hindu." So there are, most unfortunately, in my motherland, persons who will take up one of these Tantras and say, that the practice of this Tantra is to be obeyed; he who does not do so is no more orthodox in his views. Therefore it is better for us to remember that in the Upanishads is the primary authority, even the *Grihya* and *Srauta Sùtras* are subordinate to the authority of the Vedas. They are the words of the Rishis, our forefathers, and you have to believe them if you want to become a Hindu. You may even believe the most peculiar ideas about the Godhead, but if you deny the authority of the Vedas, you are a *Nàstika.*

Therein lies the difference of the scriptures of the Christians or the Buddhists; they are all Puranas, and not scriptures, because they describe the history of the deluge, and the history of kings and reigning families, and record the lives of great men, and so on. This is the work of the Puranas, and so far as they agree with the Vedas, they are good. So far as the Bible and the scriptures of other nations agree with the Vedas, they are perfectly good, but when they do not agree, they are no more to be accepted. So with the Quoran. There are many moral teachings in these, and so far as they agree with the Vedas they have the authority of the Puranas, but no more. The idea is that the Vedas were never written, the idea is they never came into existence. I was told once by a Christian missionary that their scriptures have a historial character, and therefore are true. To which I replied, "Mine have no historical character, and *therefore* they are true; yours being historical they were evidently made by some man the other day. Yours are man-made and mine are not; their non-historicality is in their favour." These are the relations of the Vedas with all the other scriptures at the present day.

We now come to the teachings of the Upanishads. Various texts are there. One is perfectly dualistic. What do I mean by dualistic? There are certain doctrines which are agreed to by all the different sects of India. First, there is the doctrine of *Samsâra*, or re-incarnation of the soul. Secondly, they all agree in their psychology; first there is the body, behind that, what they call the *Sukshma-Sharira*, the mind, and behind that even, is the Jiva. That is the great difference between Western and Indian Psychology; in the Western Psychology the mind is the soul, here it is not. The *Antahkarana*, the internal instrument, as the mind is called, is only an instrument in the hands of that Jiva, through which the Jiva works on the body, or on the external world. Here they all agree, and they all also agree that this Jiva, or Atman, Jivâtman as it is called by various sects, is eternal, without beginning; and that it is going from birth to birth, until it gets a final release. They all agree in this, and they also all agree in one other most vital point, which alone marks characteristically, most prominently, most vitally, the difference between the Indian and the Western mind, and it is this, that everything is in the soul. There is no inspiration, but properly speaking, expiration. All powers and all purity and all greatness—everything is in the soul. The Yogi would tell you that the *Siddhis—Animà, Laghimà*, and so on—that he wants to attain to, are not to be attained, in the proper sense of the word, but are already there in the soul; the work is to make them manifest. Patanjali, for instance, would tell you that even in the lowest worm that crawls under your feet, all the eightfold Yogi's powers are already existing. The difference has been made by the body. As soon as he gets a better body the powers will become manifest, but they are there. निमित्तमप्रयोजकं प्रकृतीनां वरणभेदस्तु ततः क्षेत्रिकवत् "Good and bad deeds are not the direct causes in the transformation of nature, but they act as breakers of obstacles to the evolutions of nature: as a farmer breaks the obstacles to the course of water, which then runs down by its own nature." Here Kapila gives the celebrated example of the cultivator bringing water into his field from a huge tank somewhere. The tank is already filled and the water would flood his land in a moment, only there is a mud-wall between the tank and his field. As soon as the barrier is broken, in rushes the water out of its own power and force: This mass of power and purity and perfection is in the soul already. The only difference is this *âvarana*—this veil—that has been cast over it. Once the veil is removed the soul attains to purity, and its powers become manifest. This, you ought to remember, is the great difference between Eastern and Western thought. Hence you find people teaching such awful doctrines as that we are all born sinners, and because we do not believe in such awful doctrines we are all born wicked. They never stop to think that if we are by our very nature wicked, we can never be good—for how can nature change? If it changes, it contradicts itself; it is not nature. We ought to remember this. Here the Dualist, and the Advaitist, and all others in India agree.

The next point, which all the sects in India believe in, is God. Of course their ideas of God will be different. The Dualists believe in a personal God, and a personal only. I want you to understand this word personal, a little more. This word personal does not mean that God has a body, sits on a throne somewhere, and rules this world, but personal means *Saguna*, with qualities. There are many descriptions of the personal God. This personal God as the Ruler, the Creator, the Preserver, and the Destroyer, of this universe, is believed in by all the sects. The Advaitists believe something more. They believe in a still higher phase of this personal God, which is personal-impersonal. No adjective can illustrate where there is no qualification, and the Advaitist would not give Him any qualities except the three—Sat—Chit—Ananda, Existence, Knowledge and Bliss Absolute. This is what Sankara did. But in the Upanishads themselves you find they penetrate even further, and say, nothing can be predicated of It except *neti, neti*, "not this, not this." Here all the different sects of India agree. But taking the dualistic side, as I have said, I will take Ramanuja as the typical dualist of India, the great modern representative of the dualistic systems. It is a pity that our people in Bengal know so very little about the great religious leaders in India, who have been born in other parts of the country; and for the matter of that, during the whole of the Mahommedan period, with the exception of our Chaitanya, all the great religious leaders were born in Southern India, and it is the intellect of Southern India that is really governing India now; for even Chaitanya belonged to one of these sects, a sect of the Madhvas. According to Ramanuja these three entities are eternal—God, and soul, and Nature. The souls are eternal, and they will remain eternally existing, individualised through eternity, and will retain their individuality all through. Your soul will be different from my soul through all eternity, says Ramanuja, and so will this Nature, which is an existing fact, as much existing as the existence of soul, or the existence of God—this will remain always. And God is interpenetrating, the essence of the soul. He is the *Antaryamin*; in this sense Ramanuja sometimes thinks that God is one with the soul, the essence of the soul, and these souls,—at the time of *Pralaya*, when the whole of Nature becomes what he calls *Sankuchita*, contracted,—become contracted and minute, and remain so for a time. And at the beginning of the next cycle they all come out, according to their past Karma, and undergo the effect of that Karma. Every action that makes the natural inborn purity and perfection of the soul, get contracted, is a bad action, and every action that makes it come out and expand itself, is a good action, says Ramanuja. Whatever helps to make the *Vikâsha* of the soul is good, and whatever makes it *Sankuchita* is bad. And thus the soul is going on, expanding or contracting in its actions, till, through the grace of God, comes salvation. And that grace comes to all souls, says Ramanuja, that are pure, and struggle for that grace.

There is a celebrated verse in the Srutis, आहारशुद्धौ सत्त्वशुद्धिः सत्त्वशुद्धौ ध्रुवास्मृतिः *i.e.*, "When the food is pure then the *Sattva* becomes pure; when the

Sattva is pure then the Smriti,"—the memory of the Lord, or the memory of our own perfection—if you are an Advaitist—" becomes truer, steadier, and absolute." Here is a great discussion. First of all, what is this *Sattva?* We know that according to the Sankhya—and it has been admitted by all our sects of philosophy—the body is composed of three sorts of materials—not qualities; it is the general idea that Sattva, Rajas and Tamas are qualities. Not at all, not qualities but the materials of this universe, and with *âhàra-suddhi*, when the food is pure, the *Sattva* material becomes pure. The one theme of the Vedanta is to get this Sattva. As I have told you, the soul is already pure and perfect, and it is, according to the Vedanta, covered up by Rajas and Tamas particles. The Sattva particles are the most luminous, and the effulgence of the soul penetrates through them as easily as light through glass. So if the Rajas and Tamas particles go, and leave the Sattva particles, in this state the power and purity of the soul will appear, and leave the soul more manifest.

Therefore it is necessary to have this Sattva. And the text says, "When the *âhara* becomes pure." Ramanuja takes this word, âhâra, to mean food, and he has made it one of the turning points of his philosophy. Not only so, it has affected the whole of India, and all the different sects. Therefore, it is necessary for us to understand what it means, for that, according to Ramanuja, is one of the principal factors in our life, *âhàra-suddhi*. What makes food impure, asks Ramanuja? Three sorts of defects make food impure—first, *jâti-dosha*, the defect in the very nature of the class to which the food belongs, as the smell in onions, garlic, and such like. The next is *âshraya-dosha*, the defect in the person from whom the food comes; food coming from a wicked person will make you impure. I myself have seen many great sages in India following strictly that advice all their lives. Of course they had the power to know who brought food, and even who had touched the food, and I have seen it in my own life, not once, but hundreds of times. Then *Nimitta-dosha*, the defect of impure things or influences coming in contact with food is another. We had better attend to that a little more now. It has become too prevalent in India to take food with dirt and dust and bits of hair in it. If food is taken from which these three defects have been removed, that makes *Sattva-suddhi*, purifies the *Sattva*. Religion seems to be a very easy task then. Then everyone can have religion, if it comes by eating pure food only. There is none so weak or incompetent in this world, that I know, who cannot save himself from these defects. Then comes Sankaracharya, who says this word *âhàra* means thought collected in the mind; when that becomes pure, the *Sattva* becomes pure, and not before that. You may eat what you like. If food alone would purify the *Sattva*, then feed the monkey with milk and rice all its life; would it become a great Yogi? Then the cows and the deer would be great Yogis. As has been said, if it is by bathing much that heaven is reached, the fishes will get to heaven first. If by eating vegetables a man gets to heaven, the cows and the deer will get to heaven first.

But what is the solution? Both are necessary. Of course the idea that Sankaracharya gives us of *âhâra* is the primary idea. But pure food, no doubt, helps pure thought; it has an intimate connection; both ought to be there. But the defect is, that in modern India we have forgotten the advice of Sankaracharya and taken only the "pure food" meaning. That is why people get mad with me when I say, religion has got into the kitchen, and if you had been in Madras with me you would have agreed with me. The Bengalees are better than that. In Madras they throw away food if anybody looks at it. And with all this, I do not see that the people are any the better there. If only eating this and that sort of food, and saving it from the looks of this person and that person would give them perfection, you would expect them all to be perfect men, which they are not.

Thus, although these are to be combined, and linked together to make a perfect whole, do not put the cart before the horse. There is a cry nowaday's about this and that food, and about *Varnâshrama*, and the Bengalees are the most vociferous in these cries. I would ask every one of you, what do you know about this *Varnâshrama?* Where are the four castes to-day in this country? Answer me; I do not see the four castes. Just as our Bengalee proverb has it, 'As headache without a head,' so you want to make this *Varnàshrama* here. There are not four castes here. I see only the Brâhman and the Sudra. If there are the Kshatriyas and the Vaisyas, where are they, and why do not you Brâhmans order them to take the *Yajnopavita* and study the Vedas, as every Hindu ought to do?—and if the Vaisyas and the Kshatriyas do not exist, but only the Brâhmans and the Sudras, the Sastras say that the Bráhman must not live in a country, where there are only Sudras; so depart bag and baggage! Do you know what the Sastras say about people who have been eating *mlechchha* food, and living under a Government of the *mlechchhas*, as you have for the last thousand years? Do you know the penance for that? The penance would be burning one's self with his own hands. Do you want to pass as teachers, and walk like hypocrites? If you believe in your Sastras burn yourselves first like the one great Brâhman did, who went with Alexander the Great, and burnt himself because he thought he had eaten the food of a *mlechchha*. Do like that and you will see that the whole nation will be at your feet. You do not believe in your own Sastras and yet want to make others believe in them. If you think you are not able to do that in this age, admit your weakness and excuse the weakness of others, take the other castes up, give them a helping hand, let them study the Vedas, and become just as good Aryans as any other Aryans in the world and be you likewise Aryans, you Bràhmans of Bengal.

Give up this filthy *Vâmâchâra* that is killing your country. You have not seen the other parts of India. When I see how much the *Vâmâchâra* has entered our society, I find it a most disgraceful place with all its boast of culture. These *Vâmâ-châra* sects are honeycombing our society in Bengal. Those who come out in the daytime and preach most loudly about *âchâra*, it is they who carry on the horrible debauchery at night, and are backed by the most dreadful books. They are ordered by the books to do these things. You who are of Bengal know it. The Bengalee Sastras are the Vàmàchàra Tantras. They are published by the cart-load, and you poison the minds of your children with them, instead of teaching them your Srutis. Fathers of Calcutta, do you not feel ashamed that such horrible stuff as these Vâmàchâra Tantras, with translations too, should be put into the hands of your boys and girls, and their minds poisoned, and that they should be brought up with the idea that these are the Sastras of the Hindus? If you are ashamed, take them away from your children, and let them read the true Sastras, the Vedas, the Gita, the Upanishads.

According to the dualistic sects of India, the individual souls remain as individuals throughout, and God creates the universe out of pre-existing material, only as the efficient cause. According to the Advaitists, on the other hand, God is both the material, and the efficient cause of the universe. He is not only the Creator of the universe, but He creates it out of Himself. That is the Advaitist position.

There are crude dualistic sects who believe that this world has been created by God out of Himself, and at the same time God is eternally separate from the universe, and everything is eternally subordinate to the Ruler of the universe. There are sects too who also believe that out of Himself God has evolved this universe, and individuals in the long run attain to Nirvàna, to give up the finite and become the Infinite. But these sects have disappeared. The one sect of Advaitists that you see in modern India is composed of the followers of Sankara. According to Sankara, God is both the material and the efficient cause, through Maya, but not in reality. God has not become this universe, but the universe is not, and God is. This is one of the highest points to understand of Advaita Vedanta, this idea of Maya. I am afraid I have no time to discuss this one most difficult point in our philosophy. Those of you who are acquainted with Western philosophy will find something very similar in Kant. But I must warn you, those of you, who have studied Professor Max Muller's writings on Kant, that there is one idea most misleading. It was Sankara who first found out the idea of the identity of time, space and causation with Maya, and I had the good fortune to find one or two passages in Sankara's commentaries and send them to my friend the Professor. So even that idea was here in India. Now this is a peculiar theory—this Maya theory of the Advaita Vedantists. The Brahman is all that exists, but differentiation has been caused by this Maya. Unity, the one Brahman, is the ultimate, the goal, and herein is an eternal dissension again between Indian and Western thought. India has thrown this challenge to the world for thousands of years, and the challenge has been taken up by different nations, and the result is that they all succumbed and you live. This is the challenge, that this world is a delusion, that it is all Maya, that whether you eat off the ground with your fingers, or dine off golden plates, whether you live in palaces, and are one of the mightiest of monarchs or are the poorest of beggars, death is the one result; it is all the same, all Maya. That is the old Indian theme, and again and again nations are springing up trying to unsay it, to disprove it; becoming great, with enjoyment as their watchword, power in their hands, they use that power to the utmost, enjoy to the utmost, and the next moment they die. We stand for ever because we see that everything is Maya. The children of Maya live for ever, but the children of enjoyment die.

Here again is another great difference. Just as you find the attempts of Hegel and Schopenhauer in German Philosophy, so you will find the very same ideas brought forward in ancient India. Fortunately for us, Hegelianism was nipped in the bud, and not allowed to sprout and cast its baneful shoots over this motherland of ours. Hegel's one idea is that the one, the absolute, is only chaos, and that the individualised form is the greater. The world is greater than the non-world, Samsara is greater than salvation. That is the one idea, and the more you plunge into this Samsara, the more your soul is covered with the workings of life, the better you are. They say, do you not see how we build houses, cleanse the streets, enjoy the senses. Aye, behind that they may hide rancour, misery, horror—behind every bit of that enjoyment. On the other hand, our philosophers have from the very first declared that every manifestation, what you call evolution, is vain, a vain attempt of the unmanifested to manifest itself. Aye, you the almighty cause of this universe, trying to reflect yourself in little mud puddles! But after making the attempt for a time you find out it was all in vain, and beat a retreat to the place from whence you came. This is *Vairágya*, or renunciation, and the very beginning of religion. How can religion or morality begin without renunciation itself? The Alpha and Omega is renunciation; "give up," says the Veda, "give up." That is the one way, "give up." न प्रजया धनेन त्यागेनैके अमृतत्वमानशुः ।—"Neither through wealth, nor through progeny, but by giving up alone that immortality is to be reached." That is the dictate of the Indian books. Of course, there have been great givers-up of the world, even sitting on thrones, but even Janaka himself had to renounce; who was a greater renouncer than he? But in modern times we all want to be called Janakas! They are all Janakas* of children,—unclad, ill-fed, miserable children. The word Janaka can be applied to them in that sense only; they have none of the shining, God-like thoughts as the old Janaka had. These are our modern Janakas! A little less of this Janakism now, and come straight to the mark! If you can give up, you will have religion. If you cannot, you may read all the books that are in the world, from East to West, swallow all the libraries, and become the greatest of Pandits, but if you have Karma-kanda only, you are nothing; there is no spirituality. Through renunciation alone this immortality is to be reached. It is the power, the great power, that cares not even for the universe; then it is that ब्रह्माण्डम् गोष्पदायते—"The whole universe becomes likes a hollow made by a cow's foot." Renunciation, that is the flag, the banner of India, floating over the world, the one undying thought which India sends again and again as a warning to dying races, as a warning to all tyranny, as a warning to wickedness in the world. Aye, Hindus, let not your hold of that banner go. Hold it aloft. Even if you are weak, and cannot renounce, do not lower the ideal. Say I am weak and cannot renounce the world, but do not try to be hypocrites, torturing texts, and making specious arguments, and trying to throw dust in the eyes of people who ought to have known better. Do not do that, but own you are weak. For the idea is great, that of renunciation. What matters it if millions fail in the attempt, if ten soldiers, or even two, return victorious! Blessed be the millions dead! Their blood has bought the victory. This renunciation is the one ideal throughout the different Vedic sects except one, and that is the Vallabhâchârya sect in Bombay Presidency, and most of you are aware what comes where renunciation does not exist. We want orthodoxy, even the hideously orthodox, even those who smother themselves with ashes, even those who stand with their hands up-lifted. Aye, we want them, unnatural though they be, for standing for that idea of giving up, and acting as a warning to the race against succumbing to the effeminate luxuries that are creeping into India, eating into our very vitals, and tending to make the whole race a race of hypocrites. We want to have a little of asceticism. Renunciation has conquered India in days of yore, it has still to conquer India. Still it stands greatest and highest of Indian ideals,—this renunciation. The land of Buddha, the land of Ramanuja, of Ramakrishna Paramahamsa, the land of renunciation, the land where, from the days of yore, Karma-kanda was preached against, and even to-day there are hundreds who have given up everything, and become *Jivanmuktas*—aye, will that land give up its ideals? Certainly not. There may be people whose brains have become turned by the Western luxurious ideals; there may be thousands and hundreds of thousands, who have drunk deep of enjoyment, this curse of the West, the senses, the curse of the world, yet for all that, there will be other thousands in this mother-land of mine to whom religion will ever be a reality, and who will be ever ready to give up without counting the cost, if need be.

Another ideal very common in all our sects, I want to place before you; it is also a vast subject. This unique idea that religion is to be realised, is in India alone.

* The word *Janaka* lit. means a father.

[illegible]

[illegible] Such is the Guru. [illegible] himself crossed this terrible ocean [illegible] to himself, helping others to cross the [illegible] and mark, that none else can be a Guru, for [illegible] परियन्ति मूढा अन्धेनैव [illegible] in darkness, but in the pride of their hearts thinking they know everything, the fools want to help others, and they go round and round in many crooked ways, staggering to and fro, and thus like blind leading the blind, both fall into the ditch." Thus, say the Vedas. Compare that and your present custom. You are Vedantists, you are very orthodox, are you not? You are great Hindus, and very orthodox. Aye, what I want to do is to make you more orthodox. The more orthodox you are the more sensible, and the more you think of modern orthodoxy the more foolish you are. Go back to your old orthodoxy, for in those days every sound that came from these books, every pulsation, was out of a strong, steady and sincere heart; every note was true. After that came degradation, in art, in science, in religion, in everything, national degradation. We have no time to discuss the causes, but all the books written about that period breathe of the pestilence, the national decay; instead of vigour, only wails and cries. Go back, go back to the old days, when there was strength and vitality. Be strong once more, drink deep of this fountain of yore, and that is the only condition of life in India.

According to the Advaitist, this individuality which we have to-day is a delusion. This has been a hard nut to crack all over the world. Forthwith you tell a man he is not an individual, he is so much afraid that his individuality, whatever that may be, will be lost. But the Advaitist says there never has been an individuality, you have been changing every moment of your life. You were a child and thought in one way, now you are a man and think another way, again, you will be an old man and think differently. Everybody is changing. If so, where is your individuality? Certainly not in the body, or in the mind, or in thought. And beyond that is your Atman, and, says the Advaitist, this Atman is the Brahman Itself. There cannot be two Infinites. There is only one individual and it is Infinite. In plain words, we are rational beings, and we want to reason. And what is reason? More or less of classification, until you cannot go on any further. And the infinite can only find its ultimate rest when it is classified into the Infinite. Go on taking up a finite and finding its reasons, and so on, but you find rest nowhere until you reach the ultimate, or Infinite, and that Infinite, says the Advaitist, is what alone exists. Everything else is Maya, nothing else has real existence; whatever is of existence in any material thing is this Brahman; we are this Brahman, and the shape and everything else is Maya. Take away the form and shape, and you and I are all one. But we have to guard against the word, 'I.' Generally people say, 'If I am the Brahman why cannot I do this and that,' but this is using the word in a different sense. As soon as you think you are bound, no more you are Brahman the Self, who wants nothing, whose light is inside. All His pleasures and bliss are inside; perfectly satisfied with Himself, He wants nothing, expects nothing, perfectly fearless, perfectly free. That is Brahman. In That we are all one.

Now this seems, therefore, to be the great point of difference between the Dualist and the Advaitist. You find even great commentators like Sankaracharya, making meanings of texts, which, to my mind, sometimes do not seem to be justified. Sometimes you find Ramanuja dealing with texts in a way that is not very clear. The idea has been even among our Pandits that only one of these sects can be true and the rest false;—although they have the idea in the Srutis, the most wonderful idea that India has yet to give to the world,—**एकम् सद्विप्रा वहुधा वदन्ति** ।—"That which exists is One; sages call It by various names." That has been the theme, and the working out of the whole of this life-problem of the nation is the working-out of that theme—**एकम् सद्विप्रा वहुधा वदन्ति** । Yea, except a very few learned men, I mean, barring a very few spiritual men, in India, we always forget this. We forget this great idea, and you will find that there are persons among Pandits—I should think ninety-eight per cent.—who are of opinion that either the Advaitist will be true, or the Vishishtadvaitist will be true, or the Dvaitist will be true, and if you go to Benares, and sit for five minutes in one of the *ghâts* there, you will have demonstration of what I say. You will see a regular bull-fight going on, about these various sects and things.

Thus it remains. Then came one whose life was the explanation, whose life was the working out of the harmony that is the background of all the different sects of India, I mean Ramakrishna Paramahamsa. It is his life that explains that both of these are necessary, that they are like the geocentric and the heliocentric in astronomy. When a child is taught astronomy he is taught the geocentric first, and works out similar ideas of astronomy to the heliocentric. But when he comes to finer systems of astronomy, the heliocentric will be necessary, and he will understand it better. Dualism is the natural idea of the senses; as long as we are bound by the senses we are bound to see a God who is only Personal, and nothing but Personal, we are bound to see the world as it is. Says Ramanuja, "So long as you think you are a body, and you think you are a mind, and you think you are a Jiva, every act of perception will give you the three,—God, and Nature, and something as causing both." But yet, at the same time, even the idea of the body disappears where the mind itself becomes finer and finer, till it has almost disappeared, when all the different things that make us fear, make us weak, and bind us down to this body-life, have disappeared. Then and then alone one finds out the truth of that grand old teaching—What is the teaching?—

इहैव तैर्जितः सर्गो येषां साम्ये स्थितं मनः।
निर्दोषं हि समं ब्रह्म तस्माद्ब्रह्मणि ते स्थिताः॥

"Even in this life they have conquered heaven, whose minds are firm-fixed on the sameness of everything, for God is pure, and the same to all, and therefore, such are said to be living in God."

समं पश्यन् हि सर्वत्र समवस्थितमीश्वरं।
न हिनस्त्यात्मनात्मानं ततो याति परां गतिम्॥

"Thus seeing the Lord the same everywhere, he, the sage, does not hurt the Self by the self, and so goes to the highest goal."

THOUGHTS ON THE GITA.

During his sojourn in Calcutta in 1897, Swamiji used to stay for the most part at the Math, the headquarters of the Ramakrishna Mission, located then at Alumbazar. During this time several young men, who had been preparing themselves for sometime previously, gathered round him and took the vows of Brahmacharyam and Sannyas, and Swamiji began to train them for future work, by holding classes on the Gita and Vedanta, and initiating them into the practices of meditation. In one of these classes he talked eloquently in Bengali on the Gita. The following is the translation of the summary of the discourse as it was entered in the Math diary :—

The book known as the Gita forms a part of the Mahabharata. In understanding the Gita properly, several things are very important to know. First, whether it formed a part of the Mahabharata, i.e., whether the authorship attributed to Veda Vyâsa was true, or if it was merely interpolated within the great epic; secondly, whether there was any historical personality of the name of Krishna; thirdly, whether the great war of Kurukshetra as mentioned in the Gita actually took place; and fourthly, whether Arjuna and others were real historical persons.

Now in the first place, let us see what grounds there are for such enquiry. We know that there were many who went by the name of Veda-Vyâsa; and among them who was the real author of the Gita—the Bâdarâyana Vyasa or Dvaipâyana Vyâsa? 'Vyâsa' was only a title. Any one who composed a new Purâna was known by the name of Vyása, like the word, Vikramâditya, which was also a general name. Another point is, the book, Gita, was not much known to the generality of people, before Sankaracharya made it famous by writing his great commentary on it. Long before that, there was current, according to many, the commentary on it by Bodhâyana. If this could be proved, it would go a long way no doubt, to establish the antiquity of the Gita and the authorship of Vyâsa. But the Bodhâyana Bhâshya on the Vedanta Sutras—from which Ramanuja compiled his Sri-Bhâshya, which Sankaracharya mentions and even quotes in part here and there in his own commentary, and which was so greatly discussed by the Swami Dayananda—not a copy even of that Bodhâyana Bháshya could I find while travelling throughout India. It is said that even Ramanuja compiled his Bháshya from a worm-eaten manuscript which he happened to find. When even this great Bodhâyana Bhâshya on the Vedanta Sutras is so much enshrouded in the darkness of uncertainty, it is simply useless to try to establish the existence of the Bodháyana Bháshya on the Gita. Some infer that Sankaracharya was the author of the Gita, and that it was he who foisted it into the body of the Mahabharata.

Then as to the second point in question, much doubt exists about the personality of Krishna. In one place in the Chhandogya Upanishad we find mention of Krishna, the son of Devaki, who received spiritual instruction from one Ghoranâmâ, a Yogi. In the Mahabharata, Krishna is the king of Dwaraka; and in the Vishnu Purana we find a description of Krishna playing with the Gopis. Again in the Bhagavatam, the account of his *Ràshlilà* is detailed at length. In very ancient times in our country, there was in vogue an Utsab called *Madanotsab* (celebration in honour of Cupid). That very thing was transformed into *Dôl* and thrust upon the shoulders c

Krishna. Who can be so bold as to assert that the *Ràshlilà* and other things connected with him were not similarly fastened upon him? In ancient times, there was very little tendency in our country to find out truths by historical research. So any one could say what he thought best without substantiating it with proper facts and evidence. Another thing, in those ancient times, there was very little hankering after name and fame in men. So it often happened that one man composed a book and made it pass current in the name of his Guru or of some one else. In such cases it is very hazardous for the investigator of historical facts to get at the truth. In ancient times they had no knowledge whatever of geography—imagination ran riot, and so we meet with such fantastic creations of the brain as sweet-ocean, milk-ocean, clarified-butter ocean, curd-ocean, &c.! In the Puranas, we find one living ten thousand years, another a hundred thousand years! But the Vedas say,—शतायुर्वैपुरुषः।—"Man lives a hundred years." Whom shall we follow here? So, to reach a correct conclusion in the case of Krishna is well nigh impossible.

It is human nature to build round the real character of a great man all sorts of imaginary superhuman attributes. As regards Krishna the same must have happened, but it seems quite probable that he was a king. Quite probable I said, because in ancient times in our country it was chiefly the kings who exerted themselves most in the preaching of Brahma-Jnana. Another point to be especially noted here is, that whoever might have been the author of the Gita, we find its teachings the same as those in the whole of the Mahabharata. From this we can safely infer that in the age of the Mahabharata some great man arose and preached the Brahma-Jnana in this new garb to the then existing society. Another fact comes to the fore that in the olden days, as one sect after another arose, there also came into existence and use among them, one new scripture or another. It happened too, that in the lapse of time both the sect and its scripture died out, or the sect ceased to exist but its scripture remained. Similarly it was quite probable that the Gita was the scripture of such a sect, which had embodied its high and noble ideas, in this sacred book.

Now to the third point, bearing on the subject of the Kurukshetra War, no special evidence in support of it can be adduced. But there is no doubt that there was a war fought between the Kurus and the Pánchâlas. Another thing: How could there be so much discussion about Jnana, Bhakti and Yoga on the battle-field, where the huge army stood in battle array ready to fight, just waiting for the last signal? And was any shorthand writer present there to note down every word spoken between Krishna and Arjuna, in the din and turmoil of the battle-field? According to some, this Kurukshetra War is only an allegory. When we sum up its esoteric significance, it means the war which is constantly going on within man between the tendencies of good and bad. This meaning too, may not be irrational.

About the fourth point, there is enough ground of doubt as regards the historicity of Arjuna and others, and it is this:—Satapatha Brâhmana is a very ancient book. In it are mentioned somewhere all the names of those who were the performers of the Ashvamedha Yajna, but in those places there is not only no mention but no hint even of the names of Arjuna and others, though it speaks of Janmejaya, the son of Parikshit, and grandson of Arjuna. Yet in the Mahabharata and other books it is stated that Yudhishthira, Arjuna and others celebrated the Ashvamedha sacrifice.

One thing should be especially remembered here, that there is no connection between these historical researches and our real aim which is, the knowledge that leads to the acquirement of Dharma. Even if the historicity of the whole thing is proved to be absolutely false to-day, it will not in the least be any loss to us. Then what is the use of so much historical research, you may ask. It has its use, because we have to get at the truth; it will not do for us to remain bound by wrong ideas due to ignorance. In this country people think very little of the importance of such enquiries. Many of the sects believe that in order to preach a good thing which may be beneficial to many, there is no harm in telling an untruth, if that helps such preaching, or in other words, the end justifies the means. Hence we find many of our Tantras beginning with,—'Mahâdeva said to Pârvati.' But our duty should be to convince ourselves of the truth, to believe in truth only. Such is the power of superstition, or faith in old traditions without enquiry into its truth, that it keeps men bound hand and foot, so much so, that even Jesus the Christ, Mahommed and other great men believed in many such superstitions and could not shake them off. You have to keep your eye always fixed on truth only, and shun all superstitions completely.

Now it is for us to see, what there is in the Gita. If we study the Upanishads we notice, in wandering through the mazes of many irrelevent subjects, suddenly the introduction of the discussion of a great truth, just as in the midst of a huge wilderness a traveller unexpectedly comes across here and there an exquisitely beautiful rose, with its leaves, thorns, roots, all entangled. Compared to that, the Gita is like these truths beautifully arranged together in their proper places—like a fine garland or a bouquet of the choicest flowers. The Upanishads deal elaborately with Shraddhâ in many places, but hardly mentions Bhakti. In the Gita on the other hand, the subject of Bhakti is not only again and again dealt with, but in it, the innate spirit of Bhakti has attained its culmination.

Now let us see some of the main points discussed in the Gita. Wherein lies the originality of the Gita, which distinguishes it from all preceding scriptures? It is this: Though before its advent, Yoga, Jnana, Bhakti, &c., had each its strong adherents, they all quarrelled among themselves, each claiming superiority for his own path of devotion; no one ever tried to seek for reconciliation among these different paths. It was the author of the Gita who for the first time tried to harmonise these. He took the best from what all the sects then existing had to offer, and threaded them in the Gita. But even where Krishna failed to show a complete reconciliation (*Samanvya*) among these warring sects, it was fully accomplished by Ramakrishna Paramahamsa in this nineteenth century.

The next is, Nishkâma Karma or work without desire or attachment. People nowadays understand what is meant by this in various ways. Some say, what is implied by being unattached is to become purposeless! If that were its real meaning, then heartless brutes and the walls would be the best exponents of the performers of Nishkâma Karma. Many others again, give the example of Janaka, and wish themselves to be equally recognised as past-masters in the practice of Nishkâma Karma! Janaka did not acquire that distinction by bringing forth children, but these people all want to be Janakas, with the sole qualification of being the fathers of a brood of children! No! The true Nishkâma Karmi (performer of work without desire) is neither to be like a brute, nor to be inert, nor heartless. He is not Tâmasic but of pure Sattva. His heart is so full of love and sympathy, that he can embrace the whole world with his love. The world at large cannot generally comprehend his all-embracing love and sympathy.

The reconciliation of the different paths of Dharma, and work without desire or attachment—these are the two special characteristics of the Gita.

R

Let us now read a little from the second chapter.

संजय उवाच ॥
तं तथा कृपयाविष्टमश्रुपूर्णाकुलेक्षणम् ।
विषीदन्तमिदं वाक्यमुवाच मधुसूदनः ॥१॥
श्रीभगवानुवाच ॥
कुतस्त्वा कश्मलमिदं विषमे समुपस्थितम् ।
अनार्यजुष्टमस्वर्ग्यमकीर्तिकरमर्जुन ॥२॥
क्लैब्यं मास्म गमः पार्थ नैतत्त्वय्युपपद्यते ।
क्षुद्रं हृदयदौर्बल्यं त्यक्त्वोत्तिष्ठ परंतप ॥३॥

"Sanjaya said:

To him who was thus overwhelmed with pity and sorrowing, and whose eyes were dimmed with tears, Madhusudana spoke these words:

The Blessed Lord said:

In such a strait, whence comes upon thee, O Arjuna, this dejection, un-Arya-like, disgraceful, and contrary to the attainment of heaven?

Yield not to unmanliness, O son of Prithà! Ill doth it become thee. Cast off this mean faint-heartedness and arise, O scorcher of thine enemies!"

In the slokas beginning with तं तथा कृपयाविष्टं, how poetically—how beautifully has Arjuna's real position been painted! Then Sri Krishna advises Arjuna; and in the words क्लैब्यं मास्म गमः पार्थ &c., why is he goading Arjuna to fight? Because it was not that the disinclination of Arjuna to fight arose out of the overwhelming predominance of pure Sattva Guna; it was all Tamas that brought on this unwillingness. The nature of a man of Sattva Guna is, that he is equally calm in all situations in life—whether it be prosperity or adversity. But Arjuna was afraid, he was overwhelmed with pity. That he had the instinct and the inclination to fight is proved by the simple fact, that he came to the battle-field with no other purpose than that. Frequently in our lives also such things are seen to happen. Many people think they are Sáttvic by nature, but they are really nothing but Támasic. Many living in an uncleanly way regard themselves as Paramahamsas! Why? Because the Shastras say that Paramahamsas live like one inert, or mad, or like an unclean spirit. Paramahamsas are compared to children, but here it should be understood that the comparison is one-sided. The Paramahamsa and the child are not one and non-different. They only appear similar, being at the two extremes of a pole, as it were. One has reached to a state beyond Jnanam, and the other has not got even an inkling of Jnanam. The quickest and the gentlest vibrations of the molecular atoms of light are both beyond the reach of our spectacular vision; but in the one it is intense heat, and in the other it may be said to be almost without any heat. So it is with the opposite qualities of the Sattva and the Tamas. They seem in some respects no doubt to be the same, but there is a world of difference between them. The Tamoguna loves very much to array herself in the garb of the Sattva. Here, in Arjuna, the mighty warrior, she has come under the guise of Dayá (pity)!

In order to remove this delusion which had overtaken Arjuna, what did the Bhagavàn say? As I always preach that you should not decry a man by calling him a sinner but that you should draw his attention to the omnipotent power that is in him, in the same way does the Bhagaván speak to Arjuna: "नैतत्त्वय्युपपद्यते"—It doth not befit thee! Thou art that Atman imperishable, beyond all evil. Having forgotten thy real nature, thou hast, by thinking thyself a sinner, as one afflicted with bodily evils and mental grief,—thou hast made thyself so,—this doth not befit thee! So says the Bhagaván: "क्लैब्यं मास्म गमः पार्थ"—Yield not to unmanliness, O son of Prithá! There is in the world neither sin nor misery, neither disease nor grief; if there is anything in the world which can be called sin, it is this—"fear"; know that any work which brings out the latent power in thee, is Punya; and that which makes thy body and mind weak is, verily, sin. Shake off this weakness, this faint-heartedness! "क्लैब्यं मास्म गमः पार्थ," Thou art a hero, a *Vira;* "this is unbecoming of thee." If you, my sons, can proclaim this message to the world—"क्लैब्यं मास्म गमः पार्थ नैतत्त्वय्युपपद्यते"—then all this disease, grief, sin and sorrow will vanish from off the face of the earth in three days. All these ideas of weakness will be nowhere. Now it is everywhere—this current of the vibration of fear. Reverse the current; bring in the opposite vibration, and behold the magic transformation! Thou art omnipotent;—go, go to the mouth of the cannon, fear not! Hate not the most abject sinner, look not to his exterior. Turn thy gaze inward, where resides the Paramatman. Proclaim to the whole world with trumpet voice: "There is no sin in thee, there is no misery in thee; thou art the reservoir of omnipotent power. Arise, awake, and manifest the Divinity within!"

If one reads this one sloka,—क्लैब्यं मास्म गमः पार्थ नैतत्त्वय्युपपद्यते । क्षुद्रं हृदयदौर्बल्यं त्यक्त्वोत्तिष्ठ परंतप ॥—he gets all the merits of reading the entire Gita; for in this one sloka lies imbedded the whole Message of the Gita.

ADDRESS OF WELCOME AT ALMORA AND SWAMIJI'S REPLY.

On his arrival at Almora, Swamiji received an Address of Welcome in Hindi from the citizens of Almora, of which the following is a translation :—

Great-souled one.—Since the time we heard that, after gaining spiritual conquest in the West, you had started from England for your motherland, India, we were naturally desirous of having the pleasure of seeing you. By the grace of the Almighty, that auspicious moment has at last come. The saying of the great poet and the prince of Bhaktas, Tulsidas—"A person who intensely loves another is sure to find him," has been fully realised to-day, We have assembled here to welcome you with sincere devotion, You have highly obliged us by your kindly taking so much trouble in paying a visit to this town again. We can hardly thank you enough for your kindness. Blessed are you! Blessed, blessed is the revered Gurudeva who initiated you into Yoga. Blessed is the land of Bhárata where, even in this fearful Kaliyuga, there exist leaders of Aryan families like yourself. Even at an early period of life, you have by your simplicity, sincerity, character, philanthropy, severe discipline, conduct, and the preaching of knowledge, acquired that immaculate fame throughout the world, of which we feel so proud,

In truth, you have accomplished that difficult task which no one ever undertook in this country since the days of Sri Sankaracharya. Which of us ever dreamt that a descendant of the old Indian Aryans, by dint of *tapas*, would prove to the learned people of England and America the superiority of the ancient Indian Religion over other creeds, In the World's Parliament of Religions held in Chicago, before the representatives of different religions assembled there, you so ably advocated the superiority of the ancient religion of India, that their eyes were opened, In that great assembly, learned speakers defended their respective religions in their own way, but you surpassed them all, You completely established that no religion can compete with the religion of the Vedas, Not only this, but by preaching the ancient wisdom at various places in the continents aforesaid, you have attracted many learned men towards the ancient Aryan religion and philosophy. In England, too, you have planted the banner of the ancient religion, which it is impossible now to remove,

Up to this time, the modern civilised nations of Europe and America were entirely ignorant of the genuine nature of our religion, but you have with your spiritual teaching opened their eyes, by which they have come to know that the ancient religion, which owing to their ignorance they used to brand "as a religion of subtleties of conceited people, or a mass of discourses meant for fools," is a mine of gems, Certainly, "It is better to have a virtuous and accomplished son than to have hundreds of foolish ones," "It is the moon that singly with its light dispels all darkness and not all the stars put together." It is only the life of a good and virtuous son like yourself that is really useful to the world, Mother India is consoled in her decayed state by the presence of pious sons like you. Many have crossed the seas and run to and fro, but it was only through the reward of your past good Karma that you have proved the greatness of our religion, beyond the seas. You have made it the sole aim of your life by word, thought and deed, to impart spiritual instruction to humanity. You are always ready to give religious instruction.

We have heard with great pleasure that you intend establishing a *Math* (Monastery) here, and we sincerely pray that your efforts in this direction may be crowned with success. The great Sankaracharya also after his spiritual conquest, established a *Math* at Badarikásrama in the Himalayas for the protection of the ancient religion. Similarly, if your desire is also fulfilled, India will be greatly benefited. By the establishment of the *Math*, we Kumaonees will derive special spiritual advantages, and we shall not see the ancient religion gradually disappearing from our midst.

From time immemorial, this part of the country has been the land of asceticism. The greatest of the Indian sages passed their time in piety and asceticism in this land, but that has become a thing of the past. We earnestly hope that by the establishment of the *Math* you will kindly make us realise it again. It was this sacred land which enjoyed the celebrity all over India, of having true religion, Karma, discipline, and fair dealing, all of which seem to have been decaying by the efflux of time. And we hope that by your noble exertions this land will revert to its ancient religious state.

We cannot adequately express the joy we have felt at your arrival here. May you live long, enjoying perfect health and leading a philanthropic life! May your spiritual powers be ever on the increase, so that through your endeavours the unhappy state of India may soon disappear!

Two other addresses were presented, to which the Swami made the following brief reply:—

This is the land of dreams of our forefathers, in which was born Pàrvati, the Mother of India. This is the holy land, where every ardent soul in India wants to come at the end of its life, and to close the last chapter of its mortal career here. On the tops of the mountains of this blessed land, in the depths of its caves, on the banks of its rushing torrents, have been thought out the most wonderful thoughts, a little bit of which has drawn so much admiration even from foreigners, and which have been pronounced by the most competent of judges to be incomparable. This is the land which, since my very childhood, I have been dreaming of passing my life in, and as all of you are aware, I have attempted again and again to live here, and although the time was not ripe, and I had work to do and was whirled outside of this holy place, yet it is the hope of my life to end my days somewhere in this Father of mountains, where Rishis lived, where philosophy was born. Perhaps, my friends, I shall not be able to do it, in the way that I had planned before—how I wish that silence, that unknownness would be given to me,—yet I sincerely pray and hope, and almost believe that my last days will be spent here, of all places on earth.

Inhabitants of this holy land, accept my gratitude for the kind praise that has fallen from you for my little work in the West. But, at the same time, my mind does not want to speak of that, either in the East or in the West. As peak after peak of this Father of mountains began to appear before my sight, all the propensities to work, that ferment that had been going on in my brain for years, seemed to quiet down, and instead of talking about what had been done, and what was going to be done, the mind reverted to that one eternal theme which the Himalayas always teach us, that one theme which is reverberating in the very atmosphere of the place, the one theme the murmur of whose dreams I hear, the one thing that I hear in the rushing whirlpools of its rivers—renunciation! सर्वं वस्तु भयान्वितं भुवि नृणां वैराग्यमेवाभयं—"Everything in this life is fraught with fear. It is renunciation alone that makes one fearless." Yes, this is the land of renunciation.

The time will not permit me, and the circumstances are not fitting to speak to you fully. I shall have to conclude, therefore, by pointing out to you that the Himalayas stand for that renunciation, and the grand lesson we shall ever teach to humanity will be, renunciation. As our forefathers used to be attracted towards it in the latter days of their lives, so, strong souls from all quarters of this earth, in time to come, will be attracted to this Father of mountains, when all this fight between sects, and all those differences in dogmas, will not be remembered any more, and quarrels between your religion and my religion will have vanished altogether, when mankind will understand that there is but one eternal religion, and that is, the perception of the Divine within, and the rest is mere froth: such ardent souls will come here knowing that the world is but vanity of vanities, knowing that everything is useless except the worship of the Lord and the Lord alone.

Friends, you have been very kind to allude to an idea of mine, which is to start a centre in the Himalayas, and perhaps I have sufficiently explained why it should be so, why above all others, this is the spot which I want to select as one of the great centres to teach this universal religion. These mountains are associated with the best memories of our race; if these Himalayas are taken away from the history of religious India, there will be very little left behind. Here, therefore, must be one of those centres, not merely of activity, but more of calmness, of meditation, and of peace, and I hope some day to realise it. I hope also to meet you at other times, and have better opportunities of talking to you. For the present, let me thank you again for all the kindness that has been shown to me, and let me take it as not only kindness shown to me in person, but as to one who represents our religion; may it never leave our hearts. May we always remain as pure as we are at the present moment, and as enthusiastic for spirituality as we are just now.

VEDIC TEACHING IN THEORY AND PRACTICE.

When the Swami's visit was drawing to a close, his friends in Almora invited him to give a lecture in Hindi. He consented to make the attempt for the first time. He began slowly, and soon warmed to his theme, and found himself building his phrases and almost his words as he went along. Those best acquainted with the difficulties and limitations of the Hindi language as a medium for oratory, expressed their opinion that a triumph had been achieved, probably unique of its kind; as well as being profoundly interesting; and the lecturer had proved by his masterly use of it, that the language had in it undreamt of possibilities of development in the direction of oratory.

The subject was "Vedic Teaching in Theory and Practice." A short historical sketch of the rise of the worship of the tribal God, and its spread through conquest of other tribes, was followed by an account of the Vedas. Their nature, character and teaching were briefly touched upon. Then the Swami spoke about the soul, comparing the Western method, which seeks for the solution of vital and religious mysteries in the outside world, with the Eastern method, which, finding no answer in nature outside, turns its enquiry within. He justly claimed for his nation the glory of being the discoverers of the introspective method peculiar to themselves, and of having given to humanity the priceless treasures of spirituality, which are the result of that method alone. Passing from this theme, naturally so dear to the heart of a Hindu, the Swami reached the climax of his power as a spiritual teacher when he described the relation of the soul to God, its aspiration and real unity with God. For sometime it seemed as though the Teacher, his words, his audience, and the spirit pervading them all, were one. No longer was there any consciousness of "I" and "Thou," of "This" or "That." The different units collected there, were for the time being lost and merged into the spiritual radiance which emanated so powerfully from the great Teacher, and held them all, more than spell-bound.

Those that have frequently heard him will recall and recognise a similar experience,—a moment when he ceases to be Swami Vivekananda lecturing to critical and attentive hearers,—all details and personalities are lost, names and forms disappear, only the Spirit remains, uniting Speaker, Hearer, and spoken Word.

BHAKTI.

(Delivered at Sialkote, Punjab.)

In response to invitations from the Punjab and Kashmir, the Swami Vivekananda travelled through those parts. He stayed in Kashmir for over a month and his work there was very much appreciated by the Máharajah and his brothers. He then spent a few days in visiting Murree, Rawalpindi and Jammu, and at each of these places he delivered lectures. Subsequently, he visited Sialkote and lectured twice, once in English and once in Hindi. The subject of the Swamiji's Hindi lecture was Bhakti, a summary of which, translated into English is given below :—

The various religions that exist in the world, although they differ in the form of the worship they take, are really one. In some places, the people build temples and worship in them ; in some, they worship fire, in others they prostrate themselves before idols, while there are many who do not believe at all in God. All are true, for, if you look to the real words, the real religion, and the truths in each of them, they are all alike. In some religions God is not worshipped, nay, His existence is not believed in, but good and worthy men are worshipped as if they were Gods. The example worthy of illustration in this case is Buddhism. Bhakti is everywhere, whether directed to God, or to noble persons. *Upásaná* in the form of Bhakti is everywhere supreme and Bhakti is more easily attained than Jnána. The latter requires favourable circumstances and strenuous practice. Yoga cannot be properly practised unless a man is physically very healthy, and free from all worldly attachments. But Bhakti can be more easily practised by persons in every condition of life. Sándilya Rishi who wrote about Bhakti, says, that *Parama Anurága* in *Ishvara* is Bhakti. Prahláda speaks to the same effect. If a man does not get food one day, he is troubled, if his son dies how agonising it is to him. The true Bhakta feels the same pangs in his heart when he yearns after God. The great quality of Bhakti is that it cleanses the mind, and the firmly established Bhakti in the *Parameshvara* is alone sufficient to purify the *chitta.* " O God, Thy names are innumerable, but in every name Thy power is manifest, and every name is pregnant with deep and mighty significance." We should think of God always and not consider time and place for doing so.

The different names under which God is worshipped are apparently different. One thinks that his method of worshipping God is the most efficacious, and another thinks that his is the more potent process of attaining salvation. But look at the true basis of all, and it is one. The Shaivas call Shiva the most powerful ; the Vaishnavas hold to their all-powerful Vishnu ; the worshippers of Devi will not yield to any in their idea that their Devi is the most omnipotent Power in the universe. Leave inimical thoughts aside if you want to have permanent Bhakti. Hatred is a thing which greatly impedes the course of Bhakti, and the man who hates none reaches God. Even then the Bhakti of one's own *Ishta* is necessary. Hanuman says, " Shiva, Vishnu, Ráma, I know, are all one and the same, but after all, the lotus-eyed Ráma is my best treasure." The *Bháva*, or the peculiarities which are born with a person, must remain with him. That is the sole reason why the world cannot be of one religion ;

and God forbid that there should be one religion only; the world would be a chaos and not a cosmos; a man must follow the tendencies peculiar to himself; and if he gets a teacher to tell him more and to advance the knowledge of his own *Bháva*, he will progress. That *Bháva* is to be cultivated. We should let a person go the way he intends to go, but if we try to force him into another path, he will lose what he has already attained and will become worthless. As the face of one person does not resemble that of another, so the *Prakriti* of one differs from that of another, and why should he not be allowed to act accordingly. A river flows in a certain direction, and if you direct the course into a regular channel the current becomes more rapid and the force is increased, but try to divert it from its proper course and you will see the result; the volume as well as the force will be lessened. This life is very important and it therefore ought to be guided in the way one's *Bháva* prompts him. In India there was no enmity and every religion was left unmolested, so religion has accordingly lived. It ought to be remembered that quarrels about religion arise from thinking that one has the truth, and whoever does not believe as one does is a fool; while another thinks that the other is a hypocrite, for if he were not so, he would follow him.

If God wished that people should follow one religion, why have so many religions sprung up? Methods have been vainly tried, to force one religion upon everyone. Even when a sword was lifted to make all people follow one religion, history tells us that ten religions sprang up in its place. One religion cannot suit all. *Játi* is the product of two forces, action and reaction, which make a man think. If such forces did not exercise a man's mind he would be incapable of thinking. Man is a creature who thinks; *Manushya* is a being with *Manas*, and as soon as this leaves him, his thinking power goes, and he becomes nothing better than an animal. Who would like such a man? God forbid that any such state should come upon the people of India. Variety in unity is necessary to keep man as man. Variety ought to be preserved in everything; for as long as there is variety the world will exist. Of course variety does not merely mean that one is small and the other is great, but if all play their parts equally well in their respective position in life, the variety is still preserved. In every religion there have been men good and able, thus making the religion to which they belonged worthy of respect, and as there are such people in every religion, there ought to be no hatred for any sect whatsoever Then, the question can be asked, should we respect that religion which advocates vice? The answer will be certainly in the negative, and such a religion ought to be expelled at once, because it is productive of harm. All religion is to be based upon *niti* (law), and *àchàra* (personal purity) is to be counted superior to Dharma. In this connection it ought to be known that *àchàra* means purity inside and outside. External purity can be attained by cleansing the body with water and other things, which are recommended in the Shástras. The internal man is to be purified by not speaking falsehood, by not drinking, by not doing immoral acts, and by doing good to others. If you do not commit any sin, if you do not tell lies, if you do not drink, gamble or commit theft, it is good. But that is only your duty and you cannot be applauded for it. Some *paropakára* is also to be done. As you do good to yourself, so you must do good to others. Here I shall say something about *Bhojan* (the laws relating to eating). All the old customs have faded away and nothing but a vague notion of not eating with this man and not eating with that man has been left among our countrymen. *Shuchi* (purity by touch) is *the* only basic relic left of the good rules laid down hundreds of

S

years ago. Three kinds of food are forbidden in the Shástras. First, *Játi-dosha*,—which means the defect that is in the food itself, as in garlic or onions. If a man eats too much of them it creates passion, and he may be led to commit immoralities, hateful both to God and man. Second, eating in unclean places. We ought to select some place quite neat and clean in which to take our food. Thirdly, we should avoid eating food touched by a wicked man, because contact with such produces bad ideas in us. Even if one be a son of a Bráhman, but is profligate and immoral in his habits, we should not eat food from his hands.

But the spirit of these observances is gone. What is left is this, that we cannot eat from the hands of any man who is not of the highest caste, even though he be the most wise and holy person. The disregard of those old rules is ever to be found in the confectioner's shop. If you look there you will find flies hovering all over the confectionery, and the dust from the road blowing upon the sweetmeats, and the confectioner himself in a dress that is not very clean and neat. Purchasers should declare with one voice that they will not buy sweets unless they are kept in glass-cases in the *halwar's* shop. That would have the salutary effect of preventing flies from conveying cholera and other plague germs to the sweets. We ought to improve, but instead of improving we have gone back. Manu says that we should not spit in water, but we throw all sorts of filth into the rivers. Considering all these things we find that the purification of one's outer self is very necessary. The Shâstrakâras knew that very well. But now the real spirit of this observance of *Shuchi* and *Ashuchi* is lost and the letter only remains. Thieves, drunkards, and criminals can be our caste-fellows, but if a good and noble man eats food with a person of a lower caste, who is quite as respectable as himself, he will be out-casted and lost for ever. This custom has been the bane of our country. It ought therefore to be distinctly understood that sin is got by coming in contact with sinness, and nobility in the company of good persons; and keeping aloof from the wicked is the external purification. The internal purification is a task much more severe. It consists in speaking the truth, serving the poor, helping the needy, &c. Do we always speak the truth? What happens is often this. People go to the house of a rich person for some business of their own and flatter him by calling him benefactor of the poor, and so forth; even though that man may cut the throat of a poor man coming to his house. What is this? Nothing but falsehood. And it is this that pollutes the mind. It is therefore truly said, that whatever a man says who has purified his inner self for twelve years without entertaining a single vicious idea during that period, is sure to come true. This is the power of truth, and one who has cleansed both the inner and the outer self, is alone capable of Bhakti. But the beauty is that Bhakti itself cleanses the mind to a great extent. Although the Jews, Mahommedans and Christians do not set so much importance upon the excessive external purification of the body as the Hindus do, still they have it in some form or other; they find that to a certain extent it is always required. Among the Jews, idol worship is condemned, but they had a temple, in which was kept a chest which they called an ark, in which the Tables of the Law were preserved, and above the chest were two figures of angels with wings outstretched, between which the Divine Presence was supposed to manifest Itself as a cloud That temple has long since been destroyed, but the new temples are made exactly after the old fashion, and in the chest religious books are kept. The Roman Catholics and the Greek Christians have idol worship in certain forms. The image of Jesus, and those of his father and mother, are worshipped. Among Protestants there is no idol worship, yet they worship God in a personal form, which takes the place of an idol. Among Parsees and Iranians fire-worship is carried on to a great extent. Among Mahommedans the Prophets and great and noble persons are worshipped, and they turn their faces towards the Kaaba when they pray. These things show that men at the first stage of religious development, have to make use of something external, and when the inner self becomes purified they turn to more abstract conceptions. When Brahman is united with Jiva, and Jnana is practised, it is *Madhyama*. *Japa* is the *adhama* (lowest form), and external worship is the *adhama* of *adhama*, that is, the lowest of the low. But it should be distinctly understood that even in practising the last there is no sin. Everybody ought to do what he is able to do, and if he be dissuaded from that he will do it in some other way in order to attain his end. So we should not speak ill of a man who worships idols. He is in that stage of growth, and therefore must have them; wise men should try to help forward such men, and to get them to do better. But there is no use in quarrelling about these various sorts of worship.

Some persons worship God for the sake of obtaining wealth, others because they want to have a son; and they think themselves *Bhágavats*. This is no Bhakti, and they are not true *Bhágavats*. When a Sadhu comes who professes that he can make gold, they run to him, and they still consider themselves *Bhágavats*. It is not Bhakti if we worship God with the desire for a son; it is not Bhakti if we worship with the desire to be rich; it is not Bhakti even if we have a desire for *Swarga*; it is not Bhakti if a man worships with the desire of being saved from the tortures of hell. Bhakti is not the outcome of fear or greediness. He is the true *Bhágavat* who says—"O God, I do not want a beautiful wife, I do not want knowledge, nor salvation, let me be born and die hundreds of times, what I want is that I should be ever engaged in Thy service." It is at this stage, and when a man sees God in everything, and everything in God, that he attains perfect Bhakti. It is then that he sees Vishnu incarnated in everything, from the microbe to Brahmá, and it is then that he sees God manifesting Himself in everything, it is then that he feels that there is nothing without God, and it is then and then alone that thinking himself to be the most insignificant of all beings he worships God with the true spirit of a Bhakta. He then leaves *Tirthas* and external forms of worship far behind him, he sees every man to be the most perfect *Devàlaya*. Bhakti is described in several ways in the *Shástras*. We say that God is our Father. In the same way we call Him Mother, and so on. These relationships are conceived in order to strengthen Bhakti in us, and make us feel nearer and dearer to God. Hence these names are justifiable in one way, and that is, that the words are simply words of endearment, the outcome of the fond love which a true *Bhágavat* feels for God. Take the story of Rádha and Krishna in *Ráslila*. The story simply exemplifies the true spirit of a Bhakta, because no love in the world exceeds that existing between a man and a woman. Where there is such intense love, there is no fear, no other attachment save that one which binds that pair in an inseparable and all-absorbing bond. But with regard to parents, love is accompanied with fear due to the reverence we have for them. Why should we care whether God created anything or not, what have we to do with the fact that He is our preserver. He is our only Beloved, and we should adore Him devoid of all thoughts of fear. A man loves God only when he has no other desire, when he thinks of nothing else and when he is mad after Him. That love which a man has for his beloved can illustrate the love we ought to have for God. Krishna is the God and Rádha loves Him; read those books which describe that story, and then you can imagine the way you should love God. But how many understand this? How can people, who are vicious to their very core, and have no idea of what morality is, understand all this? When people drive all sorts of worldly thoughts from their minds and live in a clear moral and spiritual atmosphere, it is then they understand the abstrusest of thoughts even if they be uneducated. But how few are there of that nature? There is not a single religion which cannot be perverted by man. For example, he may think that the Atman is quite separate from the body, and so, when committing sins with the body his Atman is unaffected. If religions were truly followed there would not have been a single man, whether Hindu, Mahommedan, or Christian, who would not have been all purity. But men are guided by their own Prakriti, whether good or bad; there is no gainsaying that. But in the world, there are always some who get intoxicated when they hear of God, and weep tears of joy when they read of God; such men are true Bhaktas.

At the initial stage of religious development a man thinks of God as his Master and himself as His servant. He feels indebted to Him for providing for his daily wants, and so forth. Put such thoughts aside. There is but one attractive power, and that is God; and it is in obedience to that attractive power that the sun and the moon, and everything else moves. Everything in this world, whether good or bad, belongs to God. Whatever occurs in our life, whether good or bad, is bringing us to Him. One man kills another because of some selfish purpose. But the motive behind is love, whether for himself or for any one else. Whether we do good or evil, the propeller is love. When a tiger kills a buffalo, it is because he or his cubs are hungry.

God is Love personified. He is apparent in everything. Everybody is drawn to Him whether he knows it or not. When a woman loves her husband, she does not understand that it is the Divine in her husband that is the great attractive power. The God of Love is the one thing to be worshipped. So long as we think of Him only as the Creator, and Preserver, we can offer Him external worship, but when we get beyond all that, and think Him to be Love Incarnate, seeing Him in all things and all things in Him, it is then that Supreme Bhakti is attained.

THE COMMON BASES OF HINDUISM.

On his arrival at Lahore on 5th November 1897, the Swamiji was accorded a grand reception by the leaders, both of the Arya Samaj and of the Sanatan Dharma Sabha. During his brief stay in Lahore Swamiji delivered three lectures. The first of these was on "The Common Bases of Hinduism"; the second on "Bhakti"; and the third one was the famous lecture on "The Vedanta." On the first occasion he spoke as follows:—

This is the land which is held to be the holiest even in holy Aryavarta; this is the Brahmavarta of which our great Manu speaks. This is the land from whence arose that mighty aspiration after the Spirit, aye, which in times to come, as history shows, was to deluge the world. This is the land where, like its mighty rivers, spiritual aspirations have arisen and joined their strength, till they travelled over the length and breadth of the world, and declared themselves with a voice of thunder. This is the land which had first to bear the brunt of all inroads and invasions into India; this heroic land had first to bare its bosom to every onslaught of the outer barbarians into Aryavarta. This is the land which, after all its sufferings, has not yet entirely lost its glory and its strength. Here it was that in later times the gentle Nának preached his marvellous love for the world. Here it was that his broad heart was opened, and his arms outstretched to embrace the whole world, not only of Hindus, but of Mahommedans too. Here it was that one of the last and one of the most glorious of our race, Guru Govinda Singh, after shedding his blood, and that of his dearest and nearest, for the cause of religion, even when deserted by those for whom this blood was shed, retired into the South to die like a wounded lion struck to the heart, and without a word against his country, without a single word of murmur, disappeared.

Here, in this ancient land of ours, children of the land of five rivers, I stand before you, not as a teacher—for I know very little to teach, but as one who has come from the East to exchange words of greeting with the brothers of the West, to compare notes. Here am I, not to find out differences that exist among us, but to find where we agree. Here am I trying to understand on what ground we may always remain brothers, upon what foundations the voice that has spoken from eternity may become stronger and stronger as it grows. Here am I trying to propose to you something of constructive work and not destructive. For criticism the days are past, and we are waiting for constructive work. The world needs, at times, criticisms, even fierce ones; but that is only for a time and the work for eternity is progress and construction, and not criticism and destruction. For the last hundred years or so, there has been a flood of criticism all over this land of ours, where the full play of Western Science has been let loose upon all the dark spots, and as a result the corners and the holes have become much more prominent than anything else. Naturally enough there arose mighty intellects all over the land, great and glorious, with the love of truth and justice in their hearts; in their hearts, the love of their country, and above all, an intense love for their religion and their God; and because these mighty souls felt so deeply, because they loved so deeply, they criticised everything they thought was wrong. Glory unto these mighty spirits of the past! They have done so much good; but the voice of the present day is coming to us, telling, "Enough!" There has been enough of criticism, there has been enough of fault-finding, the time has come for the rebuilding, the reconstructing; the time has come for us to gather all our scattered forces, to concentrate them into one focus, and through that, to lead the nation on its onward march, which for centuries almost, has been stopped. The house has been cleansed; let it be inhabited anew. The road has been cleared: march ahead, children of the Aryas!

Gentlemen, this is the motive that brings me before you, and, at the start, I may declare to you that I belong to no party and no sect. They are all great and glorious to me, I love them all, and all my life I have been attempting to find what is good and true in them. Therefore, it is my proposal to-night to bring before you points where we are agreed, to find out if we can, a ground of agreement; and if through the grace of the Lord such a state of things be possible, let us take it up, and from theory carry it out into practice. We are Hindus. I do not use the word Hindu in any bad sense at all, nor do I agree with those that think there is any bad meaning in it. In old times, it simply meant people who lived on the other side of the Indus, to-day a good many among those who hate us may have put a bad interpretation upon it, but names are nothing. Upon us depends whether the name Hindu will stand for everything that is glorious, everything that is spiritual, or whether it will remain a name of opprobrium, one designating the down-trodden, the worthless, the heathen. If at present the word Hindu means anything bad, never mind; by our action let us be ready to show that this is the highest word that any language can invent. It has been one of the principles of my life not to be ashamed of my own ancestors. I am one of the proudest men ever born, but let me tell you frankly, it is not for myself, but on account of my ancestry. The more I have studied the past, the more I have looked back, more and more has this pride come to me, and it has given me the strength and courage of conviction, raised me up from the dust of the earth, and set me working out that great plan laid out by those great ancestors of ours. Children of those ancient Aryans, through the grace of the Lord may you have the same pride, may that faith in your ancestors come into your blood, may it become a part and parcel of your lives, may it work towards the salvation of the world!

Before trying to find out the precise point where we are all agreed, the common ground of our national life, one thing we must remember. Just as there is an individuality in every man, so there is a national individuality. As one man differs from another in certain particulars, in certain characteristics of his own, so one race differs from another in certain other characteristics; and just as it is the mission of every man to fulfil a certain purpose in the economy of nature, just as it is a particular line set out for him by his own past Karma, so it is with nations—each nation has a destiny to fulfil, each nation has a message to deliver, each nation has a mission to accomplish. Therefore, from the very start, we must have to understand the mission of our own race, the destiny it has to fulfil, the place it has to occupy in the march of nations, the note which it has to contribute to the harmony of races. In our country, when children, we hear stories how that some serpents have jewels in their heads, [illegible]ever one may do with the serpent, so long as the jewel is there, the serpent [illegible] killed. We hear stories of giants and ogres who had souls living in [illegible]le birds, and so long as the bird was safe, there was no power on earth to [illegible] giants, you might hack them to pieces, or do what you liked to them, the [illegible]ld not die. So with nations, there is a certain point where the life of a [illegible]nites, where lies the nationality of the nation, and until that is touched, that nation cannot die. In the light of this we can [illegible] phenomenon that the history of the world has [illegible] barbarian conquest has rolled over this devoted [illegible] has rent the skies for hundreds of years, and [illegible] be his last. This is the most suffering and the most [illegible] lands of the world. Yet we still stand practically [illegible] culties again and again if necessary, and not only so, [illegible] we are not only strong, but ready to go out, for the sign of [illegible]

We find to-day that our ideas and thoughts are no [illegible] bounds of India, but whether we will it or not, they are [illegible] the literature of nations, taking their place among nations, and [illegible] commanding, dictatorial position. Behind this we find [illegible] great contribution to the sum-total of the world's progress from India [illegible] the noblest, the sublimest theme that can occupy the mind of man [illegible] and spirituality. Our ancestors tried many other things; they, [illegible] first went to bring out the secrets of external Nature, as we all know, and [illegible] gigantic brains that marvellous race could have done miracles in that line of [illegible] the world yet cannot dream. But they gave it up for something higher; something better rings out from the pages of the Vedas:—"That science is the greatest [illegible] makes us know Him who never changes!" The science of Nature, changeful, evanescent, the world of death, of woe, of misery, may be great, great indeed; but the science of Him who changes not, the Blissful One, where alone is peace, where alone is life eternal, where alone is perfection, where alone all misery ceases,—that, according to our ancestors, was the sublimest science of all. After all, sciences that can give us only bread and clothes and power over our fellowmen, sciences that can only teach us how to conquer our fellow-beings, to rule over them, which teach the strong to domineer over the weak,—those they could have discovered if they willed; but praise be unto the Lord, they caught at once the other side, which was grander, infinitely higher, infinitely more blissful, till it has become the national characteristic, till it has come down to us, inherited from father to son for thousands of years, till it has become a part and parcel of us, till it tingles in every drop of blood that runs through our veins, till it has become our second nature, till the name of religion and Hindu have become one. This is the national characteristic, and this cannot be touched. Barbarians with sword and fire, barbarians bringing barbarous religions, could [illegible] of them touch the core, not one could touch the 'jewel,' not one had the [illegible] the 'bird' which the soul of the race inhabited. This, therefore, is the vital [illegible] race, and so long as that remains there is no power under the sun that can kill the race. All the tortures and the miseries of the world will pass over without hurting us, and we shall come out of the flames like Prahlád, so long as we hold on to this grandest of all our inheritances, spirituality. If a Hindu is not spiritual I do not call him a Hindu. In other countries a man may be political first, and then he may have a little religion, but here in India the first and the foremost duty of our [illegible] is to be spiritual first, and then, if there is time, let other things come. Bearing [illegible] in mind we shall be in a better position to understand why, for our national [illegible] we must first seek out at the present day, all the spiritual forces of the race, [illegible] done in days of yore, and will be done in all times to come. National [illegible] in India must be a gathering up of its scattered spiritual forces. A nation in [illegible] must be a union of those whose hearts beat to the same spiritual tune.

There have been sects enough in this country. There are sects enough, and there will be enough in the future, because this has been the peculiarity of our religion, that in abstract principles so much latitude has been given, that although afterwards so much detail has been worked out, all these details are the working out of principles, broad as the skies above our heads, eternal as Nature herself. Sects, therefore, as a matter of course, must exist here, but what need not exist, is sectarian quarrel. Sects must be, but sectarianism need not. The world would not be the better for sectarianism, but the world cannot move on without having sects. One set of men cannot do everything. The almost infinite mass of energy in the world cannot be managed by a small number of people. Here, at once we see the necessity that forced this division of labour upon us—the division into sects,—for the use of spiritual forces let there be sects, but is there any need that we should quarrel, when our most ancient books declare that this differentiation is only apparent, that in spite of all these differences there is a thread of harmony, that beautiful unity, running through them all? Our most ancient books have declared: *Ekam sat viprá bahudhá vadanti.*—"That which exists is One; sages call Him by various names." Therefore, if there are these sectarian struggles, if there are these fights among the different sects, if there is jealousy and hatred between the different sects in India, the land where all sects have always been honoured, it is a shame on us who dare to call ourselves the descendants of those fathers.

There are certain great principles in which, I think, we are—whether Vaishnavas, Saivas, Sáktas or Gânapatyas, whether belonging to the ancient Vedantists, or the modern ones, whether belonging to the old rigid sects, or the modern reform ones—we are all one, and whoever calls himself a Hindu, believes in certain principles. Of course there is a difference in the interpretation, in the explanation, of these principles, and that difference should be there, and it should be allowed, for our standard is not to bind every man down to our own position; it would be a sin, to force every man to work out our own interpretation of things, and to live by our own methods. Perhaps all who are here will agree on the first point, that we believe the Vedas to be the eternal teachings of the secrets of Religion. We all believe that this holy literature is without beginning and without end, coeval with Nature, which is without beginning and without end; and that all our religious differences, all our religious struggles must end when we stand in the presence of that holy book; we are all agreed that this is the last court of appeal in all our spiritual differences. We may take different points of view as to what the Vedas are. There may be one sect which regards one portion as more sacred than another, but that matters little, so long as we say that we are all brothers in the Vedas, that out of these venerable, eternal, marvellous books, has come everything that we possess to-day, good, holy, and pure. Well, therefore, if we believe in all this, let this principle first of all be preached broadcast throughout the length and breadth of the land. If this be true, let the Vedas have that prominence which they always deserve, and which we all believe in; first then the Vedas. The second point we all believe in is God, the creating, the preserving Power of the whole universe, and unto whom it periodically returns, to come out at other periods and manifest this wonderful phenomenon, called the universe. We may differ as to our conception of God. One may believe in a God who is entirely personal, another may believe in a God who is personal and yet not human, and yet another may believe in a God who is entirely impersonal, and all may get their support from the Vedas. Still we are all believers in God; that is to say, that man who does not believe in a most marvellous Infinite Power, from which everything has come, in which everything lives, and to which everything must in the end return, cannot be called a Hindu. If that be so, let us try to preach that idea all over the land. Preach whatever conception you have to give, there is no difference, we are not going to fight over it, but to preach God; that is all we want. One idea may be better than another, but, mind you, not one of them is bad. One is good, another is better, and again another may be the best, but the word bad does not enter the category of our religion. Therefore, may the Lord bless them all who preach the name of God in whatever form they like. The more He is preached, the better for this race. Let our children be brought up in this idea, let this idea enter the homes of the poorest and the lowest, as well as of the richest and the highest,—the idea of the name of God.

The third idea that I will present before you is, that, unlike all other races of the world, we do not believe that this world was created only so many thousand years ago, and is going to be destroyed eternally, on a certain day. Nor do we believe that the human soul has been created along with this universe just out of nothing. Here is another point I think we are all able to agree upon. We believe in Nature being without beginning and without end, only at psychological periods this gross material of the outer universe goes back to its finer state, thus to remain for a certain period, again to be projected outside, to manifest all this infinite panorama we call Nature; this wave-like motion is going on even before time began, through eternity, and will remain for an infinite period of time. Next, all Hindus believe that man is not only a gross material body, not only that within this there is the finer body, the mind, but there is something yet greater; for the body changes, so does the mind, but something beyond, the Atman—I cannot translate the word to you, for any translation will be wrong—that there is something beyond even this fine body, which is the Atman of man, which has neither beginning nor end, which knows not what death is. And then this peculiar idea different from that of all other races of men, that this Atman inhabits body after body until there is no more interest for it to continue to do so, and it becomes free, not to be born again. I refer to the theory of *Samsâra* and the theory of eternal souls taught by our Shastras. This is another point where we all agree, whatever sect we may belong to. There may be differences as to the relation between the soul and God. According to one sect the soul may be eternally different from God, according to another it may be a spark of that infinite fire, yet again according to others it may be one with that Infinite. It does not matter what our interpretation is, but so long as we hold on to the one basic belief that the soul is infinite, that this soul was never created, and therefore will never die, that it had to pass and evolve into various bodies, till it attained perfection in the human one—to that we are all agreed. And then comes the most differentiating, the grandest, and the most wonderful discovery in the realms of spirituality that has ever been made. Some of you, perhaps, who have been studying Western thought, may have observed already, that there is another radical difference severing at one stroke all that is Western from all that is Eastern. It is this that we hold, whether we are Sáktas, Sauras, or Vaishnavas, even whether we are Bauddhas or Jainas, we all hold in India that the soul is by its nature pure and perfect, infinite in power and blessed. Only, according to the Dualist, this natural blissfulness of the soul has become contracted by past bad work and, through the grace of God, it is again going to open out and show its perfection, while according to the Monist, even this idea of contraction is a partial mistake, it is the veil of Mayâ that causes us to think the soul has lost its powers, but the powers are there fully manifest. Whatever the difference may be, we come to the central core, and there is at once an irreconcilable difference between all that is Western and Eastern. The Eastern is looking inward for all that is great and good. When we worship, we close our eyes and try to find God within. The Western is looking up outside for his God. To the Westerns their religious books have been inspired, while with us our books have been expired; breath-like they came, the breath of God, out of the hearts of sages they sprang, the *Mantra-drashtâs*.

This is one great point to understand, and, my friends, my brethren, let me tell you, this is the one point we shall have to insist upon in the future. For I am firmly convinced, and I beg you to understand this one fact,—no good comes out of the man who day and night thinks he is nobody. If a man, day and night thinks he is miserable, low and nothing, nothing he becomes. If you say yea, yea, I am, I am, so shall you be; and if you say I am not, think that you are not, and day and night meditate upon the fact that you are nothing, aye, nothing shall you be. That is the great fact which you ought to remember. We are the children of the Almighty, we are sparks of the infinite, divine fire. How can we be nothings? We are everything, ready to do everything, we can do everything, and man must do everything. This faith in themselves was in the hearts of our ancestors, this faith in themselves was the motive power that pushed them forward and forward in the march of civilisation, and if there has been degeneration, if there has been defect, mark my words, you will find that degradation to have started on the day our people lost this faith in themselves. Losing faith in one's self means losing faith in God. Do you believe in that Infinite, good Providence working in and through you? If you believe that this Omnipresent One, the *Antaryâmin*, is present in every atom, is through and through, *Ota-Prota*, as the Sanskrit word goes, penetrating your body, mind and soul, how can you lose heart? I may be a little bubble of water, and you may be a mountain-high wave; never mind! The infinite ocean is the background of me as well as of you. Mine is also that infinite ocean of life, of power, of spirituality, as well as yours. I am already joined,—from my very birth, from the very fact of my life—I am in Yoga with that infinite life, and infinite goodness, and infinite power, as you are, mountain-high though you may be. Therefore, my brethren, teach this life-saving, great, ennobling, grand doctrine to your children, even from their very birth. You need not teach them Advaitism; teach them Dvaitism, or any 'ism' you please, but we have seen that this is the common 'ism' all through India; this marvellous doctrine of the soul, the perfection of the soul, is commonly believed in by all sects. As says our great philosopher Kapila, if purity has not been the nature of the soul, it can never attain purity afterwards, for anything that was not perfect by nature, even if it attained to perfection, that perfection would go away again. If impurity is the nature of man, then man will have to remain impure, even though he may be pure for five minutes. The time will come when this purity will wash out, pass away, and the old natural impurity will have its sway once more. Therefore, say all our philosophers, good is our nature, perfection is our nature, not imperfection, not impurity,—and we should remember that. Remember the beautiful example of the great sage who when he was dying, asked his mind to remember all his mighty deeds and all his mighty thoughts. There you do not find that he was teaching his mind to remember all his weakness and all his follies. Follies there are, weakness there must be, but remember your real nature always,—that is the only way to cure the weakness, that is the only way to cure the follies.

It seems that these few points are common among all the various religious sects in India, and perhaps in future upon this common platform, conservative and liberal religionists, old type and new type, may shake hands. Above all, there is another thing to remember, which I am sorry we forget from time to time, that religion, in India, means realisation and nothing short of that. "Believe in the doctrine and you are safe," can never be taught to us, for we do not believe in that; you are what you make yourselves. You are, by the grace of God and your own exertions, what you are. Mere believing in certain theories and doctrines will not help you much. The mighty word that came out from the sky of spirituality in India was *Anubhuti*, realisation, and ours are the only books which declare again and again: "The Lord is to be *seen*." Bold, brave words indeed, but true to their very core; every sound, every vibration is true. Religion is to be realised, not only heard; it is not only that some doctrine should be learnt like a parrot. Not only is there intellectual assent; that is nothing; but it must come into us. Aye, and therefore the greatest proof that we have of the existence of a God is not because our reason says so, but because God has been seen by the ancients as well as by the moderns. We believe in the soul not only because there are good reasons to prove its existence, but, above all, because there have been in the past, thousands in India, there yet are still many who have realised, and there will be thousands in the future, who will realise, and see their own souls. And there is no salvation for man until he sees God, realises his own soul. Therefore, above all, let us understand this, and the more we understand it the less we shall have of sectarianism in India, for it is only that man who has realised God and seen Him, who is religious. In him the knots have been cut asunder, in him alone the doubts have subsided; he alone has become free from the fruits of action, who has seen Him who is nearest of the near and farthest of the far. Aye, we often mistake mere prattle for religious truth, mere intellectual perorations for great spiritual realisation, and then comes sectarianism, then comes fight. If we once understand that this realisation is the only religion, we shall look into our own hearts and find how far we are towards realising the truths of religion. Then we shall understand that we ourselves are groping in darkness, and are leading others to grope in the same darkness, then we shall cease from sectarianism, quarrel and fight. Ask a man who wants to start a sectarian fight, "Have you seen God? Have you seen the Atman? If you have not, what right have you to preach His name,—you walking in darkness to lead me into the same darkness,—the blind leading the blind, and both falling into the ditch?"

Therefore, take more thought before you go and find fault with others. Let them follow their own path to realisation so long as they struggle to see truth in their own hearts; and when the broad, naked truth will be seen, then they will find that wonderful blissfulness which marvellously enough has been testified to by every seer in India, by everyone who has realised the truth. Then words of love alone will come out of that heart, for it has already been touched by Him who is the essence of Love Himself. Then and then alone, all sectarian quarrels will cease, and we shall be in a position to understand, to bring to our hearts, to embrace, to intensely love the very word Hindu, and every one who bears that name. Mark me, then and then alone, you are a Hindu, when the very name sends through you a galvanic shock of strength.

Then and then alone, you are a Hindu when every man who bears the name, from any country, speaking our language or any other language, becomes at once the nearest and the dearest to you. Then and then alone, you are a Hindu when the distress of anyone bearing that name comes to your heart and makes you feel as if your own son were in distress. Then and then alone, you are a Hindu when you will be ready to bear everything for them, like the great example I have quoted at the beginning of this lecture, of your great Guru Govind Singh. Driven out from this country, fighting against its oppressors, after having shed his own blood for the defence of the Hindu religion, after having seen his children killed on the battle-field, —aye, this example of the great Guru, left even by those for whose sake he was shedding his blood and the blood of his own nearest and dearest,—he, the wounded lion retired from the field calmly to die in the South, but not a word of curse escaped his lips against those who had ungratefully forsaken him! Mark me, every one of you will have to be a Govind Singh, if you want to do good to your country. You may see thousands of defects in your countrymen, but mark their Hindu blood. They are the first Gods you will have to worship, even if they do everything to hurt you; even if everyone of them send out a curse to you, you send out to them words of love. If they drive you out, retire to die in silence like that mighty lion, like Govind Singh. Such a man is worthy the name of Hindu; such an ideal ought to be before us always. All our hatchets let us bury; send out this grand current of love all round.

Let them talk of India's regeneration as they like; let me tell you as one who has been working—at least trying to work—all his life, that there is no regeneration for India until you be spiritual. Not only so, but upon it depends the welfare of the whole world. For I must tell you frankly that the very foundations of Western civilisation have been shaken to their base. The mightiest buildings, if built upon the loose sand foundations of materialism, must come to grief one day, must totter to their destruction some day. The history of the world is our witness. Nation after nation has arisen and based its greatness upon materialism—man was all matter, it declared. Aye, in Western language, a man gives up the ghost, but in our language a man gives up his body. The Western man is a body first, and then he has a soul; with us a man is a soul and spirit, and he has a body. Therein lies a world of difference. All such civilisations, therefore, as have been based upon such sand foundations as material comfort and all that, have disappeared one after the other, after short lives, from the face of the world; but the civilisation of India and the other nations that have stood at India's feet to listen and learn, namely, Japan and China, live even to the present day, and there are signs even of revival among them. Their lives are like that of the Phœnix, a thousand times destroyed, but ready to spring up again more glorious. But a materialistic civilisation once dashed down, never can come up again; that building once thrown down, is broken into pieces once for all. Therefore have patience and wait, the future is in store for us.

Do not be in a hurry, do not go out to imitate anybody else. This is another great lesson we have to remember; imitation is not civilisation. I may deck myself out in a Raja's dress; but will that make me a Raja? An ass in a lion's skin never makes a lion. Imitation, cowardly imitation, never makes for progress. It is verily the sign of awful degradation in a man. Aye, when a man has begun to hate himself, then the last blow has come. When a man has begun to be ashamed of his ancestors, the end has come. Here am I, one of the least of the Hindu race, yet proud of my race, proud of my ancestors. I am proud to call myself a Hindu, I am proud that I am one of your unworthy servants. I am proud that I am a countryman of yours, you the descendants of the sages, you the descendants of the most glorious Rishis the world ever saw. Therefore have faith in yourselves, be proud of your ancestors, instead of being ashamed of them. And do not imitate; do not imitate! Whenever you are under the thumb of others, you lose your own independence. If you are working, even in spiritual things at the dictation of others, slowly you lose all faculty even of thought. Bring out through your own exertions what you have, but do not imitate, yet take what is good from others. We have to learn from others. You put the seed in the ground, and give it plenty of earth, and air, and water to feed upon; when the seed grows into the plant, and into a gigantic tree, does it become the earth, does it become the air, or does it become the water? It becomes the mighty plant, the mighty tree, after its own nature, having absorbed everything that was given to it. Let that be your position. We have indeed many things to learn from others, yea, that man who refuses to learn is already dead.

Declares our Manu: आददीत परां विद्यां प्रयत्नादवरादपि। अन्त्यादपि परं धर्मं स्त्रीरत्नं दुष्कुलादपि॥ "Take the jewel of a woman for your wife, though she be of inferior descent. Learn supreme knowledge with service even from the man of low birth; and even from the Chandála, learn by serving him the way to salvation." Learn every thing that is good from others, but bring it in, and in your own way absorb it; do not become others. Do not be dragged away out of this Indian life; do not for a moment think that it would be better for India if all the Indians dressed, ate and behaved like another race. You know the difficulty of giving up a habit of a few years. The Lord knows how many thousands of years are in your blood; this national specialised life has been flowing in one way, the Lord knows for how many thousands of years; and do you mean to say that that mighty stream, which has nearly reached its ocean, can go back to the snows of its Himalayas again? That is impossible! The struggle to do so would only break it. Therefore, make way for the life-current of the nation. Take away the blocks that bar the way to the progress of this mighty river, cleanse its path, clear the channel, and out it will rush by its own natural impulse, and the nation will go on careering and progressing.

These are the lines which I beg to suggest to you for spiritual work in India. There are many other great problems which, for want of time, I cannot bring before you this night. For instance, there is the wonderful question of caste. I have been studying this question, its *pros* and *cons*, all my life; I have studied it in nearly every province in India. I have mixed with people of all castes nearly in every part of the country, and I am too bewildered in my own mind to grasp even the very significance of it. The more I try to study it, the more I get bewildered. Still, at last I find that a little glimmer of light is before me, I begin to feel its significance just now. Then there is the other great problem about eating and drinking. That is a great problem indeed. It is not so useless a thing as we generally think. I have come to the conclusion that the insistence which we make now about eating and drinking, is most curious and is just going against what the Shástras required, that is to say, we come to grief by neglecting the proper purity of the food we eat and drink; we have lost the true spirit of it.

There are several other questions which I want to bring before you, and show how these problems can be solved, how to work out the ideas; but unfortunately the meeting could not come to order until very late, and I do not wish to detain you any longer now. I will therefore keep my ideas about caste and other things for a future occasion.

Now, one word more and I will finish about these spiritual ideas. Religion for a long time has come to be statical in India, what we want is to make it dynamical. I want it to be brought into the life of everybody. Religion, as it always has been in the past, must enter the palaces of kings as well as the homes of the poorest peasants in the land. Religion, the common inheritance, the universal birthright of the race, must be brought free to the door of everybody. Religion in India must be made as free and as easy of access as is God's air. And this is the kind of work we have to bring about in India, but not by getting up little sects and fighting on points of difference. Let us preach where we all agree, and leave the differences to remedy themselves. As I have said to the Indian people again and again, if there is the darkness of centuries in a room, and we go into the room and begin to cry, "Oh, it is dark, it is dark!" will the darkness go? Bring in the light and the darkness will vanish at once. This is the secret of reforming men. Suggest to them higher things; believe in man first. Why start with the belief that man is degraded and degenerated? I have never failed in my faith in man in any case, even taking him at his worst. Wherever I had faith in man, though at first the prospect was not always bright, yet it triumphed in the long run. Have faith in man, whether he appears to you to be a very learned one or a most ignorant one. Have faith in man, whether he appears to be an angel or the very devil himself. Have faith in man first, and then having faith in him, believe that if there are defects in him, if he makes mistakes, if he embraces the crudest and the vilest doctrines, believe that it is not from his real nature that they come, but from the want of higher ideals. If a man goes towards what is false, it is because he cannot get what is true. Therefore the only method of correcting what is false is by supplying him with what is true. Do this, and let him compare. You give him the truth, and there your work is done. Let him compare it in his own mind with what he has already in him; and, mark my words, if you have really given him the truth, the false must vanish, light must dispel darkness and truth will bring the good out. This is the way if you want to reform the country spiritually; this is the way, and not by fighting, not even by telling people that what they are doing is bad. Put the good before them, see how eagerly they take it, see how the Divine that never dies, that is always living in the human, comes up awakened and stretches out its hand for all that is good, and all that is glorious.

May He who is the Creator, the Preserver and the Protector of our race, the God of our forefathers, whether called by the name of Vishnu, or Shiva, or Shakti, or Ganapati, whether He is worshipped as Saguna or as Nirguna, whether He is worshipped as personal, or as impersonal, may He whom our forefathers knew and addressed by the words—एकम् सद्विप्रा बहुधा वदन्ति—"That which exists is One; sages call Him by various names"—may He enter into us with His mighty love, may He shower His blessings on us, may He make us understand each other, may He make us work for each other with real love, with intense love for truth, and may not the least desire for our own personal fame, our own personal prestige, our own personal advantage, enter into this great work of the spiritual regeneration of India.

BHAKTI.

In his second lecture on Bhakti, Swamiji was very emphatic in his insistence upon practical work being more necessary in India than mere theory, of which he believed the country has had enough and to spare. The starving millions, he urged, cannot live on metaphysical speculations, what they require is bread. He suggested that the best religion for to-day is, that every man should, according to his means, go out into the streets, to search for one, two, six or twelve "hungry Nârâyans," take them into his house, feed them, clothe them, and offer them all the worship he would give to his *Ishta Devatâ*. Man is the highest temple of God, and the worship of God through man is therefore of the highest. In such work he should always remember that according to the Hindu religion, the receiver is greater than the giver, because, for the time being, the receiver is God Himself. He added that he had seen charity in many countries, and the reason for its failure was the spirit in which it was carried out. The spirit elsewhere was, "Here, take this and go away." Charity belied its name so long as it was given to gain name, or the applause of the world. In conclusion, he again urged the young men of Lahore, to create at once an association of an entirely unsectarian character, for working during the evenings, among "the poor Nàràyans"—the giving of food, the nursing of the sick, and the education of the ignorant, on simple and popular lines.

THE VEDANTA.

(Delivered at Lahore on the 12th November 1897.)

Two worlds there are in which we live, one the external, the other, internal. Human progress has been made, from days of yore, almost in parallel lines along both these worlds. The search began in the external, and man at first wanted to get answers for all the deep problems from outside nature. Man wanted to satisfy his thirst for the beautiful and the sublime from all that surrounded him; he wanted to express himself and all that was within him in the language of the concrete; and grand indeed were the answers he got, most marvellous ideas of God and worship, and most rapturous expressions of the beautiful. Sublime ideas came from the external world indeed. But the other, opening out for humanity later, laid out before him an universe yet sublimer, yet more beautiful, and infinitely more expansive. In the Karma-kanda portion of the Vedas, we find the most wonderful ideas of religion inculcated, we find the most wonderful ideas about an over-ruling Creator, Preserver and Destroyer of the universe presented before us, in language sometimes the most soul-stirring. Most of you perhaps remember that most wonderful *sloka* in the Rig Veda Samhita where you get the description of chaos, perhaps the sublimest that has ever been attempted yet. In spite of all this, we find it is only a painting of the sublime outside, we find that yet it is gross, that something of matter yet clings to it. Yet we find that it is only the expression of the Infinite in the language of matter, in the language of the finite, it is the infinite of the muscles and not of the mind; it is the infinite of space, and not of thought. Therefore in the second portion or Jnana-kanda, we find there is altogether a different procedure. The first was a search in external nature for the truths of the universe; it was an attempt to get the solution of the deep problems of life from the material world. यस्यैते हिमवन्तो महित्वा—"Whose glory these Himalayas declare." This is a grand idea, but yet it was not grand enough for India. The Indian mind had to fall back, and the research took a different direction altogether, from the external the search came to the internal, from matter to mind. There arose the cry, "When a man dies, what becomes of him?" अस्तीत्येके नायमस्तीति चैके &c. "Some say that he exists, others, that he is gone; say, O king of Death, what is Truth?" An entirely different procedure we find here. The Indian mind got all that could be had from the external world, but it did not feel satisfied with that; it wanted to search further, to dive into its own soul, and the final answer came.

The Upanishads, or the Vedanta or the Aranyakas, or *Rahasya*, is the name of this portion of the Vedas. Here we find at once that religion has got rid of all external formalities. Here we find at once that spiritual things are told not in the language of matter, but in the language of the spirit, the superfine, in the language of the superfine. No more any grossness attaches to it, no more is there any compromise with things of worldly concern.. Bold, brave, beyond the conception of the present day, stand the giant minds of the sages of the Upanishads, declaring the noblest truths that have ever been preached to humanity, without any compromise, without any fear. This, my countrymen, I want to lay before you. Even the Jnana-kanda of the Vedas is a vast ocean; many lives are necessary to understand even a little of it. Truly has it been said of the Upanishads, by Ramanuja, that the Vedanta is the head, the shoulders, the crested form of the Vedas, and surely enough the Upanishads have become the Bible of modern India. The Hindus have the greatest respect for the Karma-kanda of the Vedas, but, for all practical purposes, we know that for ages by Sruti has been meant the Upanishads, and the Upanishads alone. We know that all our great philosophers, either Vyasa, Patanjali, Gautama, and even the father of all philosophy, the great Kapila himself, whenever they wanted an authority for what they wrote, everyone of them found it in the Upanishads, and nowhere else, for therein are the truths that remain for ever.

There are truths that are true only in a certain line, in a certain direction, under certain circumstances, and for certain times, those that are founded on the institutions of the times. There are other truths which are based on the nature of man himself, and which must endure so long as man himself endures. These are the truths that alone can be universal, and in spite of all the changes that have come to India, as to our social surroundings, our methods of dress, our manner of eating, our modes of worship,—these universal truths of the Srutis, the marvellous Vedantic ideas, stand out in their own sublimity, immovable, unvanquishable, deathless, and immortal. Yet the germs of all the ideas that were developed in the Upanishads had been taught already in the Karma-kanda. The idea of the cosmos, which all sects of Vedantists had to take for granted, the psychology which has formed the common basis of all the Indian schools of thought, had there been worked out already and presented before the world. A few words, therefore, about the Karma-kanda are necessary before we begin the spiritual portion of the Vedanta, and first of all I should like to explain the sense in which I use the word Vedanta.

Unfortunately there is the mistaken notion in modern India, that the word Vedanta has reference only to the Advaita system, but you must always remember that in modern India, the three *Prasthânas* are considered equally important in the study of all the systems of religion. First of all there are the Revelations, the Srutis, by which I mean the Upanishads. Secondly, among our philosophies, the Sutras of Vyasa have the greatest prominence, on account of their being the consummation of all the preceding systems of philosophy. These systems are not contradictory to one another, but one is based on another, and there is a gradual unfolding of the theme which culminates in the Sutras of Vyasa. Then, between the Upanishads and the Sutras, which are the systematising of the marvellous truths of the Vedanta, comes in Sri Gita, the divine commentary on the Vedanta. The Upanishads, the Vyasa Sutras, and the Gita, therefore, have been taken up by every sect in India that wants to claim authority for orthodoxy, whether Dualist, or Vaishnavist, or Advaitist; the authorities of each of these are the three *Prasthânas*. We find that a Sankaracharya, or a Ramanuja, or a Madhwacharya, or a Vallabhacharya, or a Chaitanya,—any one who wanted to propound a new sect—had to take up these three systems and write only a new commentary on them. Therefore it would be wrong to confine the word Vedanta only to one system, which has arisen out of the Upanishads. All these are covered by the word Vedanta. The Visishtadvaitist has as much right to be called a Vedantist as the Advaitist; in fact I will go a little further and say that what we really mean by the word Hindu is really the same as Vedantist. I want you to note, that these three systems have been current in India almost from time immemorial—for you must not believe that Sankara was the inventor of the Advaita system; it existed ages before Sankara was born; he was one of its last representatives. So with the Visishtadvaita system; it existed ages before Ramanuja appeared, as we already know from the commentaries he has written; so with the Dualistic systems that have existed side by side with the others. And with my little knowledge, I have come to the conclusion that they do not contradict each other. Just as in the case of the six *Darshanas*, we find they are a gradual unfolding of the grand principles, whose music beginning far back in the soft low notes, ends in the triumphant blast of the Advaita, so also in these three systems we find the gradual working up of the human mind towards higher and higher ideals, till everything is merged in that wonderful unity which is reached in the Advaita system. Therefore these three are not contradictory. On the other hand I am bound to tell you, that this has been a mistake committed by not a few. We find that an Advaitist teacher keeps intact those texts which especially teach Advaitism, and tries to interpret the Dualistic or Qualified-non-dualistic texts into his own meaning. Similarly we find Dualistic teachers trying to read their Dualistic meaning into Advaitic texts. Our Gurus were great men, yet there is a saying as, "Even the faults of a Guru must be told." I am of opinion that in this only they were mistaken. We need not go into text torturing, we need not go into any sort of religious dishonesty, we need not go into any sort of grammatical twaddle, we need not go about trying to put our own ideas into texts which were never meant for them, but the work is plain and becomes easier, once you understand the marvellous doctrine of *Adhikárabheda*.

It is true that the Upanishads have this one theme before them, कस्मिन्नु भगवो विज्ञाते सर्वमिदं विज्ञातं भवति।—"What is that knowing which we know everything else?" In modern language, the theme of the Upanishads is to find an ultimate unity of things. Knowledge is nothing but finding unity in the midst of diversity. Every science is based upon this; all human knowledge is based upon the finding of unity in the midst of diversity; and if it is the task of small fragments of human knowledge, which we call our sciences, to find unity in the midst of a few different phenomena, the task becomes stupendous when the theme before us is to find unity in the midst of this marvellously diversified universe, where prevail unnumbered differences in name and form, in matter and spirit,—each thought differing from every other thought, each form differing from every other form. Yet, to harmonise these many planes and unending *lokas*, in the midst of this infinite variety to find unity, is the theme of the Upanishads. On the other hand, the old idea of *Arundhati Nyáya* applies. To show a man the fine star Arundhati, one takes the big and brilliant star nearest to it, upon which he is asked to fix his eyes first, and then it becomes quite easy to direct his sight to Arundhati. This is the task before us, and to prove my idea I have simply to show you the Upanishads, and you will see it. Nearly every chapter begins with Dualistic teaching, *upásaná*. Later on, God is first taught as some one who is the Creator of this universe, its Preserver, and unto whom everything goes at last. He is one to be worshipped, the Ruler, the Guide of nature, external and internal, yet as if He were something outside of nature and external. One step further, and we find the same teacher teaching that this God is not outside of nature, but immanent in nature. And at last both ideas are discarded, and whatever is real is He; there is no difference. तत्त्वमसि श्वेतकेतो—"Svetaketu, That thou art." That Immanent One is at last declared to be the same that is in the human soul. Here is no compromise; here is no fear of other's opinions. Truth, bold truth, has been taught in bold language, and we need not fear to preach the truth in the same bold language to-day, and, by the grace of God, I hope at least to be the one who dares to be that bold preacher.

To go back to our preliminaries. There are first two things to be understood,—one, the psychological aspect common to all the Vedantic schools, and the other, the cosmological aspect. I will first take up the latter. To-day we find wonderful discoveries of modern science coming upon us like bolts from the blue, opening our eyes to marvels we never dreamt of. But many of these are only re-discoveries of what had been found ages ago. It was only the other day that modern science found that even in the midst of the variety of forces there is unity. It has just discovered that what it calls heat, magnetism, electricity, and so forth, are all convertible into one unit force, and as such, it expresses all these by one name, whatever you may choose to call it. But this has been done even in the Samhita; old and ancient as it is, in it we meet with this very idea of force I was referring to. All the forces, whether you call them gravitation, or attraction, or repulsion, whether expressing themselves as heat, or electricity, or magnetism, are nothing, but the variations of that unit energy. Whether they express themselves as thought, reflected from *antahkarana*, the inner organs of man, or from one organ, the unit from which they spring is what is called the Pràna. Again, what is Prána? Prána is *spandana* or vibration. When all this universe shall have resolved back into its primal state, what becomes of this infinite force? Do they think that it becomes extinct? Of course not. If it became extinct, what would be the cause of the next wave, because the motion is going in wave forms, rising, falling, rising again, falling again? Here is the word *srishti*, which expresses the universe. Mark that the word does not mean creation. I am helpless in talking English; I have to translate the Sanskrit words as best as I can. It is *srishti*, projection. Everything becomes finer and finer and is resolved back to the primal state from which it sprang, and there it remains for a time, quiescent, ready to spring forth again. That is *srishti*, projection. And what becomes of all these forces, the Pránas? They are resolved back into the primal Prána, and this Prána becomes almost motionless—not entirely motionless,—but almost motionless,—and that is what is described in the Vedic *Sukta*. "It vibrated without vibrations"—*ánidavátam*. There are many difficult texts in the Upanishads to understand, especially in the use of technical phrases. For instance, the word *váyu*, to move; many times it means air and many times motion, and often people confuse one with the other. We must guard against that. And what becomes of what you call matter? The forces permeate all matter; they all dissolve into ether, from which they again come out; and the first to come out is *ákásha*. Whether you translate it as ether, or anything else, the idea is that this *ákásha* is the primal form of matter. This *ákásha* vibrates under the action of Prána, and when the next *srishti* is coming up, as the vibration becomes quicker, the *ákásha* is lashed into all these wave forms which we call suns, and moons, and systems.

We read again :—**यदिदं किंच जगत् सर्वं प्राण एजति निःसृतम्।**—

"Everything in this universe has been projected, Prána vibrating." You must mark the word *ejati*, because it comes from *eja*, to vibrate, *nihsritam* projected, *yadidam kincha*—whatever is this universe.

This is a part of the cosmological side. There are many details working into it. For instance, how the process takes place, how there is first ether, and how from the ether come other things, how that ether begins to vibrate, and from that *váyu* comes. But the one idea is here, that it is from the finer that the grosser has come. Gross matter is the last to emerge and the most external, and this gross matter had the finer matter before it. Yet we see that the whole thing has been resolved into two, but there is not yet a final unity. There is the unity of force, Prána; there is the unity of matter called *ákásha*. Is there any unity to be found among them again? Can they be melted into one? Our modern science is mute here, it has not yet found its way out; and if it is doing so, just as it has been slowly finding the same old Prâna and the same ancient *ákásha*, it will have to move along the same lines. The next unity is the omnipresent impersonal being known by its old mythological name as Brahmâ, the four-headed Brahmâ, and psychologically called Mahat. This is where the two unite. What is called your mind is only a bit of this Mahat caught in the trap of the brain, and the sum total of all brains caught in the meshes of Mahat is what you call *samashti*, the aggregate, the universal. Analysis had to go further; it was not yet complete. Here we were each one of us, as it were, a microcosm, and the world taken altogether is the macrocosm. But whatever is in the *vyashti*, the particular, we may safely conjecture that a similar thing is happening also outside. If we had the power to analyse our own minds we might safely conjecture that the same thing is happening in the cosmic mind. What is this mind is the question. In modern times in Western countries, as physical science is making rapid progress, as physiology is step by step conquering stronghold after stronghold of old religions, the Western people do not know where to stand, because to their great despair, modern physiology at every step has identified the mind with the brain. But we in India have known that always. That was the first proposition the Hindu boy should learn, that the mind is matter, only finer. The body is gross, and behind the body is what we call the *sukshma sharira*, the fine body or mind. This is also material, only finer; and it is not the Atman. I will not translate this word to you in English, because the idea does not exist in Europe; it is untranslatable. The modern attempt of German philosophers is to translate the word Atman by the word 'Self,' and until that word is universally accepted it is impossible to use it. So, call it as Self or anything, it is our Atman. This Atman is the real man behind. It is the Atman that uses the material mind as its instrument, its *antahkarana*, as is the psychological term for the mind. And the mind by means of a series of internal organs works the visible organs of the body. What is this mind? It was only the other day that Western philosophers have come to know that the eyes are not the real organs of vision, but that behind these are other organs, the *indriyas*, and if these are destroyed, a man may have a thousand eyes, like Indra, but there will be no sight for him. Aye, your philosophy starts with this assumption, that by vision is not meant the external vision. The real vision belongs to the internal organs, the brain centres inside. You may call them what you like, but it is not that the *indriyas* are the eyes, or the nose, or the ears. And the sum total of all these *indriyas* plus the *manas*, *buddhi*, *chitta*, *ahamkâra*, &c., is what is called the mind, and if the modern physiologist comes to tell you that the brain is what is called the mind, and that the brain is formed of so many organs, you need not be afraid at all; tell him that your philosophers knew it always; it is one of the very first principles of your religion.

Well then, we have to understand now what is meant by this *manas*, *buddhi*, *chitta*, *ahamkâra*, etc. First of all, let us take *chitta*; it is the mind-stuff;—a part of the Mahat—it is the generic name for the mind itself, including all its various states. Suppose on a summer evening, there is a lake, smooth and calm, without a ripple on its surface. And suppose some one throws a stone into this lake. What happens? First there is the action, the blow given to the water; next, the water rises and sends a reaction towards the stone, and that reaction takes the form of a wave. First the water vibrates a little, and immediately sends back a reaction in the form of a wave. The *chitta* let us compare to this lake, and the external objects are like the stones thrown into it. As soon as it comes in contact with any external object by means of these *indriyas*—the *indriyas* must be there to carry these external objects inside—there is a vibration, what is called the *manas*, indecisive. Next there is a reaction, the determinative faculty, *buddhi*, and along with this *buddhi* flashes the idea of *aham* and the external object. Suppose there is a mosquito sitting upon my hand. This sensation is carried to my *chitta* and it vibrates a little; this is the psychological *manas*. Then there is a reaction, and immediately comes the idea that I have a mosquito on my hand, and that I shall have to drive it off. Thus these stones are thrown into the lake, but in the case of the lake every blow that comes to it is from the external world, while in the case of the lake of the mind, the blows may either come from the external world, or the internal world. This whole series is what is called the *antahkarana*. Along with it, you ought to understand one thing more that will help us in understanding the Advaita system later on. It is this. All of you must have seen pearls and most of you know how pearls are formed. A grain of sand enters into the shell of a pearl-oyster, and sets up an irritation there, and the oyster's body reacts towards the irritation and covers the little particle with its own juice. That crystallises and forms the pearl. So the whole universe is like that, it is the pearl which is being formed by us. What we get from the external world is simply the blow. Even to be conscious of that blow we have to react, and as soon as we react, we really project a portion of our own mind towards the blow, and when we come to know of it, it is really our own mind as it has been shaped by the blow. Therefore, it is clear even to those who want to believe in a hard and fast realism of an external world, and which they cannot but admit in these days of physiology,—that supposing we represent the external world by "X," what we really know is "X" plus mind, and this mind-element is so great that it has covered the whole of that "X," which has remained unknown and unknowable throughout, and therefore, if there is an external world it is always unknown and unknowable. What we know of it is, as it is moulded, formed, fashioned by our own mind. So with the internal world. The same applies to our own soul, the Atman. In order to know the Atman we shall have to know it through the mind, and therefore what little we know of this Atman is simply the Atman plus the mind. That is to say, the Atman covered over, fashioned, and moulded by the mind, and nothing more. We shall return to this a little later, but we will remember it here.

The next thing to understand is this. The question arose, that this body is the name of one continuous stream of matter; every moment we are adding material to it, and every moment material is being thrown off by it, like a river continually flowing, vast masses of water always changing places; yet all the same, we take up the whole thing in imagination, and call it the same river. What do we call the river? Every moment the water is changing, the shore is changing, every moment the environment is changing; what is the river then? It is the name of this series of changes. So with the mind. That is the great *Kshanika Vijnâna Vâda* doctrine, most difficult to understand, but most rigorously and logically worked out in the Buddhistic philosophy, and this arose also in India in opposition to some part of the Vedanta. That had to be answered, and we will see how, later on, it could only be answered by Advaitism and by nothing else. We will see also how, in spite of people's curious notions about Advaitism, people's fright about Advaitism, it is the salvation of the world, because therein alone is to be found the reason of things. Dualism and other isms are very good as means of worship, very satisfying to the mind, and maybe, they have helped the mind onward; but if man wants to be rational and religious at the same time, Advaita is the one system in the world for him. Well now, we will regard the mind as a similar river, continually filling itself at one end, and emptying itself at the other end. Where is that unity which we call the Atman? The idea is this, that in spite of this continuous change in the body, and in spite of this continuous change in the mind, there is in us something that is unchangeable, our ideas of things are unchangeable. When rays of light coming from different quarters, fall upon a screen, or a wall, or upon something that is not changeable, then and then alone it is possible for them to form a unity, then and then alone it is possible for them to form one complete whole. Where is this unity in the human organs, falling upon which, as it were, the various ideas will come to unity and become one complete whole? This certainly cannot be the mind itself, seeing that it also changes. Therefore there must be something which is neither the body nor the mind, something which changes not, something permanent, upon which all our ideas, our sensations fall to form a unity, and a complete whole, and this is the real soul, the Atman, of man. And seeing that everything material, whether you call it fine matter, or mind, must be changeful, seeing that what you call gross matter, the external world, must also be changeful in comparison to that,—this unchangeable something cannot be of material substance,—therefore it is spiritual, that is to say, it is not matter; it is indestructible, unchangeable.

Next will come another question—apart from those old arguments which only rise in the external world, the arguments in support of Design—who created this external world, who created matter, &c.? The idea here is to know truth only from the inner nature of man, and the question arises just in the same way as it arose about the soul. Taking for granted that there is a soul, unchangeable, in each man, which is neither the mind, nor the body, there is still a unity of idea among the souls, a unity of feeling, of sympathy. How is it possible that my soul can act upon your soul, where is the medium through which it can work, where is the medium through which it can act? How is it I can feel anything about your souls? What is it that is in touch both with your soul, and with my soul? Therefore there is a metaphysical necessity of admitting another soul, for it must be a soul which acts in contact with all the different souls, and in and through matter; one Soul which covers and interpenetrates all the infinite number of souls in the world, in and through which they live, in and through which they sympathise, and love, and work for one another. And this universal Soul is Paramâtman, the Lord God of the universe. Again, it follows that because the soul is not made of matter, since it is spiritual, it cannot obey the laws of matter, it cannot be judged by the laws of matter. It is therefore unconquerable, birthless, deathless and changeless.

नैनं छिन्दन्ति शस्त्राणि नैनं दहति पावकः।
न चैनं क्लेदयंत्यापो न शोषयति मारुतः॥
नित्यः सर्वगतः स्थाणुरचलोऽयं सनातनः॥

"This Self weapons cannot pierce, nor fire can burn, water cannot melt, nor air can dry up. Changeless, all-pervading, unmoving, immovable, eternal is this Self of man." We learn according to the Gita and the Vedanta, that this individual Self is also *vibhu*, and according to Kapila, is omnipresent. Of course there are sects in India who hold that the Self is *anu*, infinitely small; but what they mean is *anu* in manifestation; its real nature is *vibhu*, all-pervading.

There comes another idea, startling perhaps, yet a characteristically Indian idea, and if there is any idea that is common to all our sects, it is this. Therefore I beg you to pay attention to this one idea and to remember it, for this is the very foundation of everything that we have in India. The idea is this. You have heard of the doctrine of physical evolution preached in the Western world, by the German and the English savants. It tells us that the bodies of the different animals are really one, the differences that we see are but different expressions of the same series, that from the lowest worm to the highest and the most saintly man it is but one, the one changing into the other, and so on, going up and up, higher and higher, until it attains perfection. We had that idea also. Declares our Yogi Patanjali—जात्यन्तरपरिनामः प्रकृत्यापूरात् । One species—the *jàti* is species—changes into another species—evolution; *parinàmah* means one thing changing into another, just as one species changes into another. Where do we differ from the Europeans? Patanjali says, *Prakrityàpûràt*—"By the infilling of nature." The European says, it is competition, natural and sexual selection, &c., that forces one body to take the form of another. But here is another idea, a still better analysis, going deeper into the thing, and saying—"By the infilling of nature." What is meant by this infilling of nature? We admit that the amœba goes higher and higher until it becomes a Buddha; we admit that, but we are, at the same time, as much certain that you cannot get an amount of work out of a machine unless you have put it in in some shape or other. The sum total of the energy remains the same, whatever the forms it may take. If you want a mass of energy at one end you have got to put it in at the other end, it may be in another form, but the amount of energy that should be produced of it must be the same. Therefore, if a Buddha is the one end of the change, the very amœba must have been the Buddha also. If the Buddha is the evolved amœba, the amœba was the involved Buddha also. If this universe is the manifestation of an almost infinite amount of energy, when this universe was in a state of *pralaya*, it must have represented the same amount of involved energy. It cannot have been otherwise. As such it follows that every soul is infinite. From the lowest worm that crawls under our feet to the noblest and greatest saints, all have this infinite power, infinite purity, and infinite everything. Only, the difference is in the degree of manifestation. The worm is only manifesting just a little bit of that energy; you have manifested more, another god-man has manifested still more; that is all the difference. But that infinite power is there all the same. Says Patanjali:—ततः क्षेत्रिकवत् । "Just as the peasant irrigating his field." Through a little corner of his field he brings water from a reservoir somewhere, and perhaps he has got a little lock that prevents the water from rushing into his field. When he wants water he has simply to open the lock, and in rushes the water of its own power. The power has not to be added, it is already there in the reservoir. So every one of us, every being, has as his own background such a reservoir of strength, infinite power, infinite purity, infinite bliss, and existence infinite,—only these locks, these bodies, are hindering us from expressing what we really are to the fullest.

And as these bodies become more and more finely organised, as the *tamoguna* becomes the *rajoguna*, and as the *rajoguna* becomes *sattva guna*, more and more of this power and purity becomes manifest, and therefore it is that our people have been so careful about eating and drinking, and the food question. It may be that the original ideas have been lost, just as with our marriage—which, though not belonging to the subject, I may take as an example. If I have another opportunity I will talk to you about these; but let me tell you now that the ideas behind our marriage system are the only ideas through which there can be a real civilisation. There cannot be anything else. If a man or a woman were allowed the freedom to take up any man or woman as wife or husband, if individual pleasure, if satisfaction of animal instincts, were to be allowed to run loose in society, the result must be evil, evil children, wicked and demoniacal. Aye, man in every country is, on the one hand, producing these brutal children, and on the other hand multiplying the police force to keep these brutes down. The question is not how to destroy evil that way, but how to prevent the very birth of evil, and so long as you live in society your marriage certainly affects every member of it; and therefore society has the right to dictate whom you shall marry, and whom you shall not. And great ideas of this kind have been behind the system of marriage here; what they call the astrological *jâti* of the bride and bridegroom. And in passing I may remark, that according to Manu a child who is born of lust is not an Aryan. The child whose very conception and whose death is according to the rules of the Vedas, such is an Aryan. Yes, and less of these Aryan children are being produced in every country, and the result is the mass of evil which we call *Kali Yuga*. But we have lost all these ideals; it is true we cannot carry all these ideas to the fullest length now, it is perfectly true we have made almost a caricature of some of these great ideas. It is lamentably true that the fathers and mothers are not what they were in old times, neither is society so educated as it used to be, neither has society that love for individuals that it used to have. But, however faulty the working out may be, the principle is sound; and if its application has become defective, if one method has failed, take up the principle and work it out better; why kill the principle? The same applies to the food question; the work and details are bad, very bad indeed, but that does not hurt the principle. The principle is eternal and must be there. Work it out afresh, and make a re-formed application.

This is the one great idea of the Atman which every one of our sects in India has to believe, only, as we will find, the Dualists preach that this Atman by evil works becomes *Sankuchita*, i.e., all its powers and its nature become contracted, and by good works again that nature expands. And the Advaitist says, that the Atman never expands nor contracts, but seems to do so, it appears to have become contracted. That is all the difference, but all have the one idea that our Atman has all the powers already, not that anything will come to it from outside, not that anything will drop into it from the skies. Mark you, your Vedas are not inspired, but expired, not that they came from anywhere outside, but they are the eternal laws living in every soul. The Vedas are in the soul of the ant, in the soul of the god. The ant has only to evolve and get the body of a sage or a Rishi, and the Vedas will come out, eternal laws expressing themselves. This is the one great idea to understand, that our power is already ours, our salvation is already within us. Say either that it has become contracted, or say that it has been covered with the evil of Màyà, it matters little; the idea is there already; you must have to believe in that, believe in the possibility of everybody; even in the lowest man there is the same possibility as in the Buddha. This is the doctrine of the Atman.

But now comes a tremendous fight. Here are the Buddhists, who equally analyse the body into a material stream and as equally analyse the mind into another. And as about this Atman they state that it is unnecessary; so we need not assume the Atman at all. What use of a substance, and qualities adhering to the substance? We say *gunas*, qualities, and qualities alone. It is illogical to assume two causes where one will explain the whole thing. And the fight went on, and all the theories which held the doctrine of substance were thrown to the ground by the Buddhists. There was a break-up all along the line of those who held on to the doctrine of substance and qualities, that you have a soul, and I have a soul, and every one has a soul separate from the mind and body, and that each one is an individual. So far we have seen that the idea of Dualism is all right; for there is the body, there is then the fine body—the mind, there is this Atman, and in and through all the Atmans, is that Paramâtman, God. The difficulty is here, that this Atman and Paramâtman are both so-called substance, to which the mind and body and so-called substances adhere like so many qualities. Nobody has ever seen a substance, none can ever conceive; what is the use of thinking of this substance? Why not become a *Kshanikavâdin*, and say that whatever exists is this succession of mental currents and nothing more. They do not adhere to each other, they do not form a unit, one is chasing the other, like waves in the ocean, never complete, never forming one unit-whole. Man is a succession of waves, and when one goes away it generates another, and the cessation of these wave-forms is what is called *Nirvâna.* You see that Dualism is mute before this, it is impossible that it can bring up any argument, and the Dualistic God also cannot be retained here. The idea of a God that is omnipresent, and yet is a Person who creates without hands, and moves without feet, and so on, and who has created the universe as a *khumbhakâra* (potter) creates a *ghata*, the Buddhist declares, is childish, and that if this is God, he is going to fight this God and not worship it. This universe is full of misery; if it is the work of a God, we are going to fight this God. And secondly, this God is illogical and impossible, as all of you are aware. We need not go into the defects of the 'design' theory, as all our *Kshanikas* had to show, and so this personal God fell to pieces.

Truth, and nothing but truth, is the watchword of the Advaitist. *Satyameva jayate nânritam satyenaiva panthâ vitato Devayâna.*—"Truth alone triumphs, and not untruth. Through truth alone the way to *Devayâna* lies." Everybody marches forward under that banner; aye, but it is only to crush the weaker man's position by his own. You come with your Dualistic idea of God to pick a quarrel with a poor man who is worshipping an image, and you think you are wonderfully rational, you can confound him, but if he turns round and shatters your own personal God, and calls that an imaginary ideal, where are you? You fall back on faith and so on, or raise the cry of Atheism, the old cry of a weak man—whosoever defeats him is an atheist. If you are to be rational, be rational all along the line, and if not, allow others the same privilege which you ask for yourselves. How can you prove the existence of this God? On the other hand it can be almost disproved. There is not a shadow of proof as to His existence, and there are very strong arguments to the contrary. How will you prove His existence, with your God, and His *gunas*, and an infinite number of souls which are substance, and each soul an individual? In what are you an individual? You are not as a body, for you know to-day better than even the Buddhists of old knew, that what may have been matter in the sun has just now become matter in you, and will go out and become matter in the plants; then where is your individuality, Mr. so and so? The same applies to the mind. Where is your individuality? You have one thought to-night and another to-morrow. You do not think the same way as you thought when you were a child, and old men do not think the same way as they did when they were young. Where is your individuality then? Do not say it is in consciousness, this *ahamkára*, because this only covers a small part of your existence. While I am talking to you, all my organs are working and I am not conscious of it. If consciousness is the proof of existence they do not exist then, because I am not conscious of them. Where are you then with your personal God theories? How can you prove such a God? Again, the Buddhists will stand up and declare not only is it illogical, but immoral, for it teaches man to be a coward and to seek assistance outside, and nobody can give him such help. Here is the universe, man made it; why then depend on an imaginary being outside, whom nobody ever saw or felt, or got help from? Why then do you make cowards of yourselves, and teach your children that the highest state of man is to be like a dog, and go crawling before this imaginary being, saying that you are weak and impure, and that you are everything vile in this universe? On the other hand, the Buddhists may urge not only that you tell a lie, but that you bring a tremendous amount of evil upon your children, for, mark you, this world is one of hypnotisation. Whatever you tell yourself that you believe. Almost the first words the great Buddha uttered were—"What you think, that you are, what you will think, that you will be." If this is true, do not teach yourself that you are nothing, aye, that you cannot do anything unless you are helped by somebody who does not live here, but sits above the clouds. The result will be that you will be more and more weakened every day; by constantly repeating, "We are very impure, Lord, make us pure," the result will be that you will hypnotise yourselves into all sorts of vices. Aye, the Buddhists say that ninety per cent. of these vices that you see in every society are on account of this idea of a personal God; this is an awful idea of the human being that the end and aim of this expression of life, this wonderful expression of life, is to become like a dog. Says the Buddhist to the Vaishnava, if your ideal, your aim and goal is to go to the place called *Vaikuntha* where God lives, and there stand before Him with folded hands all through eternity, it is better to commit suicide than do that. The Buddhists may even urge, that that is why he is going to create annihilation, *Nirvána*, to escape this. I am putting these ideas before you as a Buddhist just for the time being, because nowadays all these Advaitic ideas are said to make you immoral, and I am trying to tell you how the other side looks. Let us face both sides boldly and bravely.

We have seen first of all that this cannot be proved, this idea of a personal God creating the world; is there any child that can believe this to-day? Because a *kumbhakára* creates a *ghata*, therefore a God created the world! If this is so, then your *kumbhakára* is God also, and if any one tells you that he acts without head and hands you may take him to a lunatic asylum. Has ever your Personal God, the Creator of the world, to whom you cry all your life, ever helped you,—is the next challenge from modern science. They will prove that any help you have had could have been got by your own exertions, and better still, you need not have spent your energy in that crying, you could have done it better without that weeping and crying. And we have seen that along with this idea of a Personal God comes tyranny and priestcraft. Tyranny and priestcraft have prevailed wherever this idea existed, and until the lie is knocked on the head, say the Buddhists, tyranny will not cease. So long as man thinks he has to cower before a supernatural being, so long there will be priests to claim rights and privileges and to make men cower before them, while these poor men will continue to ask some priest to act as interceder for them. You may do away with the Brâhmana, but mark me, that those who do so will put themselves in his place, and will be worse, because the Brâhmana has a certain amount of generosity in him, but these upstarts are always the worst of tyrannisers. If a beggar gets wealth, he thinks the whole world is a bit of straw. So these priests there must be, so long as this Personal God idea persists, and it will be impossible to think of any great morality in society. Priestcraft and tyranny go hand in hand. Why was it invented? Because some strong men in old times got people into their hands and said, you must obey us or we will destroy you. That was the long and short of it. *Sabhayam vajramudyatam.* It is the idea of the thunderer, who kills every one who does not obey him.

Next the Buddhist says, you have been so rational up to this point that you say that everything is the result of the law of Karma. You believe in an infinity of souls, and that souls are without birth or death, and this infinity of souls and the belief in the law of Karma, is perfectly logical no doubt. There cannot be a cause without an effect, the present must have had its cause in the past, and will have its effect in the future. The Hindu says the Karma is *jada* and not *chaitanya*, therefore some *chaitanya* is necessary to bring this cause to fruition. Is it so, that *chaitanya* is necessary to bring the plant to fruition? If I plant the seed and add water, no *chaitanya* is necessary. You may say there was some original *chaitanya* there, but the souls themselves were the *chaitanya*, nothing else is necessary. If human souls have it too, what necessity is there for a God, as say the Jains, who, unlike the Buddhists, believe in souls, and do not believe in God. Where are you logical, where are you moral? And when you criticise Advaitism and fear that it will make for immorality, just read a little of what has been done in India by Dualistic sects. If there have been twenty thousand Advaitist blackguards, there have been more than twenty thousand Dvaitist blackguards. Generally speaking, there will be more Dvaitist blackguards, because it takes a better type of mind to understand Advaitism, and Advaitists can scarcely be frightened into anything. What remains for you Hindus, then? There is no help for you out of the clutches of the Buddhist. You may quote the Vedas, but he does not believe in them. He will say, "My *Tripitakas* say otherwise, and they are without beginning or end, not even written by Buddha, for Buddha says he is only reciting them; they are eternal." And he adds, that yours are wrong, ours are the true Vedas, yours are manufactured by the Brâhman priests, therefore out with them. How do you escape?

Here is the way to get out. Take up the first objection, the metaphysical one, that substance and qualities are different. Says the Advaitist, they are not. There is no difference between substance and qualities. You know the old illustration, how the rope is taken for the snake, and when you see the snake you do not see the rope at all, the rope has vanished. Dividing the thing into substance and quality, is a metaphysical something in the brains of philosophers, for never can there be an effect outside. You see substance if you are an ordinary man, and qualities if you are a great Yogi, but you never see both at the same time. So, Buddhists, your quarrel about substance and qualities has been but a miscalculation which does not stand in fact. But, if substance is unqualified, there can only be one. If you take qualities off from the soul, and show that these qualities are in the mind, really superimposed on the soul, then there can never be two souls, for it is qualification that makes the difference between one soul and another. How do you know that one soul is different from the other? Owing to certain differentiating marks, certain qualities. And where qualities do not exist how can there be differentiation? Therefore there are not two souls, there is but One, and your *Paramátman* is unnecessary, it is this very soul. That One is called *Paramátman,* that very One is called *jivátman,* and so on; and you Dualists, such as the Sánkhya and others, who say that the soul is *vibhu,* omnipresent, how can you make two infinites? There can be only one. What else? This One is the one Infinite Atman, everything else is Its manifestation. There the Buddhist stops, but there it does not end. The Advaitist position is not merely a weak one of criticism. The Advaitist criticises others when they come too near him, and just throws them away, that is all, but he propounds his own position. He is the only one that criticises, and does not stop with criticism and showing books. Here you are. You say the universe is a thing of continuous motion. In *vyashti* everything is moving, you are moving, the table is moving, motion everywhere; it is *samsára,* continuous motion; it is *jagat.* Therefore there cannot be an individuality in this *jagat,* because individuality means that which does not change; there cannot be any changeful individuality, it is a contradiction in terms. There is no such thing as individuality in this little world of ours, the *jagat.* Thought and feeling, mind and body, men and animals and plants are in a continuous state of flux. But suppose you take the universe as a unit whole; can it change or move? Certainly not. Motion is possible in comparison with something which is a little less in motion, or entirely motionless. The universe as a whole, therefore, is motionless, unchangeable. You are, therefore, an individual then, and then alone, when you are the whole of it, when the realisation of "I am the universe" comes. That is why the Vedantist says that so long as there are two, fear does not cease. It is only when one does not see another, does not feel another, when it is all one,—then alone fear ceases, then alone death vanishes, then alone *samsára* vanishes. Advaita teaches us therefore that man is individual in being universal, and not in being particular. You are immortal only when you are the whole. You are fearless and deathless only when you are the universe; and then, that which you call the universe is the same as that you call God, the same that you call existence, the same that you call the whole. It is the one undivided Existence which is taken to be the manifold world as we see it and others also who are in the same state of mind as we. People who have done a little better Karma and get a better state of mind, when they die, look upon it as *svarga,* and see Indras and so forth. People still higher will see it, the very same thing, as *Brahma Loka,* and the perfect ones will neither see the earth nor the heavens, nor any *Loka* at all. This universe will have vanished, and Brahman will be in its stead.

Can we know this Brahman? I have told you of the painting of the Infinite in the Samhita. Here we shall find another side shown, the infinite internal. That was the infinite of the muscles. Here we shall have the infinite of thought. There, the Infinite was attempted to be painted in language positive; here, that language failed, and the attempt has been to paint it in language negative. Here is this universe, and even admitting that it is Brahman, can we know it? No! No! You must understand this one thing again very clearly. Again and again this doubt will come to you, if this is Brahman, how can we know it? *Vijnátáramare kena vijániyát*—"By what can the knower be known"? How can the knower be known? The eyes see everything; can they see themselves? They cannot. The very fact of knowledge is a degradation. Children of the Aryas, you must remember this, for herein lies a big story. All the Western temptations that come to you, have their metaphysical basis on that one thing—there is nothing higher than sense-knowledge. In the East, we say in our Vedas that this knowledge is lower than the thing itself, because it is always a limitation. When you want to know a thing, it immediately becomes limited by your mind. They say, refer back to that instance of the oyster making a pearl and see how knowledge is limitation, gathering a thing, bringing it into consciousness, and not knowing it as a whole. This is true about all knowledge, and can it be less so about the Infinite? Can you thus limit Him who is the substance of all knowledge, Him who is the *Sákshi*, the Witness, without whom you cannot have any knowledge, Him who has no qualities, who is the Witness of the whole universe, the Witness in our own souls? How can you know Him? By what means can you bind Him up? Everything, the whole universe, is such a false attempt. This Infinite Atman is, as it were, trying to see his own face, and all, from the lowest animals, to the highest of gods, are like so many mirrors to reflect himself in, and he is taking up still others, finding them insufficient, until in the human body he comes to know that it is the finite of the finite, all is finite, there cannot be any expression of the Infinite in the finite. Then comes the retrograde march, and this is what is called renunciation, *vairágyam*. Back from the senses, back! do not go to the senses, is the watchword of *vairágyam*. This is the watchword of all morality, this is the watchword of all well-being; for you must remember that with us the universe begins in *tapasyá*, in renunciation; and as you go back and back, all the forms are being manifested before you, and they are left aside one after the other until you remain what you really are. This is *moksha*, or liberation.

This idea we have to understand.—*Vijnátáramare kena vijániyát.* "How to know the knower;" the knower cannot be known, because if it were known it will not be the knower. If you look at your eyes in a mirror, the reflection is no more your eyes, but something else, only a reflection. Then if this Soul, this Universal, Infinite Being which you are, is only a witness, what good is it? It cannot live, and move about, and enjoy the world, as we do. People cannot understand how the witness can enjoy. "Oh," they say "you Hindus have become quiescent, and good for nothing, through this doctrine, that you are witnesses!" First of all, it is only the witness that can enjoy. If there is a wrestling match, who enjoys it, those who take part in it, or those who are looking on, the outsiders? The more and more you are the witness of anything in life, the more you enjoy it. And this is *ánandam*, and therefore infinite bliss can only be yours when you have become the witness of this universe, then alone you are a *mukta* purusha. It is the witness alone that can work without any desire, without any idea of going to heaven, without any idea of blame, without any idea of praise. The witness alone enjoys, and none else.

Coming to the moral aspect, there is one thing between the metaphysical and the moral aspect of Advaitism; it is the theory of Maya. Everyone of these points in the Advaita system requires years to understand and months to explain. Therefore you will excuse me if I only just touch them *en passant*. This theory of Maya has been the most difficult thing to understand in all ages. Let me tell you in a few words that it is surely no theory, it is the combination of the three ideas *Desha-kála-nimitta* —space, time, and causation—and this time and space and cause have been further reduced into *náma rúpa*. Suppose there is a wave in the ocean. The wave is distinct from the ocean only in its form and name, and this form and this name cannot have any separate existence from the wave; they exist only with the wave. The wave may subside, but the same amount of water remains, even if the name and form that were on the wave vanish for ever. So this Maya is what makes the difference between me and you, between all animals and man, between gods and men. In fact, it is this Maya that causes the Atman to be caught, as it were, in so many millions of beings, and these are distinguishable only through name and form. If you leave it alone, let name and form go, all this variety vanishes for ever, and you are what you really are. This is Maya. It is again no theory, but a statement of facts. When the realist states that this table exists, what he means is, that this table has an independent existence of its own, that it does not depend on the existence of anything else in the universe, and if this whole universe be destroyed and annihilated this table will remain just as it is now. A little thought will show you that it cannot be so. Everything here in the sense-world is dependent and inter-dependent, relative and co-relative, the existence of one depending on the other. There are three steps, therefore, in our knowledge of things; the first is, that each thing is individual, and separate from every other; and the next step is to find that there is a relation and co-relation between all things; and the third is that there is only one thing which we see as many. The first idea of God with the ignorant is that this God is somewhere outside the universe, that is to say, the conception of God is extremely human; He does just what a man does, only on a bigger and higher scale. And we have seen how that idea of God is proved in a few words to be unreasonable and insufficient. And the next idea is the idea of a power we see manifested everywhere. This is the real personal God we get in the *Chandi*, but, mark me, not a God that you make the reservoir of all good qualities only. You cannot have two Gods, God and Satan; you must have only one, and dare to call Him good and bad, but have only one, and take the logical consequences. We read in the *Chandi*—"We salute Thee, O Divine Mother, who lives in every being as peace. We salute Thee, O Divine Mother who lives in all beings as purity." At the same time we must take the whole consequence of calling Him the All-formed. "All this bliss, O Gárgi, wherever there is bliss there is a portion of the Divine." You may use it how you like. In this light before me, you may give a poor man a hundred rupees, and another man may forge your name, but the light will be the same for both. This is the second stage; and the third is that God is neither outside nature nor inside nature, but God and nature and soul and universe are all convertible terms. You never see two things; it is your metaphysical words that have deluded you. You assume that you are a body and have a soul, and that you are both together. How can that be? Try in your own mind. If there is a Yogi among you, he knows himself as *chaitanya*, for him the body has vanished. An ordinary man thinks of himself as a body; the idea of spirit has vanished from him; but because the metaphysical ideas exist that man has a body and a soul and all these things, you think they are all simultaneously there. One thing at a time. Do not talk of God when you see matter; you see the effect and the effect alone, and the cause you cannot see, and the moment you can see the cause the effect will have vanished. Where is this world then, and who has taken it off?

"One that is present always as consciousness, the bliss absolute, beyond all bounds, beyond all compare, beyond all qualities, ever-free, limitless as the sky, without parts, the absolute, the perfect,—such a Brahman, O sage, O learned one, shines in the heart of the Jnânin, in Samâdhi."

Where all the changes of Nature cease for ever, thought beyond all thoughts, who is equal to all yet having no equal, immeasurable, whom the Vedas declare, who is the essence in what we call our existence, the perfect,—such a Brahman, O sage, O learned one, shines in the heart of the Jnânin in Samâdhi."

"Beyond all birth and death, the Infinite One, incomparable, like the whole universe deluged in water in *mahâpralaya*,—water above, water beneath, water on all sides, and on the face of that water not a wave, not a ripple,—silent and calm, all visions have died out, all fights and quarrels and the war of fools and saints have ceased for ever;—such a Brahman, O sage, O learned one, shines in the heart of the Jnânin in *samâdhi*."

That also comes, and when that comes the world has vanished.

We have seen then, that this Brahman, this Reality is unknown and unknowable, not in the sense of the agnostic, but because to know Him would be a blasphemy, because you are He already. We have also seen that this Brahman is not this table and yet is this table. Take off the name and form, and whatever is reality is He. He is the reality in everything.

"Thou art the woman, thou the man, thou art the boy, and the girl as well, thou the old man supportest thyself on a stick, thou art all in all in the Universe." That is the theme of Advaitism. A few words more. Herein lies, we find, the explanation of the essence of things. We have seen how here alone we can take a firm stand against all the onrush of logic and scientific knowledge. Here at last reason has a firm foundation, and, at the same time, the Indian Vedantist does not curse the preceding steps; he looks back and he blesses them, and he knows that they were true, only wrongly perceived, and wrongly stated. They were the same truth, only seen through the glass of Maya, distorted it may be,—yet truth, and nothing but truth. The same God whom the ignorant man saw outside nature, the same whom the little-knowing man saw as interpenetrating the universe, and the same whom the sage realises as his own self, as the whole universe itself,—all are One and the same Being, the same entity seen from different standpoints of view, seen through different glasses of Maya, perceived by different minds, and all the difference was caused by that. Not only so, but one view must lead to the other. What is the difference between science and common knowledge? Go out into the streets in the dark, and if something unusual is happening there, ask one of the passers-by, what is the cause of it. It is ten to one that he will tell you it is a ghost causing the phenomenon. He is always going after ghosts and spirits outside, because it is the nature of ignorance to seek for causes outside of effects. If a stone falls it has been thrown by a devil or a ghost, says the ignorant man, but the scientific man says it is the law of nature, the law of gravitation.

What is the fight between science and religion everywhere? Religions are encumbered with such a mass of explanations which are outside—one angel is in charge of the sun, another of the moon, and so on *ad infinitum;* every change is caused by a spirit, the one common point of agreement being that they are all outside the thing; while science means that the cause of a thing is sought out by the nature of the thing itself. As step by step science is progressing, it has taken the explanation of natural phenomena out of the hands of spirits and angels. Because Advaitism has done likewise in spiritual matters, it is the most scientific religion. This universe has not been created by any extra-cosmic God, nor is it the work of any outside genius. It is the self-creating, self-dissolving, self-manifesting, One Infinite Existence, the Brahman. *Tattvamasi, Svetaketo*—"That Thou art, O Svetaketu!" Thus you see that this, and this alone, and none else, can be the only scientific religion. And with all the prattle about science that is going on daily at the present time in modern half-educated India, with all the talk about rationalism and reason that I hear every day, I expect that whole sects of you will come over and dare to be Advaitists, and dare to preach it to the world in the words of Buddha, *Bahujana hitâya bahujana Sukhâya*—"For the good of many, for the happiness of many." If you do not, I take you for cowards. If you cannot get over your cowardice, if your fear is your excuse, allow the same liberty to others, do not try to break up the poor idol-worshipper, do not call him a devil, do not go about preaching to every man that does not agree entirely with you; know first, that you are cowards yourselves, and if society frightens you, if your own superstitions of the past frighten you so much, how much more will these superstitions frighten and bind down those who are ignorant? That is the Advaita position. Have mercy on others. Would to God that the whole world were Advaitists to-morrow, not only in theory, but in realisation. But if that cannot be, let us do the next best thing; let us take the ignorant by the hand, lead them always step by step just as they can go, and know that every step in all religious growth in India has been progressive. It is not from bad to good, but from good to better.

Something more has to be told about the moral relation. Our boys blithely talk nowadays, they learn from somebody—the Lord knows from whom—that Advaita makes people immoral, because if we are all one and all God, what need of morality will there be at all! In the first place, that is the argument of the brute, who can only be kept down by the whip. If you are such brutes commit suicide, rather than pass for human beings, who have to be kept down by the whip. If the whip is taken away, you will all be demons! You ought all to be killed, if such is the case; there is no help for you; you must always be living under this whip and rod, and there is no salvation, no escape for you. In the second place, Advaita and Advaita alone explains morality. Every religion preaches that the essence of all morality is to do good to others. And why? Be unselfish. And why should I? Some God has said it? He is not for me. Some texts have declared it? Let them; that is nothing to me; let them all tell it. And if they do, what is it to me? Each one for himself, and somebody take the hindermost; that is all the morality in the world, at least with many. What is the reason that I should be moral? You cannot explain it except when you come to know the truth as given in the Gita—"He, who sees every one in himself, and himself in everyone, thus seeing the same God living in all, he, the sage no more kills the self by the self." Know through Advaita that whoever you hurt you hurt yourself; they are all you. Whether you know it or not, through all hands you work, through all feet you move, you are the king enjoying in the palace, you are the beggar leading that miserable existence in the street; you are in the ignorant as well as in the learned, you are in the man who is weak, and you are in the strong; know this and be sympathetic. And that is why we must not hurt others. That is why I do not even care whether I have to starve, because there will be millions of mouths eating at the same time, and they are all mine. Therefore I should not care what becomes of me and mine, for the whole universe is mine, I am enjoying all the bliss at the same time; and who can kill me, or the universe? Herein is morality. Here, in Advaita alone, is morality explained. The others teach it, but cannot give you its reason. Then, so far about explanation.

What is the gain? It is strength. Take off that veil of hypnotism which you have cast upon the world, send not out thoughts and words of weakness unto humanity. Know that all sins and all evils can be summed up in that one word, weakness. It is weakness that is the motive power in all evil doing; it is weakness that is the source of all selfishness; it is weakness that makes men injure others; it is weakness that makes them manifest what they are not in reality. Let them all know what they are; let them repeat day and night what they are. *Soham*—Let them suck it in with their mothers' milk, this idea of strength—I am He, I am He. This is to be heard first.—श्रोतव्योमन्तव्यो निदिध्यासितव्य: etc. And then let them think of it, and out of that thought, out of that heart will proceed works such as the world has never seen. What has to be done? Aye, this Advaita is said by some to be impracticable; that is to say, it is not yet manifesting itself on the material plane. To a certain extent that is true, for, remember the saying of the Vedas—

ओमित्येकाक्षरं ब्रह्म ओमित्येकाक्षरं परं।
ओमित्येकाक्षरं ज्ञात्वा यो यदिच्छति तस्य तत्॥

"Om, this is the great secret; Om, this is the greatest possession; he who knows the secret of this Om, whatever he desires that he gets." Aye, therefore first know the secret of this Om, that you are the Om; know the secret of this *Tattvamasi*, and then and then alone, whatever you want shall come to you. If you want to be great materially, believe that you are so. I may be a little bubble, and you may be a wave mountain-high, but know that for both of us the infinite ocean is the background, the infinite Brahman is our magazine of power and strength, and we can draw as much as we like, both of us, I the bubble and you the mountain-high wave. Believe therefore in yourselves. The secret of Advaita is—Believe in yourselves first, and then believe in anything else. In the history of the world, you will find that only those nations that have believed in themselves have become great and strong. In the history of each nation, you will always find that only those individuals who have believed in themselves have become great and strong. Here, to India, came an Englishman who was only a clerk, and for want of funds and other reasons he twice tried to blow his brains out, and when he failed, he believed in himself, he believed that he was born to do great things, and that man became Lord Clive, the founder of the Empire. If he had believed the *pádris* and gone crawling all his life—"Oh Lord I am weak, and I am low"—where would he have been? In a lunatic asylum. You also are made lunatics with these evil teachings. I have seen all the world over, the bad effects of these weak teachings of humility destroying the human race. Our children are brought up in this way, and is it a wonder that they become semi-lunatics.

This is teaching on the practical side. Believe, therefore, in yourselves, and if you want material wealth, work it out; it will come to you. If you want to be intellectual, work it out on the intellectual plane, and intellectual giants you shall be. And if you want to attain to freedom, work it out on the spiritual plane, and free you shall be, and shall enter into *Nirvána*, the blissful. But one defect which lay in the Advaita was, its being worked out so long on the spiritual plane only, and nowhere else; now, the time has come when you have to make it practical. It shall no more be a *Rahasya*, a secret, it shall no more live with monks in caves and forests, and in the Himalayas; it must come down to the daily, everyday life of the people; it shall be worked out in the palace of the king, in the cave of the recluse, it shall be worked out in the cottage of the poor, by the beggar in the street, everywhere, anywhere it can be worked out. Therefore do not fear whether you are a woman or a Sudra, for this religion is so great, says Lord Krishna, that even the least done, brings a great amount of good.

Therefore, children of the Aryas, do not sit idle ; awake, arise, and stop not till the goal is reached. The time has come when this Advaita is to be worked out practically. Let us bring it down from heaven unto the earth ; this is the present dispensation. Aye, the voices of our forefathers of old are telling us to bring it down from heaven to the earth. Let your teachings permeate the world, till they have entered into every pore of society, till they have become the common property of everybody, till they have become part and parcel of our lives, till they have entered into our veins and tingle with every drop of blood there.

Aye, you may be astonished to hear, that as practical Vedantists the Americans are better than we are. I used to stand on the sea-shore at New York, and look at the emigrants coming from different countries, crushed, down-trodden, hopeless, unable to look a man in the face, with a little bundle of clothes as all their possession, and these all in rags ; if they saw a policeman they were afraid and tried to get to the other side of the footpath. And, mark you, in six months those very men were walking erect, well-clothed, looking everybody in the face ; and what made this wonderful difference ? Say, this man comes from Armenia, or somewhere else where he was crushed down beyond all recognition, where everybody told him he was a born slave, and born to remain in a low state all his life, and where at the least move on his part he was trodden upon. There everything told him as it were, "Slave ! you are a slave, remain so. Hopeless you were born, hopeless you must remain." Even the very air murmured round him as it were, "There is no hope for you, hopeless and a slave you must remain"; while the strong man crushed the life out of him. And when he landed in the streets of New York, he found a gentleman, well-dressed, shaking him by the hand ; it made no difference that the one was in rags and the other well-clad. He went a step further and saw a restaurant, that there were gentlemen dining at a table, and he was asked to take a seat at the corner of the same table. He went about, and found a new life, that there was a place where he was a man among men. Perhaps he went to Washington, shook hands with the President of the United States, and perhaps there he saw men coming from distant villages, peasants, and ill-clad, all shaking hands with the President. Then the veil of Maya slipped away from him. He is Brahman, he who has been hypnotised into slavery and weakness, is once more awake, and he rises up and finds himself a man, in a world of men. Aye, in this country of ours, the very birthplace of the Vedanta, our masses have been hypnotised for ages into that state. To touch them is pollution ; to sit with them is pollution ! Hopeless they were born ; hopeless they must remain ! And the result is that they have been sinking, sinking, sinking, and have come to the last stage to which a human being can come. For what country is there in the world where man has to sleep with the cattle ; and for this blame nobody else, do not commit the mistake of the ignorant. The effect is here and the cause is here too. We are to blame. Stand up, be bold, and take the blame on your own shoulders. Do not go about throwing mud at others ; for all the faults you suffer from you are the sole and only cause.

Young men of Lahore, understand this, therefore, this great sin, hereditary and national, is on your shoulders. There is no hope for us. You may make thousands of societies, twenty thousand political assemblages, fifty thousand institutions. These will be of no use until there is that sympathy, that love, that heart, that thinks for all ; until Buddha's heart comes once more into India, until the words of Lord Krishna are brought to their practical use, there is no hope for us. You go on imitating the Europeans and their societies and their assemblages, but let me tell you a story, a fact that I saw with my own eyes. A company of Burmans was taken over to London by some persons here, who turned out to be Eurasians. They exhibited these people in London, took all the money, and then took these Burmans over to the Continent, and left them there for good or evil. These poor people did not know a word of any European language, but the English Consul in Austria sent them over to London. They were helpless in London, without knowing anyone. But an English lady got to know of them, took these foreigners from Burma into her own house, gave them her own clothes, her bed, and everything, and then sent the news to the papers. And, mark you, the next day the whole nation was, as it were, roused. Money poured in and these people were helped out and sent back to Burma. On this sort of sympathy are based all their political and other institutions; it is the rock-foundation of love, for themselves at least. They may not love the world; and the Burmans may be their enemies, but in England, it goes without saying, there is this great love for their own people, for truth and justice and charity to the stranger at the door. I should be the most ungrateful man if I did not tell you how wonderfully and how hospitably I was received in every country in the West. Where is the heart here to build upon? No sooner do we start a little joint-stock company than we try to cheat each other, and the whole thing comes down with a crash. You talk of imitating the English, and building up as big a nation as they are. But where are the foundations? Ours are only sand, and therefore the building comes down with a crash in no time.

Therefore, young men of Lahore, raise once more that mighty banner of Advaita, for on no other ground can you have that wonderful love, until you see that the same Lord is present everywhere. Unfurl that banner of love! "Arise, awake and stop not till the goal is reached." Arise, arise once more, for nothing can be done without renunciation. If you want to help others, your little self must go. In the words of the Christians—you cannot serve God and Mammon at the same time. Have *Vairágyam*—your ancestors gave up the world for doing great things. At the present time there are men who give up the world to help their own salvation. Throw away everything, even your own salvation, and go and help others. Aye, you are always talking bold words, but here is practical Vedanta before you. Give up this little life of yours. What matters it if you die of starvation, you and I and thousands like us, so long as this nation lives? The nation is sinking, the curse of unnumbered millions is on our heads;—those to whom we have been giving ditch-water to drink when they have been dying of thirst and while the perennial river of water was flowing past; the unnumbered millions whom we have allowed to starve in sight of plenty; the unnumbered millions to whom we have talked of Advaita and whom we have hated with all our strength; the unnumbered millions for whom we have invented the doctrine of *Lokáchára*;—to whom we have talked theoretically that we are all the same, and all are one with the same Lord, without even an ounce of practice. "Yet, my friends, it must be only in the mind and never in practice!" Wipe off this blot. "Arise and awake." What matters it if this little life goes; everyone has to die, the saint or the sinner, the rich or the poor. The body never remains for anyone. Arise and awake and be perfectly sincere. Our insincerity in India is awful; what we want is character, that steadiness and character that make a man cling on to a thing like grim death.

"Let the sages blame or let them praise, let Lakshmi come to-day or let her go away, let death come just now, or in a hundred years; he indeed is the sage who does not make one false step from the right path." Arise and awake, for the time is passing and all our energies will be frittered away in vain talking. Arise and awake, let minor things, and quarrels over little details, and fights over little doctrines be thrown aside, for here is the greatest of all works, here are the sinking millions. When the Mahommedans first came into India, what great numbers of Hindus were here; but mark, how to-day they have dwindled down. Every day they will become less and less till the whole disappear. Let them disappear, but with them will disappear the marvellous ideas, of which, with all their defects and all their misrepresenta tions, they still stand as representatives. And with them will disappear this marvellous Advaita, the crest-jewel of all spiritual thought. Therefore, arise, awake, with your hands stretched out to protect the spirituality of the world. And first of all, work it out for your own country. What we want is, not so much spirituality as a little of the bringing down of the Advaita into the material world. First bread and then religion. We stuff them too much with religion, when the poor fellows have been starving. No dogmas will satisfy the craving of hunger. There are two curses here, first our weakness, secondly, our hatred, our dried-up hearts. You may talk doctrines by the millions, you may have sects by the hundreds of millions; aye, but it is nothing until you have the heart to feel, feel for them as your Veda teaches you, till you find that they are parts of your own bodies, till you realise that you and they, the poor and the rich, the saint and the sinner, are all parts of One Infinite Whole, which you call Brahman.

Gentlemen, I have tried to place before you a few of the most brilliant points of the Advaita system, and now the time has come when it should be carried into practice, not only in this country but everywhere. Modern Science and its sledge-hammer blows are pulverising the porcelain foundations of all Dualistic religions everywhere. Not only here are the Dualists torturing texts till they will extend no longer,—for texts are not India-rubber,—it is not only here that they are trying to get into the nooks and corners to protect themselves, it is still more so in Europe and America. And even there something of this idea will have to go from India. It has already got there. It will have to grow and increase, and save their civilisations too. For, in the West, the old order of things is vanishing, giving way to a new order of things, which is the worship of gold, the worship of Mammon. Thus, this old crude system of religion was better than the modern system, namely,—competition and gold. No nation, however strong, can stand on such foundations, and the history of the world tells us that all that had such foundations are dead and gone. In the first place we have to stop the in-coming of such a wave in India. Therefore, preach the Advaita to every one, so that religion may withstand the shock of modern science. Not only so, you will have to help others; your thought will help out Europe and America. But above all, let me once more remind you that here is need of practical work, and the first part of that is, that you should go to the sinking millions of India, and take them by the hand, remembering the words of the Lord Krishna:—

इहैव तैर्जितः सर्गो येषां साम्ये स्थितं मनः ।
निर्दोषं हि समं ब्रह्म तस्मात् ब्रह्मणि ते स्थिताः ॥

"Even in this life they have conquered heaven whose minds are firmed-fixed on the sameness of everything, for God is pure and the same to all; therefore, such are said to be living in God."

VEDANTISM.

At Khetri on 20th December 1897, Swami Vivekananda delivered a lecture on Vedantism, in the hall of the Maharaja's bungalow in which he lodged with his disciples. The Swami was introduced by the Rajaji, who was the president of the meeting, and spoke for more than an hour and a half. The Swami was at his best, and it was a matter of regret that no shorthand writer was present to report this interesting lecture at length. The following is a summary from notes taken down at the time:—

Two nations of yore, namely the Greek and the Aryan, placed in different environments and circumstances,—the former, surrounded by all that was beautiful, sweet, and tempting in Nature, with an invigorating climate, and the latter, surrounded on every side by all that was sublime, and born and nurtured in a climate which did not allow of much physical exercise,—developed two peculiar and different ideals of civilisation. The study of the Greeks was the outer infinite, while that of the Aryans was the inner infinite;—one studied the macrocosm, and the other, the microcosm. Each had its distinct part to play in the civilisation of the world. Not that one was required to borrow from the other, but if they compared notes both would be the gainers. The Aryans were by nature an analytical race. In the sciences of mathematics and grammar wonderful fruits were gained, and by the analysis of mind the full tree was developed. In Pythagoras, Socrates, Plato, and the Egyptian neo-Platonists, we can find traces of Indian thought.

The Swami then traced in detail the influence of Indian thought on Europe, and showed how at different periods Spain, Germany, and other European countries, were greatly influenced by it. The Indian prince, Dârâ Shuko, translated the Upanishads into Persian, and a Latin translation of the same was seen by Schopenhauer, whose philosophy was moulded by these. Next to him, the philosophy of Kant also shows traces of the teachings of the Upanishads. In Europe it is the interest in comparative philology that attracts scholars to the study of Sanskrit, though there are men like Deussen who take interest in philosophy for its own sake. The Swami hoped that in future much more interest would be taken in the study of Sanskrit. He then showed that the word "Hindu" in former times was full of meaning, as referring to the people living beyond the Sindhu, or the Indus; it is now meaningless, representing neither the nation, nor their religion, for on this side of the Indus, various nations professing different religions live at the present day.

The Swami then dwelt at length on the Vedas, and stated that they were not spoken by any person, but the ideas were evolving slowly and slowly until they were embodied in book form, and then that book became the authority. He said, that various religions were embodied in books; the power of books seemed to be infinite. The Hindus have their Vedas, and will have to hold on to them for thousands of years more, but their ideas about them are to be changed and built anew on a solid foundation of rock. The Vedas, he said, were a huge literature. Ninety-nine per cent. of them were missing; they were in the keeping of certain families, with whose extinction the books were lost. But still, those that are left now, could not be contained even in a large hall like that. They were written in language, archaic and simple; their grammar was very crude, so much so, that it was said that some part of the Vedas had no meaning.

He then dilated on the two portions of the Vedas—the Karma-kandam and the Jnana-kandam. The Karma-kandam, he said, were the Samhitas and the Brâhmanas. The Brâhmanas dealt with sacrifices. The Samhitas were songs composed in *chhandas* known as Anushthup, Trishtup, Jagati, &c. Generally they praised deities such as Varuna or Indra, and the question arose who were these deities, and if any theory was raised about them they were smashed up by other theories, and so on it went.

The Swami then proceeded to explain different ideas of worship. With the ancient Babylonians, the soul was only a double, having no individuality of its own and not able to break its connection with the body. This double was believed to suffer hunger and thirst, feelings and emotions like that of the old body. Another idea was, that if the first body was injured the double would be injured also; when the first was annihilated, the double also perished; so the tendency grew to preserve the body, and thus mummies, tombs, and graves came into existence. The Egyptians, the Babylonians, and the Jews never got any farther than this idea of the double; they did not reach to the idea of the Atman beyond.

Prof. Max Müller's opinion was, that not the least trace of ancestral worship could be found in the Rig-Veda. There we do not meet with the horrid sight of mummies staring stark and blank at us. There the gods were friendly to man; communion between the worshipper and the worshipped was healthy. There was no moroseness, no want of simple joy, no lack of smiles, or light in the eyes. The Swami said that, dwelling on the Vedas he even seemed to hear the laughter of the gods. The Vedic Rishis might not have had finish in their expression but they were men of culture and heart, and we are brutes in comparison to them. Swamiji then recited several Mantras in confirmation of what he had just said. "Carry him to the place where the Fathers live, where there is no grief or sorrow." &c. Thus the idea arose that the sooner the dead body was cremated the better. By and by they came to know that there was a finer body that went to a place where there was all joy and no sorrow. In the semitic type of religion there was tribulation and fear; it was thought that if a man saw God, he would die. But according to the Rig-Veda, when a man saw God face to face then began his real life.

Now the question came to be asked, what were these gods. Sometimes Indra came and helped man; sometimes Indra drank too much Soma. Now and again, adjectives such as, all-powerful, all-pervading, were attributed to him; the same was the case with Varuna. In this way it went on, and some of these Mantras depicting the characteristics of these gods were marvellous, and the language was exceedingly grand. The speaker here repeated the famous *Násadiya Sukta*, which describes the Pralaya state, and in which occurs the idea of 'Darkness covering darkness,' and asked, if the persons that described these sublime ideas in such poetic thought were uncivilised and uncultured, what can we call ourselves? It was not for him, Swamiji said, to criticise or pass any judgment on those Rishis and their Gods—Indra, or Varuna. All this was like a panorama, unfolding one scene after another, and behind them all as a background stood out "एकंसद्विप्रा बहुधा वदन्ति।" "That which exists is One; sages call It variously." The whole thing was most mystical, marvellous, and exquisitely beautiful. It seemed even yet quite unapproachable,—

the veil was so thin that it would rend, as it were, at the least touch and vanish like a mirage.

Continuing he said, that one thing seemed to him quite clear and possible, that Aryans too, like the Greeks, went to outside Nature for their solution, that Nature tempted them outside, led them step by step to the outward world, beautiful and good. But here in India anything which was not sublime, counted for nothing. It never occurred to the Greeks to pry into the secrets after death. But here from the beginning was asked again and again, "What am I?" "What will become of me after death?" There the Greek thought,—the man died and went to heaven. What was meant by going to heaven? It meant going outside of everything; there was nothing inside, everything was outside; his search was all directed outside, nay, he himself was, as it were, outside himself. And when he went to a place which was very much like this world minus all its sorrows, he thought he had got everything that was desirable and was satisfied; and there all ideas of religion stopped. But this did not satisfy the Hindu mind; in its analysis, these heavens were all included within the material universe. "Whatever comes by combination" the Hindus said, "dies of annihilation." They asked external Nature, "Do you know what is soul?" and Nature answered, "No." "Is there any God?" Nature answered, "I do not know." Then they turned away from Nature. They understood that external Nature, however great and grand, was limited in space and time. Then there arose another voice; new sublime thoughts dawned in their minds. That voice said—"*Neti, Neti,*" "Not this, Not this." All the different gods were now reduced into one; suns, moons, and stars,—nay, the whole universe—were one, and upon this new ideal, spiritual basis of religion was built.

न तत्र सूर्यो भाति न चन्द्रतारकं नेमा विद्युतो भान्ति कुतोऽयमग्निः ।
तमेव भान्तमनुभाति सर्वं तस्य भासा सर्वमिदं विभाति ॥

"There the sun doth not shine, neither the moon, nor stars, nor lightning, what to speak of this fire. He shining, everything doth shine. Through Him everything shineth." No more is there that limited, crude, personal idea; no more is there that little idea of God sitting in judgment; no more is that search outside, but henceforth it is directed inside. Thus the Upanishads became the Bible of India. It was a vast literature, these Upanishads, and all the schools holding different opinions in India came to be established on the foundation of the Upanishads.

The Swami passed on to the Dualistic, Qualified Dualistic, and Advaitic theories, and reconciled them by saying, that each one of these was like a step, by which one passed before the other was reached; the final evolution to Advaitism was the natural outcome, and the last step was "Tattvamasi." He pointed out where even the great commentators, Sankaracharya, Ramanujacharya and Madhwacharya had committed mistakes. Each one believed in the Upanishads as the sole authority, but thought that they preached one thing, one path only. Thus Sankaracharya committed the mistake in supposing that the whole of the Upanishads taught one thing, which was Advaitism, and nothing else; and wherever a passage bearing distinctly the Dvaita idea occurred, he broke and tortured the meaning to make it support his own theory. So with Ramanuja and Madhwacharya when pure Advaitic texts occurred. It was perfectly true that the Upanishads had one thing to teach, but that was taught as going up from one step to another. Swamiji regretted, that in modern India the spirit of religion is gone; only the externals remain; the people are neither Hindus, nor Vedantists; they are merely don't-touchists; the kitchen is their temple and *handi bartans* (cooking pots) are their *devatá* (object of worship). This state of thing must go. The sooner it is given up the better for our religion. Let the Upanishads shine in their glory, and at the same time let not quarrels exist amongst different sects.

As Swamiji was not keeping good health, he felt exhausted at this stage of his speech ; so he took a little rest of half an hour, during which time the whole audience waited patiently to hear the rest of the lecture. He came out and spoke again for another half hour, and explained that knowledge was the finding of unity in diversity, and the highest point in every science was reached when it found the one unity underlying all variety. This was as true in physical science, as in the spiritual.

THE INFLUENCE OF INDIAN SPIRITUAL THOUGHT IN ENGLAND.

The Swami Vivekananda presided at a meeting at which the Sister Nivedita (Miss M. E. Noble) delivered a lecture on, "The Influence of Indian Spiritual Thought in England," on the 11th March, 1898, at the Star Theatre, Calcutta. Swami Vivekananda on rising to introduce Miss Noble spoke as follows :—

LADIES AND GENTLEMEN,—

When I was travelling through the Eastern parts of Asia, one thing especially struck me, that is, the prevalence of Indian spiritual thought in Eastern Asiatic countries. You may imagine the surprise with which I noticed written on the walls of Chinese and Japanese temples, some well-known Sanskrit Mantras, and possibly it will please you all the more to know, that they were all in old Bengali characters, standing even in the present day, as a monument of missionary energy and zeal displayed by our forefathers of Bengal.

Apart from these Asiatic countries, the work of India's spiritual thought is so wide-spread and unmistakable that even in Western countries, going deep below the surface, I found traces of the same influence still present. It has now become an historical fact that the spiritual ideas of the Indian people travelled towards both the East and the West in days gone by. Everybody knows now how much the world owes to India's spirituality, and what a potent factor in the present and the past of humanity have been the spiritual powers of India. These have taken place in the past. I find another most remarkable phenomenon, and that is, that the most stupendous powers of civilisation and progress towards humanity, and social progress, have been effected by that wonderful race—I mean the Anglo-Saxon. I may go further and tell you, that had it not been for the power of the Anglo-Saxons we should not have met here to-day to discuss as we are doing, the influence of our Indian spiritual thought. And coming back to our own country, coming from the West to the East, I see the same Anglo-Saxon powers working here with all their defects, but retaining their peculiarly characteristic good features, and I believe that at last the grand result is achieved. The British idea of expansion and progress is forcing us up, and let us remember that the civilisation of the West has been drawn from the fountain of the Greeks, and that the great idea of Greek civilisation is that of *expression.* In India, we *think*—but unfortunately sometimes we think so deeply that there is no power left for expression. Gradually therefore, it came to pass that our force of expression did not manifest itself before the world, and what is the result of that ? The result is this—we worked to hide everything we had. It began first with individuals as a faculty of hiding, and it ended by becoming a national habit of hiding—there is such lack of power of expression with us that we are now considered a dead nation. Without expression, how can we live ? The backbone of Western civilisation is—expansion and expression. This side of the work of the Anglo-Saxon race in India to which I draw your attention, is calculated to rouse our nation once more to express itself—and is inciting it to bring out its hidden treasures before the world by using the means of communication provided by the same mighty race. The Anglo-Saxons have created a future for India, and the space through which our ancestral ideas are now ranging is simply phenomenal. Aye, what great facilities had our forefathers when they delivered their message of truth and salvation? Aye, how did the great Buddha preach the noble doctrine of universal brotherhood? There were even then great facilities here, in our beloved India, for the attainment of real happiness, and we could easily send our ideas from one end of the world to the other. Now we have even reached the Anglo-Saxon race. This is the kind of interaction now going on, and we find that our message is heard, and not only heard but is being responded to. Already England has given us some of her great intellects to help us in our mission. Every one has heard and is perhaps familiar with my friend Miss Müller, who is now here on this platform. This lady, born of a very good family and well educated, has given her whole life to us out of love for India, and has made India her home and her family. Every one of you is familiar with the name of that noble and distinguished Englishwoman who has also given her whole life to work for the good of India and India's regeneration. I mean Mrs. Besant. To-day, we meet on this platform two ladies from America who have the same mission in their hearts; and I can assure you that they also are willing to devote their lives to do the least good to our poor country. I take this opportunity of reminding you of the name of one of our countrymen—one who has seen England and America, one in whom I have great confidence, and whom I respect and love, and who would have been present here but for an engagement elsewhere—a man working steadily and silently for the good of our country—a man of great spirituality—I mean Mr. Mohini Mohun Chatterji. And now England has sent us another gift in Miss Margaret Noble, from whom we expect much. Without any more words of mine I introduce to you Miss Noble, who will now address you.

After Sister Nivedita had finished her interesting lecture, the Swami rose and said:—

I have only a few words to say. We have an idea, that we, Indians, can do something, and amongst the Indians we Bengalees may laugh at this idea, but I do not. My mission in life is to rouse a struggle in you. Whether you are an Advaitin, whether you are a qualified-Monist or Dualist, it does not matter much. But let me draw your attention to one thing which unfortunately we always forget, that is, "O man, have faith in yourself." That is the way by which we can have faith in God. Whether you are an Advaitist or a Dualist, whether you are a believer in the system of Yoga or a believer in Sankaracharya, whether you are a follower of Vyasa or Visvamitra, it does not matter much. But the thing is, that on this point Indian thought differs from that of all the rest of the world. Let us remember for a moment that, whereas in every other religion and in every other country, the power of the soul is entirely ignored—the soul is thought of as almost powerless, weak, and inert, we in India consider the soul to be eternal, and hold that it will remain perfect through all eternity. We should always bear in mind the teachings of the Upanishads.

Remember your great mission in life. We Indians, and especially those of Bengal, have been invaded by a vast amount of foreign ideas that are eating into the very vitals of our national religion. Why are we so backward nowadays? Why are ninety-nine per cent. of us made up of entirely foreign ideas and elements? This has to be thrown out if we want to rise in the scale of nations. If we want to rise, we must also remember that we have many things to learn from the West. We should learn from the West her arts and her sciences. From the West we have to learn the sciences of physical nature, while on the other hand the West has to come to us to learn and assimilate religion and spiritual knowledge. We Hindus must believe that we are the teachers of the world. We have been clamouring here for getting political rights and many other such things. Very well; rights and privileges and other things can only come through friendship, and friendship can only be expected between two equals. When one of the parties is a beggar, what friendship can there be? It is all very well to speak so, but I say that without mutual co-operation we can never make ourselves strong men. So, I must call upon you to go out to England and America, not as beggars but as teachers of religion. The law of exchange must be applied to the best of our power. If we have to learn from them the ways and methods of making ourselves happy in this life, why, in return, should we not give them the methods and ways that would make them happy for all eternity? Above all, work for the good of humanity. Give up the so-called boast of your narrow orthodox life. Death is waiting for every one, and mark you this—the most marvellous historical fact—that all the nations of the world have to sit down patiently at the feet of India to learn the eternal truths embodied in her literature. India dies not. China dies not. Japan dies not. Therefore, we must always remember the backbone of our spirituality, and to do that we must have a guide who will show the path to us, that path about which I am talking just now. If any of you do not believe it, if there be a Hindu boy amongst us who is not ready to believe that his religion is pure spirituality, I do not call him a Hindu. I remember in one of the villages of Cashmere, while talking to an old Mahommedan lady, I asked her in a mild voice, "What religion is yours?" She replied in her own language, "Praise the Lord! By the mercy of God, I am a Musalmân." And then I asked a Hindu, "What is your religion?" He plainly replied—"I am a Hindu." I remember that grand word of the Katha Upanishad—"*Shraddhâ*," or marvellous faith. An instance of *Shraddhâ* can be found in the life of Nachiketas. To preach the doctrine of *Shraddhâ* or genuine faith is the mission of my life. Let me repeat to you that this faith is one of the potent factors of humanity, and of all religions. First, have faith in yourselves. Know that one may be considered a little bubble and another may be mountain-high, but behind both the bubble and the mountain, there is the infinite ocean. Therefore, there is hope for every one. There is salvation for every one. Every one must sooner or later get rid of the bonds of Maya. This is the first thing to do. Infinite hope begets infinite aspiration. If that faith comes to us, it will bring back our national life as it was in the days of Vyasa and Arjuna—the days when all our sublime doctrines of humanity were preached. To-day we are far behindhand in spiritual insight and spiritual thoughts. India has plenty of spirituality, so much so that her spiritual greatness has made India the greatest nation of the existing races of the world; and if traditions and hopes are to be believed, these days will come back once more to us, and that depends upon you. You, young men of Bengal, do not look up to the rich and great men who have money. The poor did all the great and gigantic work of the world. You, poor men of Bengal, come up, you can do everything, and you must do everything. Many will follow your example, poor though you are. Be steady, and, above all, be pure and sincere to the backbone. Have faith in your destiny. You, young men of Bengal, are to work out the salvation of India. Mark that, whether you believe it or not. Do not think that it will be done to-day or to-morrow. I believe in it as I believe in my own body and my own soul. Therefore, my heart goes to you—young men of Bengal. It depends upon you who have no money; because you are poor, therefore, you will work. Because you have nothing, therefore, you will be sincere. Because you are sincere, you will be ready to renounce all. That is what I am just now telling you. Once more I repeat this to you. This is your mission in life, this is my mission in life. I do not care what philosophy you take up; only I am ready to prove here that throughout the whole of India, there runs a mutual and cordial string of eternal faith in the perfection of humanity, and I believe in it myself. And let that faith be spread over the whole land.

SANNYAS: ITS IDEAL AND PRACTICE.

A parting Address was given to Swamiji by the junior Sannyasins of the Math (Belur), on the eve of his leaving for the West for the second time (19th June, 1899). The following is the substance of Swamiji's reply:—

This is not the time for a long lecture. But I shall speak to you in brief about a few things which I should like you to carry into practice. First, we have to understand the ideal, and then the methods by which we can make it practical. Those of you who are Sannyasins must try to do good to others, for Sannyas means that. There is no time to deliver a long discourse on 'Renunciation,' but I shall very briefly characterise it as *"the love of death."* Worldly people love life. The Sannyasin is to love death. Are we to commit suicide then? Far from it. For suicides are not lovers of death, as it is often seen that when a man trying to commit suicide fails, he never attempts it for a second time. What is the love of death then? We must die, that is certain; let us die then for a good cause. Let all our actions—eating, drinking, and everything that we do—tend towards the sacrifice of our self. You nourish your body by eating. What good is there in doing that if you do not hold it as a sacrifice to the well-being of others? You nourish your minds by reading books. There is no good in doing that unless you hold it also as a sacrifice to the whole world. It is right for you that you should serve your millions of brothers rather than aggrandise this little self. Thus you must die a gradual death. In such a death is heaven, all good is stored therein—and in its opposite is all that is diabolical and evil.

Then as to the methods of carrying the ideals into practical life. First, we have to understand that we must not have any impossible ideal. An ideal which is too high makes a nation weak and degraded. This happened after the Buddhistic and the Jain reforms. On the other hand, too much practicality is also wrong. If you have not even a little imagination, if you have no ideal to guide you, you are simply a brute. So we must not lower our ideal, neither are we to lose sight of practicality.

We must avoid the two extremes. In our country the old idea is, to sit in a cave and meditate and die. To go ahead of others in salvation is wrong. One must learn sooner or later, that one cannot get salvation if one does not try to seek the salvation of his brothers. You must try to combine in your life immense idealism with immense practicality. You must be prepared to go into deep meditation now, and the next moment you must be ready to go and cultivate these fields (Swamiji said, pointing to the meadows of the Math). You must be prepared to explain the difficult intricacies of the Shāstras now, and the next moment to go and sell the produce of the fields in the market. You must be prepared for all menial services, not only here, but elsewhere also.

The next thing to remember is, that the aim of this Institution is to make men. You must not merely learn what the Rishis taught. Those Rishis are gone, and their opinions are also gone with them. You must be Rishis yourselves. You are also men as much as the greatest men that were ever born—even our Incarnations. What can mere book-learning do? What can meditation do even? What can the Mantras and Tantras do? You must stand on your own feet. You must have this new method—the method of man-making. The true *man* is he who is strong as strength itself and yet possesses a woman's heart. You must feel for the millions of beings around you, and yet you must be strong and inflexible, and you must also possess obedience; though it may seem a little paradoxical—you must possess these apparently conflicting virtues. If your superior order you to throw yourself into a river and catch a crocodile, you must first obey and then reason with him. Even if the order be wrong, first obey and then contradict it. The bane of sects, especially in Bengal, is that if any one happens to have a different opinion he immediately starts a new sect, he has no patience to wait. So you must have a deep regard for your *Sangha.* There is no place for disobedience here. Crush it out without mercy. No disobedient members here,you must turn them out. There must not be any traitors in the camp. You must be as free as the air, and as obedient as this plant and the dog.

WHAT HAVE I LEARNT?

(Delivered at Dacca, March, 1901.)

At Dacca, Swamiji delivered two lectures in English, the first one was on, "What have I learnt?" and the second one was on, "The Religion we are born in." The following is translated from the report in Bengali by a disciple, and contains the substance of the first lecture:—

First of all, I must express my pleasure at the opportunity afforded me of coming to Eastern Bengal, to acquire an intimate knowledge of this part of the country, which I hitherto lacked, in spite of my wanderings through many civilised countries of the West; as well as my gratification at the sight of majestic rivers, wide fertile plains, and picturesque villages in this, my own country of Bengal, which I had not the good fortune of seeing for myself before. I did not know that there was everywhere in my country of Bengal—on land and water—so much beauty and charm. But this much has been my gain, that after seeing the various countries of the world I can now much more appreciate the beauties of my own land. In the same way also, in search of religion, I had travelled among various sects,—sects which had taken up the ideals of foreign nations as their own, and I had begged at the door of others, not knowing then that in the religion of my country, in our national religion, there was so much beauty and grandeur. It is now many years since I have found Hinduism to be the most perfectly satisfying religion in the world. Hence, I feel sad at heart when I see existing among my own countrymen professing a peerless faith, such a widespread indifference to our religion,—though I am very well aware of the unfavourable materialistic conditions in which they pass their lives, owing to the diffusion of European modes of thought in this, our great motherland.

There are among us at the present day, certain reformers who want to reform our religion, or rather turn it topsy-turvy, with a view to the regeneration of the Hindu nation. There are, no doubt, some thoughtful people among them, but there are also many who follow others blindly and act most foolishly, not knowing what they are about. This class of reformers are very enthusiastic in introducing foreign ideas into our religion. They have taken hold of the word 'idolatry,' and aver that Hinduism is not true, because it is idolatrous. They never seek to find out what this so-called 'idolatry' is, whether it is good or bad; only taking their clue from this word they are bold enough to shout down Hinduism as untrue. There is another class of men among us who are intent upon making out some slippery scientific explanations of any and every Hindu custom, rite, &c., and who are always talking of electricity, magnetism, air vibration and all that sort of thing. Who knows, but they will perhaps someday define God Himself as nothing but a mass of electric vibrations! However, Mother bless them all! She it is who is having Her work done in various ways through multifarious natures and tendencies.

In contradistinction to these, there is that ancient class, who say,—"I do not know, I do not care to know or understand all these your hair-splitting ratiocinations; I want God, I want the Atman, I want to go to that Beyond, where there is no universe, where there is no pleasure or pain, where dwells the Bliss Supreme";—who say, "I believe in salvation by bathing in the holy Ganges with faith";—who say,

" Whomsoever you may worship with singleness of faith and devotion as the one God of the universe, in whatsoever form, as Shiva, Rama, Vishnu, &c., you will get *Moksha*" ;—to that sturdy ancient class I am proud to belong. Then there is a sect who advise us to follow God and the world together. They are not sincere, they do not express what they feel in their hearts. What is the teaching of the Great Ones ?—" Where there is Rama, there is no *Káma*; where there is *Káma*, there Rama is not. Night and day can never exist together." The voice of the ancient sages proclaim to us that, " If you desire to attain God, you will have to renounce '*Káma-Kánchana*' (lust and possession). This Samsára is unreal, hollow, void of substance. Unless you give it up, you can never reach God, try however you may. If you cannot do that, own that you are weak, but by no means lower the Ideal. Do not cover the corrupting corpse with leaves of gold !" So according to them, if you want to gain spirituality, to attain God, the first thing that you have to do is to give up this playing 'hide-and-seek with your ideas,' this dishonesty, this 'theft within the chamber of thought.'

What have I learnt ? What have I learnt from this ancient sect ? I have learnt,—

दुर्लभं त्रयमेवैतत् देवानुग्रहहेतुकं ।
मनुष्यत्वं मुमुक्षुत्वं महापुरुषसंश्रयः ॥

" Verily, these three are rare to obtain, and come only through the grace of God—human birth, desire to obtain Moksha, and the company of the great-souled ones." The first thing needed is *Manushyatvam*, human birth, because it only is favourable to the attainment of Mukti. The next is *Mumukshatvam*. Though our means of realisation vary according to the difference in sects and individuals,—though different individuals can lay claim to their special rights and means to gain knowledge, which vary according to their different stations in life,—yet it can be said in general without fear of contradiction, that without this *Mumukshatá*, realisation of God is impossible. What is *Mumukshatvam* ? It is the strong desire for Moksha—earnest yearning to get out of the sphere of pain and pleasure—utter disgust for the world. When that intense burning desire to see God comes, then you should know that you are entitled to the realisation of the Supreme.

Then another thing is necessary, and that is, the coming in direct contact with the Mahâpurushas, and thus moulding our lives according to those of the great-souled ones who have reached the Goal. Even disgust with the world and a burning desire for God are not sufficient. Initiation by the Guru is necessary. Why ? Because it is the bringing of yourself into connection with that great source of power, which has been handed down through generations, from one Guru to another, in uninterrupted succession. The devotee must seek and accept the Guru or spiritual preceptor, as his counseller, philosopher, friend and guide. In short, the Guru is the *sine qua non* of progress in the path of spirituality. Whom then shall I accept as my Guru ? श्रोत्रियोऽवृजिनोऽकामहतो यो ब्रह्मवित्तमः—" He who is versed in the Vedas, without taint, unhurt by desire, he who is best of the knowers of Brahman." *Shrotriya*—he who is not only learned in the Shâstras, but who knows their subtle secrets, who has realised their true import in their lives. " Reading merely the various scriptures they have become only parrots, and not Pandits. He indeed has become a Pandit who has gained Prema (Divine Love) by reading even one word of the Shâstras." Mere book-learned Pandits are of no avail. Nowadays, everyone wants to be a Guru ; even a poor beggar wants to make a gift of a lac of Rupees ! Then, the Guru must be without a touch of taint ; and he must be *Akámahata*—unhurt by any desire,—he has no other motive except that of purely doing good to others, he who is the ocean of mercy-without-reason, he who does not impart religious teaching with a view to gain name or fame, or anything pertaining to selfish interest. And he must be the intense knower of Brahman, that is, one who has realised Brahman, even as tangibly as an Amlaki-fruit in the palm of the hand. Such is the Guru, says the Sruti. When spiritual union is established with such a Guru, then comes realisation of God—then God-vision becomes easy of attainment.

After initiation, there should be in the aspirant after Truth, *abhyás*, or earnest and repeated attempt at practical application of the Truth by prescribed means of constant meditation upon the chosen Ideal. Even if you have a burning thirst for God, or have gained the Guru, unless you have along with it, the *abhyása*, unless you practise what you have been taught, you cannot get realisation. When all these are firmly established in you, then you will reach the Goal.

Therefore I say unto you, as Hindus, as descendants of the glorious Aryas,—Do not forget the great ideal of our religion—the great ideal of the Hindu,—which is, to go beyond this Samsâra,—not only to renounce the world, but to give up heaven too; aye, not only to give up evil, but to give up good too; and thus to go beyond all, beyond this phenomenal existence, and ultimately realise the "Sat-Chit-Anandam Brahman"—the Absolute Existence-Knowledge-Bliss, which is Brahman.

THE RELIGION WE ARE BORN IN.

At an open-air meeting, delivered at Dacca, on the 31st March 1901, the Swamiji spoke in English for two hours on the above subject before a vast audience. The following is a translation of the lecture from the Bengalee report of a disciple :—

In the remote past, our country made gigantic advances in spiritual ideas. Let us, to-day, bring before our mind's eye that ancient history. But the one great danger in meditating over long-past greatness is, that we cease to exert ourselves for new things, and content ourselves with vegetating upon that by-gone ancestral glory, and priding ourselves upon it. We should guard against that. In ancient times there were, no doubt, many Rishis and Maharshis, who came face to face with Truth. But if this recalling of our ancient greatness is to be of real benefit, we too, must become Rishis like them. Aye, not only that, but it is my firm conviction that we shall be even greater Rishis than any that our history presents to us. In the past, signal were our attainments,—I glory in them and I feel proud in thinking of them. I am not even in despair at seeing the present degradation, and I am full of hope in picturing to my mind of what is to come in the future. Why? Because I know, the seed undergoes a complete transformation, aye, the seed as seed is seemingly destroyed, before it develops into a tree. In the same way, in the midst of our present degradation lies, only dormant for a time, the potential potency of the future greatness of our religion, ready to spring up again, perhaps more mighty and glorious than ever before.

Now let us consider what are the common grounds of agreement in the religion we are born in. At first sight we undeniably find various differences among our sects. Some are Advaitists, some are Visishtadvaitists, and others are Dvaitists. Some believe in Incarnations of God, some in Image-worship, while others are upholders of the doctrine of the Formless. Then as to customs also, various differences are known to exist. The Jâts are not outcasted, even if they marry among the Mahommedans and Christians. They can enter into any Hindu temple without hindrance. In many villages in the Punjab, one who does not eat swine will hardly be considered a Hindu. In Nepal, a Brâhman can marry in the four *Varnas;* while in Bengal, a Brâhman cannot marry even among the sub-divisions of his own caste. So on and so forth. But in the midst of all these differences we note one point of unity among all Hindus, and it is this, that no Hindu eats beef. In the same way, there is a great common ground of unity underlying the various forms and sects of our religion.

First, in discussing the Scriptures, one fact stands out prominently,—that only those religions which had one or many Scriptures of their own as their basis, advanced by leaps and bounds, and survive to the present day notwithstanding all the persecution and repression hurled against them. The Greek religion, with all its beauty, died out in the absence of any Scripture to support it; but the religion of the Jews stands undiminished in its power, being based upon the authority of the Old Testament. The same is the case with the Hindu religion, with its Scripture the Vedas, the oldest in the world. The Vedas are divided into the Karma-kanda and the Jnana-kanda. Whether for good or for evil, the Karma-kanda has fallen into disuse in India, though there are some Brâhmans in the Deccan, who still perform *Yajnas* now and then with the sacrifice of goats; and also we find here and there, traces of the Vedic Kriyâ-kanda in the Mantras used in connection with our marriage and Shrâddha ceremonies, &c. But there is no chance of its being rehabilitated on its original footing. Kumarilla Bhatta once tried to do so, but he was not successful in his attempt.

The Jnana-kanda of the Vedas comprises the Upanishads and is known by the name of Vedanta, the pinnacle of the Srutis, as it is called. Wherever you find the Acharyas quoting a passage from the Srutis, it is invariably from the Upanishads. The Vedanta is now the religion of the Hindus. If any sect in India wants to have its ideas established with a firm hold on the people, it must base them on the authority of the Vedanta. They all have to do it, whether they are Dvaitists or Advaitists. Even the Vaishnavas have to go to the Gopâlatâpani Upanishad to prove the truth of their own theories. If a new sect does not find anything in the Srutis in confirmation of its own ideas, it will go even to the length of manufacturing a new Upanishad, and make it pass current as one of the old original productions. There have been many such in the past.

Now as to the Vedas, the Hindus believe that they are not mere books composed by men in some remote age. They hold them to be an accumulated mass of endless Divine Wisdom, which are sometimes manifested or at other times remain unmanifested. The Sâyanâcharya says somewhere in his works, यो वेदेभ्योऽखिलं जगत् निर्ममे। —"Who created the whole universe out of the knowledge of the Vedas." No one has ever seen the compiler of the Vedas, and it is impossible to imagine one. The Rishis were only the discoverers of the Mantras or Eternal Laws; they merely came face to face with the Vedas, the Infinite mine of knowledge, which has been there from time without beginning.

Who are these Rishis? Vâtsâyana says,—"He who has attained through proper means the direct realisation of Dharma, he alone can be a Rishi, even if he is a *Mlechchha* by birth." Thus it is that in ancient times, Vasishtha born of an illegitimate union, Vyâsa the son of a fisherman, Nârada the sôn of a maid-servant with uncertain parentage, and many others of like nature, attained to Rishihood. Truly speaking, it comes to this then, that no distinction should be made with one who has realised the Truth. If the persons just named all became Rishis, then, O ye Kulin Brâhmans of the present day, how much greater Rishis you can become! Strive after that Rishihood, stop not till you have attained the goal, and the whole world will of itself bow at your feet! Be a Rishi,—that is the secret of power.

This Veda is our only authority, and everyone has the right to it. "यथेमां वाचं कल्याणीमावदानि जनेभ्यः। ब्रह्मराजन्याभ्यां शूद्राय चार्याय च स्वाय चारणाय"॥ Thus says the *Sukla Yajur Veda*. Can you show any authority from this Veda of ours, that everyone has not the right to it? The Puranas, no doubt, say that a certain caste has the right to such and such a recension of the Vedas, or a certain caste has no right to study them, or that this portion of the Vedas is for the *Satya Yuga* and that portion is for the *Kali Yuga*. But, mark you, the Veda does not say so; it is only your Puranas that do so. But can the servant dictate to the master? The Smrtis, Puranas, Tantras—all these are acceptable only so far as they agree with the Vedas; and wherever they are contradictory, they are to be rejected as unreliable. But nowadays we have put the Puranas on even a higher pedestal than the Vedas! The study of the Vedas has almost disappeared from Bengal. How I wish that day will soon come, when in every home the Veda will be worshipped together with the Sâlagrâma, the household Deity, when the young, the old, and the women will inaugurate the worship of the Veda.

I have no faith in the theories advanced by Western Savants with regard to the Vedas. They are to-day fixing the antiquity of the Vedas at a certain period, and again to-morrow upsetting it and bringing it one thousand years forward, and so on. However, about the Puranas, I have told you that they are authoritative only in so far as they agree with the Vedas, otherwise not. In the Puranas we find many things which do not agree with the Vedas. As for instance, it is written in the Puranas that some one lived ten thousand years, another one, twenty thousand years, but in the Vedas we find—शतायुर्वै पुरुषः—"Man lives, indeed, a hundred years." Which are we to accept in this case? Certainly the Veda. Notwithstanding statements like these, I do not depreciate the Puranas. They contain many beautiful and illuminating teachings and words of wisdom on Yoga, Bhakti, Jnana, and Karma; those, of course, we should accept. Then there are the Tantras. The real meaning of the word Tantra is Shâstra, as for example, Kâpila Tantra. But the word Tantra is generally used in a limited sense. Under the sway of kings who took up Buddhism and preached broadcast the doctrine of *Ahimsâ*, the performances of the Vedic *Yâga Yajnas* became a thing of the past, and no one could kill any animal in sacrifice, for fear of the king. But subsequently amongst the Buddhists themselves—who were converts from Hinduism—the best parts of these *Yâga Yajnas* were taken up, and practised in secret. From these sprung up the Tantras. Barring some of the abominable things in the Tantras, such as the *Vâmâchara* &c., the Tantras are not so bad, as people are inclined to think. There are many high and sublime Vedantic thoughts in them. In fact, the Brâhmana portions of the Vedas were modified a little, and incorporated into the body of the Tantras. All the forms of our worship and the ceremonials of the present day, comprising the Karma-kanda, are observed in accordance with the Tantras.

Now let us discuss the principles of our religion a little. Notwithstanding the differences and controversies existing among our various sects, there are in them too, several grounds of ûnity. First, almost all of them admit the existence of three things—three entities—Ishvara, Atman, and the Jagat. Ishvara is He who is eternally creating, preserving and destroying the whole universe. Excepting the Sânkhyas, all the others believe in this. Then the doctrine of the Atman, or the re-incarnation of the soul; it maintains that innumerable individual souls having taken body after body again and again, go round and round in the wheel of birth and death according to their respective Karmas; this is *Samsâravâda* or as it is commonly called, the doctrine of re-birth. Then there is this Jagat or universe, without beginning and without end. Though some hold these three as different phases of one only, and some others as three distinctly different entities, and others again in various other ways, yet they are all unanimous in believing in these three.

Here I should ask you to remember that Hindus, from time immemorial, knew the Atman as separate from Manas, mind. But the Occidentals could never soar beyond the mind. The West knows the universe to be full of happiness, and as such, it is to them a place where they can enjoy the most; but the East is born with the conviction that this Samsâra, this ever-changing existence, is full of misery, and as such, it is nothing, nothing but unreal, not worth bartering the soul for its ephemeral joys and possessions. For this very reason, the West is ever especially adroit in organised action, and so also, the East is ever bold in search of the mysteries of the internal world.

Let us, however, turn now to one or two other aspects of Hinduism. There is the doctrine of the Incarnations of God. In the Vedas we find mention of *Matsya Avatâra*, the Fish Incarnation, only. Whether all believe in this doctrine or not is not the point; the real meaning, however, of this *Avatâravâda* is, the worship of Man,—to see God in man is the real God-vision. The Hindu does not go through Nature to Nature's God,—he goes to the God of man through Man.

Then there is, Image-worship. Except the Five Devatâs who are to be worshipped in every auspicious Karma as enjoined in our Shâstras, all the other Devatâs are merely the names of certain states held by them. But again, these five Devatâs are nothing but the different names of the one God only. This external worship of images has, however, been described in all our Shâstras as the lowest of all the low forms of worship. But that does not mean that it is a wrong thing to do. Despite the many iniquities that have found entrance into the practices of image-worship as it is in vogue now, I do not condemn it. Aye, where would I have been, if I had not been blessed with the dust of the holy feet of that orthodox, image-worshipping Brâhman!

Those reformers who preach against image-worship, or what they denounce as idolatry,—to them I say,—"Brothers! If you are fit to worship God-without-Form discarding any external help, do so, but why do you condemn others who cannot do the same? A beautiful large edifice, the glorious relic of a hoary antiquity has, out of neglect or disuse, fallen into a dilapidated condition; accumulations of dirt and dust may be lying everywhere within it; maybe, some portions are tumbling down to the ground. What will you do to it? Will you take in hand the necessary cleansing and repairs and thus restore the old, or will you pull the whole edifice down to the ground and seek to build another in its place, after a sordid modern plan whose permanence has yet to be established? We have to reform it, which truly means to make ready or perfect by necessary cleansing and repairs, not by demolishing the whole thing. There the function of reform ends. When the work of renovating the old is finished, what further necessity does it serve? Do that if you can, if not, hands off!" The band of reformers in our country want, on the contrary, to build up a separate sect of their own. They have, however, done good work; may the blessings of God be showered on their heads! But why should you, Hindus, want to separate yourselves from the great common fold? Why should you feel ashamed to take the name of Hindu, which is your greatest and most glorious possession? This national ship of ours, ye children of the Immortals, my countrymen, has been plying for ages, carrying civilisation and enriching the whole world with its inestimable treasures. For scores of shining centuries this national ship of ours has been ferrying across the ocean of life, and has taken millions of souls to the other shore, beyond all misery. But to-day it may have sprung a leak and got damaged, through your own fault or whatever cause it matters not. What would you, who have placed yourselves in it, do now? Would you go about cursing it and quarrelling among yourselves, or would you not all unite together and put your best efforts to stop the holes? Let us all gladly give our hearts' blood to do it; and if we fail in the attempt, let us all sink and die together, with blessings and not curses on our lips.

And to the Brâhmans I say,—"Vain is your pride of superiority of birth and ancestry. Shake it off. Brâhmanhood, according to your Shâstras, you have no more now, because, you have for so long lived under *Mlechchha* kings. If you at all believe in the words of your own ancestors, then go this very moment and make expiation by entering into the slow fire kindled by *Tusha* husks, like that old Kumârilla Bhatta, who with the purpose of killing the Buddhists first became a disciple of the Buddhists and then killed them, and subsequently entered the *Tushânala* to expiate his sins. If you are not bold enough to do that, then admit your weakness and stretch forth a helping hand and open the gates of knowledge, to one and all, and give the down-trodden masses once more their just and legitimate rights and privileges."

Lightning Source UK Ltd.
Milton Keynes UK
UKHW020941120920
369766UK00005B/1260

9 781375 453578